WILLIAM EVERSON
(Brother Antoninus)

THE CROOKED LINES OF GOD:
A Life Trilogy

VOLUME I
The Residual Years (1934-1948)

VOLUME II
The Veritable Years (1949-1966)

VOLUME III
The Integral Years (1966-1994)

WILLIAM EVERSON

(Brother Antoninus)

THE INTEGRAL YEARS

Poems 1966–1994

Including A Selection Of Uncollected
And Previously Unpublished Poems

Foreword by Allan Campo
Introduction by David Carpenter
Afterword by Bill Hotchkiss
Afterword by Judith Shears

BLACK SPARROW PRESS ▣ SANTA ROSA ▣ 2000

ACKNOWLEDGMENTS
Certain of these poems were originally published in the following periodicals: *Ark, Bastard Angel, Beyond Baroque 792, Brahma, Choice, Conjunctions, Hard Pressed, Kayak, Lemmings, Maryland Poetry Review, New Catholic World, Quarry, The Real World Press, Sequoia, The Sierra Journal, Sludge,* and *Sulfur.* Additionally, several of these poems were originally published in the following volumes: *Lord John Ten* (Lord John Press, Northridge, CA, 1988), *Naked Heart: Talking on Poetry, Mysticism, and the Erotic* (University of New Mexico, Albuquerque, NM, 1992), *Out of the West* (Lord John Press, Northridge, CA, 1979), *Perspectives on William Everson* (Castle Peak Editions, Murphy, OR, 1992), *Voices from the Southwest* (Northland Press, Flagstaff, AZ, 1976), and *West to the Water* (Lime Kiln Press, Santa Cruz, CA, 1972). The Everson Estate also expresses gratitude to the various publishers listed in the Bibliographical Note, who previously issued these poems in separate editions.
APPENDIX A CREDITS: The William Everson Papers (BANC MSS 82/1c), The Bancroft Library, University of California, Berkeley; Peter and Donna Thomas, Santa Cruz, CA; Northland Press, Flagstaff, AZ; University of New Mexico, Albuquerque, NM.
APPENDIX B CREDITS: The William Everson Papers (BANC MSS 82/1c) for the hitherto unpublished material contained therein; Black Sparrow Press for the Author's Note to The Engendering Flood; *Adrian Wilson, San Francisco, for the Foreword to* In Medias Res.
PHOTO ACKNOWLEDGMENT: Bancroft Library, University of California, Berkeley.
PHOTO CREDITS: Robert Turney, East Lansing, MI; John Prince, South San Francisco, CA; E. David Show, Los Altos, CA; and Allen Say.
COVER PHOTO: Robert Turney, East Lansing, MI (1980).

Black Sparrow Press books are printed on acid-free paper.

LIBRARY OF CONGRESS CATALOGING-IN-PUBLICATION DATA
Everson, William, 1912-1994
    The integral years: poems 1966-1994: including a selection of uncollected and previously unpublished poems / William Everson (Brother Antoninus); foreword by Allan Campo; introduction by David Carpenter; afterwords by Bill Hotchkiss and by Judith Shears.
        p. cm.—(The Collected Poems: v.3)
    Includes bibliographical references and index.
        ISBN 1-57423-108-1 (paperback)
        ISBN 1-57423-109-X (cloth trade)
        ISBN 1-57423-110-3 (deluxe trade)
        I. Title. II. Series: Everson, William 1912-1994. Poems: v.3.
PS3509.V65A17 2000 vol. 3   97-43682
811'.52—dc21   CIP

CONTENTS

BOOK FOUR:
THE GLYPH OF GOD (1971-1985)

I. THE MASKS OF DROUGHT

II. RENEGADE CHRISTMAS

BOOK FIVE:
DUST SHALL BE THE SERPENT'S FOOD (1975-1991)

APPENDIX A: A SELECTION OF UNCOLLECTED
AND UNPUBLISHED POEMS

from *EROS AND THANATOS*

APPENDIX B: REGARDING *DUST SHALL BE
THE SERPENT'S FOOD*

Photographs follow page 94.

BIBLIOGRAPHICAL NOTE:

This collection is comprised of the following editions, listed in the order of their respective publications. The years of composition are given in brackets.

The City Does Not Die [1969], Oyez, Berkeley, CA, 1969. [Published under the name of Brother Antoninus.]

Tendril in the Mesh [1966-1968], Cayucos Books, [Aromas, CA], 1973.

Black Hills [1970], Didymus Press, San Francisco, 1973.

Man-Fate [1969-1972], New Directions, New York, 1974.

Blackbird Sundown [1972-1973], Lord John Press, Northridge, CA, 1978. Broadside.

Rattlesnake August [1976], Santa Susanna Press (Northridge University Northridge Libraries), Northridge, CA, 1978. Portfolio.

Blame It on the Jet Stream [1973], The Lime Kiln Press, Santa Cruz, 1978.

Cutting the Firebreak [1973, 1976], The Kingfisher Press, Swanton, CA, 1978. Broadside.

Sixty Five [1977, 1980], [Labyrinth Editions], Bromer, Boston, 1980. Broadside.

The Masks of Drought [1971-1979], Black Sparrow Press, Santa Barbara, CA, 1980.

Cougar [1980], Lord John Press, Northridge, CA, 1982. Broadside.

Storm Surge [1971, 1978], J. D. Holcomb, 1983. Broadside.

In Medias Res [1975, 1981], Adrian Wilson, San Francisco, 1984.

Renegade Christmas [1977, 1980-1983], Lord John Press, Northridge, CA, 1984.

Stone Face Falls [1979], Moving Parts Press, Santa Cruz, 1984. Broadside.

The High Embrace [1977], Dawson's Book Shop, Los Angeles, 1986. Portfolio.

Mexican Standoff [1985], The Lapis Press, Emeryville, CA, 1989.

The Engendering Flood [1975-89], Black Sparrow Press, Santa Rosa, CA, 1990.

The Tarantella Rose: Six Poems by William Everson [1975], Peter and Donna Thomas, Santa Cruz, CA, 1995.

Ravaged with Joy [1969-1970], Robin Price, Publisher, Middletown, CT, 1998. [Recording of an Everson reading, accompanied by printed text.]

PREFATORY NOTE:

As title for the third volume of his *Crooked Lines of God* trilogy, William Everson had settled on *The Integral Years* by 1975, and committed himself to it in print in the "Preface" to his 1978 *The Veritable Years*. Writing there of the thesis-antithesis-synthesis dialectic that provided a perspective for the trilogy, he described the poetry that would comprise *The Integral Years* as "representing a man's effort to integrate into a synthetic whole the dichotomies that have split him, the thesis and antithesis that divide the world."

At the time, Everson was still in the process of completing the poems that would be collected as *The Masks of Drought*—itself the second volume of poetry (following the 1974 *Man-Fate*) making up this final part of the trilogy. It would be followed in the early 1980s by the five poems comprising *Renegade Christmas* and, in 1985, by the late-arriving "Mexican Standoff." Bringing this poetry together into the single *Integral Years* volume remained a work-in-progress until Everson's hospitalization in the fall of 1993 and his subsequent return to Kingfisher Flat for the remaining months of his life.

Consequently, the present volume brings together for the first time the poetic achievement of Everson's third major phase—begun in the closing years of his Dominican tenure, but mainly composed during the fifteen years that followed. The text has been amended in accord with Everson's subsequent revisions. In addition, this edition includes the five Cantos Everson had completed of his autobiographical epic poem, *Dust Shall Be the Serpent's Food*, before his illness and death caused the work to be left unfinished. An Appendix including the remaining uncollected poems and a representative selection of unpublished verse rounds out this final volume of William Everson's pursuit of his poetic vocation—a pursuit that ended only with his death on June 2, 1994.

NOTE ON TYPOGRAPHY:

Text for *The Integral Years* was partially scanned from previous editions of Everson's work, but the majority of the copy was subsequently registered on computer by Judith Shears (while Everson was still alive and could proof the copy), by Steve Sibley—and then by Allan Campo and Bill Hotchkiss, with Times New Roman text and Century Schoolbook and Moravian heads—via TrueType and Microsoft Word (6 & 7) for Windows.™ Book layout by Bill Hotchkiss, at Castle Peak Editions, Williams, Oregon. Text proofing by Allan Campo, Bill Hotchkiss, David Carpenter, Judith Shears, Lee-Marie Varner, and Elizabeth Martin-Burk.

FOREWORD:
JOURNEY'S END / THE RETURN
Allan Campo

In his 1978 Preface to *The Veritable Years*, William Everson, drawing upon Joseph Campbell's concept of "the hero's journey" as *monomyth*, provides the following perspective for the body of his poetry:

> Taken as a whole, the trilogy might be said to trace the ancient mythological journey, an amplification of the archetype represented in all rites of passage: *separation-initiation-return*. The first two lives now stand behind me as realized, and the final, inclusive one is well begun. (cited from *Veritable Years*, 98 ed., xxxvi)

To have entered upon the "final, inclusive" life is to have undertaken the *return*, without which the journey is incomplete; for it is the mission of the hero to bring something of value, the "boon," back to his people. But, as Campbell points out, the hero (and there is the hero archetype residing deep in the psyche of every individual) may not wish to enter upon his return. In that case, "the hero may have to be brought back from his supernatural adventure by assistance from without. That is to say, the world may have to come and get him."* And so it was for Everson. However sincere the man, however beneficent the means, what might have passed for his return—his poetry, his extensive public readings, his friendships, his counseling, his religious vow-taking regimen—remained insufficient. Perhaps there was yet some admixture of pride, the dilution of man and means by the condition that the return be on *his* terms. There is surrender in answering the "call" at the journey's start. There must be surrender for the journey's end.

So, the world had "to come and get him." In Everson's case, the "world" was a troubled eighteen-year-old, Susanna Rickson, brought to him for counseling in the fall of 1965. And in spite of his prudential caution (made especially needful by the fact that he was Brother Antoninus, a religious), in due time Everson fell in love with his young counselee. The love engendered intense eroticism. The relationship became a passionate fact; and Everson accepted it as such.

---

* *The Hero with a Thousand Faces*, 2nd ed. (Princeton: Princeton UP, 1968) 207.

But acceptance for two years was not enough. It was merely treading water, leading nowhere. Then, in the early months of 1968, the situational issues gained new urgency in what could be considered the pivotal period of that four year relationship. I look back upon his letters to me during those months, and they seem as nothing so much as "dispatches from the front."

> February 17. *It is true that I want desperately for the affair with Susanna to end, but that is only the head thing—I mean the mental aspect of it—my relation to the world, my reputation, my "image." Interiorly I still love and need her— not as desperately as before, but still plenty.* [That evening the two of them had dinner, and she told him it was all over, she had fallen in love with another man.] February 18. *It was due, past due. I had been praying for it in my mind for weeks but resisting it in my instinct.* [But there were loose ends for the poet.] March 2. *What I couldn't understand was—what will happen to the dark eros, that part of me that had fed so deeply and so long on her presence? Suddenly it loomed as a terrible problem at last unmasked. Can I live the celibate life, and be whole?* [Then a poem came.] March 3. *Strange, after writing...yesterday a great poem emerged—Dark Eros—the Christ as eros. It finishes the sequence to Sue* ["Tendril in the Mesh"].... *Last week was bad...but yesterday solidified everything, and I feel the basic problem is solved.* [Shortly thereafter, he left on an extended reading tour.] March 31. *[L]ast weekend Sue's new relationship broke and she was on the phone.... I crawled back into her arms, so to speak, and everything is beginning over again.* May 6. *I got back here to find the situation quite closed out. I had sensed...that she was falling back in love* [with the other man], *and she confirmed it.... So I start to close my wounds again, and let us hope for the last time.*

His hope was not to be realized. Susanna's relationship, though it engendered the birth of a son, did not last; she and Everson resumed their affair; the crucial question remained: *Can I live the celibate life, and be whole?* It was not until late in 1969 that Everson finally acknowledged the answer—*No*—and, on December 7, 1969, at the University of California, Davis, at the conclusion of his first public reading of "The Tendril in the Mesh," he announced that he was leaving the Dominican Order (a year short of his final vows) in order to marry;

the poet removed his Dominican habit, and departed. The return, long overdue and much resisted, was underway.

If "Tendril" was the sign of what it took to bring Everson to surrender his "relation to the world," so long cultivated, the poems that mark his transition back into the world, and which were collected as *Man-Fate*, reveal an evolving development away from almost anything that had gone before. While still bearing the personal voice, the confessional modality, there is a tempering as Everson works his way through the life-change he is undergoing. In these poems, there is neither the bleak prospect nor the painful urgency so often characteristic of the previous work—gone, the underlying gloom of *The Residual Years,* the spiritual anguish of *The Veritable Years.* In "A Time to Mourn" especially, there is, rather, a mulling over of a changed situation, a pondering infused with acceptance and commitment. Though the poems display restraint, feelings are palpably present. And, in the closing section, "The Narrows," we see the poet developing a new image, the frontier-jacketed persona of his return—a development to which he is not driven but at which he arrives. At the same time, the workings of the Unconscious become present—the dream episodes of "Black Hills," "The Narrows of Birth," and "The Dunes," and the fantasy that interrupts the poet's reflections in "The Scout."

The *Man-Fate* poems were written for the most part at Stinson Beach, where Everson, Susanna, and son Jude lived, in a small house just yards from the sand, for a little more than a year and a half. These poems cleared the way for Everson's full *return*—how it would truly manifest itself, what it would entail. In late summer, 1971, the family moved to Big Creek Canyon, about twenty miles north of Santa Cruz, and settled in at a spot Everson would eventually christen "Kingfisher Flat." It was four years and more before the new poems began to take shape, concurrently with the severe drought that plagued California in 1976 and 1977. And what had been germinating came to fruition in the poems collected as *The Masks of Drought* and *Renegade Christmas*— paired in this volume as Book Four, "The Glyph of God."

In the Preface Everson prepared for *The Integral Years* (which, of course, is included the present volume) he focused on the dialectical view of his life's poetic output: thesis-antithesis-synthesis—with the *Masks* poems as the validation that synthesis had been achieved. But "synthesis" smacks of a human construct, as though the individual might fashion a tangible blending of the disparate elements within reality, the polarities that create the tensions of human existence, into a synthetic harmony. True, the dialectic does have its validity. But the greater perspective derives from the overriding, self-subsistent realities of God, Nature, and the Unconscious. And these, the supremely objective *facts* that impinge upon human experience, are not, in the final analysis, subject to the individual's shaping, not reductively malleable adjuncts to the centripetal spin of human needs and human purposes.

After contending with or, often enough, struggling against these uncompromising *Facts* throughout the poetry of those *Residual* and *Veritable Years* (the needful folly of human growth), Everson attained his journey's goal—the boon his return was meant to convey—namely, the entering into harmonious relationship with these transpersonal realities, thus bringing to birth the quaternity. That is, in terms of the archetype, when the poet-hero enters into such relationship with those three realities, a foursome is created—the Jungian configuration of wholeness, within which everything (especially the poet himself) finds its proper place. Hence, the *integral* years.

The result is a series of poems quite unlike anything that preceded them. There is a new objectivity present here, for once Everson found his place, he made good on the promise of his *return*. No longer was the poet at center stage; no longer were the poems dominated by a focus on his feelings; no longer was anguished struggle or bewilderment the hallmark of his verse. He achieved a sense of objectivity, an integration of feeling, and relationship rather than confrontation. Each poem embraces the reality of what *is* and evokes the aura, the feel of wholeness.

We see the change in the presence of Nature's creatures—whether the venomous rattler, the lordly cougar, the mysterious steelhead, the frantic jays and the jubilant cats, the dreaded great horned owl. Whatever meaning or impact the poet derives from their presence and their activity, their existence supersedes his purpose. For they exist, they *matter*, quite apart from his perceptions of them.

We see the change in the awareness of God. In an unpublished introduction he prepared for *Masks of Drought*, Everson referred to "the gleam of divinity in the incidence of Nature," for God is no longer to be quarreled or pleaded with, begged from or exulted upon. God is *present*, and that is what matters.

We see the changed character of the Unconscious. No longer the hotbed of inner demons and terrifying tensions, it is the provider of meaning and direction, the individual's deep mentor.

Most importantly, we see the consequences of becoming remiss as to one's proper place within the relationships that constitute the cosmic Whole. It may be, as in the earlier "Black Hills," an almost comically punctured inflation—the poet wounded by stepping on little Jude's plastic plaything after being caught up in an excess of assumed rapture

("All Indian at last"). It may be the hair's breadth close call of "Chainsaw," the consequence of success breeding cocksureness. Or it may be the potentially fatal mishap in "Reaper" that comes as a delayed backlash from the "Cutting the Firebreak" frenzy of a decade earlier. Indeed, it is such comeuppances that give a special tang to the atmosphere and the decided bite of reality in the poems.

One of the most telling moments in these verses—constellating the integration which characterizes them—comes in the concluding lines of "Steelhead":

> Ineluctable pariah, he burns in my dream
> And calls me from sleep.
>
>   Who am hardly surprised
> To find by the water his scattered remains
> Where the raccoons flung him: tore gill from fin,
> Devoured the life-sustaining flesh, and left in the clay
> The faint skeletal imprint—as fossil
> Etched in stone spans time like myth—
> The glyph of God. (111-112)

Nature, the dream reality of the Unconscious, the "glyph" of God (that "gleam of divinity in the incidence of Nature"), and amongst them the person of the poet—amongst and in harmony with the numinous scenario—his own sense of exile ameliorated.

"Mexican Standoff"—arriving just too late to find place in *Renegade Christmas*—comes as something of an exclamation mark. The poet, again in a dream-episode, encounters the voice-personification, not simply of Death but, more to the point, Thanatos— the force of dissolution, dis-integration, the essence of what the poet's Parkinson's disease enacts. Most of all, it is the antithesis and adversary of Eros, life as passionate energy and creativity—indeed, the fundamental polarity of human existence. But the poet stands his ground. He defies (*God damn it! Take it!*); he condescends (*I wish you well of it.*); he mocks (*Are you sure / You can handle it?*); and then he thrusts home (*What are you going to do with it? / Use it?*) with the very exposure of the emptiness of the voice's threat, for Thanatos is by nature annihilatory of any use. There is no synthesis here, no erasure of polarity. What there is here is the very pronouncement of wholeness, the true stature of personhood. And even the comic awkwardness connoted by the title can be allowed to remain.

In my Foreword to the 1997 *Residual Years*, the first volume of Everson's *Life-Trilogy*, I recounted how, in 1972, at the poet's first Southern California reading appearance since leaving the Order, he read poems from thirty years earlier when, appropos his current state, "I was trying to find a place where I could stand." The poems of *Masks of Drought* and *Renegade Christmas*, the poetry of his *return*, the journey's end, demonstrate that at Kingfisher Flat (as much a state of soul as a plot of land) he at last found that place. And in so doing, he gained— regardless of the eventual marital severance, regardless of the physical debility of his Parkinson's—that personal boon of which he wrote in "The City Will Not Die":

> For to die in the place of one's happiness
> Is the last blessing of life. (25)

🔲

In terms of the editorial work involved in the preparation of this volume, previous collections, separate editions of single poems, and periodical appearances of the poetry have been consulted in order to check for errors and to note changes that have cropped up. We have also attempted to incorporate those changes that Everson made over the years—drawn from those noted in the poet's personal copies of his published work and those noted on computer hardcopies made available to him, including both the present collection of *The Integral Years* and the projected selection, *The Achievement of William Everson*.

There was no predecessor collection published for *The Integral Years* as there had been for *The Residual Years* and *The Veritable Years*. What does exist, however, is a computer text entered by Judith Shears in close and continuous consultation with Everson. This text was executed in 1989 and updated in late 1991. In late summer of 1993, Steve Sibley, who had become the poet's live-in caregiver following the breakup of Everson's marriage in September of 1992, utilized a copy of the earlier computer disc to prepare a new computer text under Everson's supervision. These texts provided us with the basic collection—just as the published predecessors for the previous volumes had done.

A particular ongoing problem in the preparation of the text of Everson's poetry was accentuated in editing the present collection. William Everson was an inveterate tinkerer with his verse—regardless of a poem's publication history or how much time had passed in the life of the poem. Generally speaking, of course, the validation of a change noted by Everson in a personal copy of a printed collection or on a manuscript version would be the inclusion of the change in a subsequently printed appearance of the affected poem. In comparison with the previous poetry, the work of *The Integral Years* has had a less extensive printing history. Therefore, the question of validating the poet's changes tended to become somewhat more problematic than in the past. The difficulty was further exacerbated by the poet's failing health and diminishing energy, so that changes were not consistently followed through from one hardcopy, say, to another.

In late October of 1993, Everson was taken seriously ill and hospitalized until his return home in December. Occupied with the formidable difficulties of his post-hospital condition and giving what energy and attention he could to supervising the proofreading of work then being prepared for publication (most especially Albert Gelpi's edition of selected poems, *The Blood of the Poet* [Seattle: Broken Moon Press, 1994]), Everson was unable to finalize either the text or the preliminaries of *The Integral Years*. Consequently, the need for editorial decisions regarding text and arrangement has been greater than it was in the previous volumes of Everson's *Life-Trilogy*.

The matter of the arrangement and division of the poetry deserves comment. The Table of Contents in the computer versions is distinguished by the simple use of sequential Roman numerals for each group of poems. The division of the poetry into "Books" (as was the case in the previous volumes, in accord with Everson's arrangement in their predecessor editions) is absent. However, there are a couple of late (July 1993) holograph pages in which the "Book" division is established—reinforcing our inclination to utilize such a division. In addition, from similar sources we found support for using "The Glyph of God" as the title for Book Four and bringing together both "The Masks of Drought" and "Renegade Christmas" as separate units within that Book. It is worth noting that preliminary preparations for the publication of *The Masks of Drought* (1980) included "The Glyph of God" as a possible title.

As to Everson's Preface, we have used the piece as he completed it in the fall of 1991. A year later, however, he revised the Preface in order to take into account a new prospect for his "Collected Poems," namely, the expansion of *Dust Shall Be the Serpent's Food* into a fourth and separate volume, instead of the earlier arrangement that would have included the completed Cantos as the final section of *The Integral Years*. Thus, the principal revision of the Preface was the addition of the following paragraph as conclusion:

Thus concludes *The Integral Years*, but not, it seems, *The Crooked Lines of God*. Another unsuspected break-in-plane has thrown the profile of my life from a trinitarian to a quaternity configuration. Although unplanned, its aesthetic form is confirmed by its fitness as the Jungian symbol of wholeness, suggesting its designation as *The Holistic Years*. It begins with the autobiographical epic *Dust Shall Be the Serpent's Food*, itself incepted by *The Engendering Flood*, Canto[s] I to IV of the masterwork. Its break-in-plane is decisive. If [*The Residual Years*], *The Veritable Years* and *The Integral Years* tell the story of my life, *The Holistic Years* must say what it means.

Given the substantially incomplete state of the autobiographical epic (only five Cantos of the projected ten were completed prior to the poet's death), we have followed Everson's earlier arrangement by placing the Cantos as the final Book of this collection. The "masterwork" serves, at the last, as epilogue. However, in addition to our Appendix A ("A Selection of Uncollected and Unpublished Poems"), we have included an Appendix B, comprised of material relevant to a consideration of the epic poem and including unpublished introductory material prepared by Everson.

The arrangement of the poems is basically chronological, with the notable exception of the poems previously published as *The Masks of Drought*, where we have maintained the order used by Everson in that book—that is, as he noted there, the poems placed in seasonal order. In his Introduction to the present volume, David Carpenter touches upon the matter of Everson's departure from strict chronology. It should also be noted that various of the poems were initiated but then set aside for an uncharacteristic two or more years before Everson took them up again and carried them through to completion. This, too, contributes to a somewhat irregular chronology.

We have attempted to arrange the text of the poems for printing in accord with Everson's desired (though not always executed) practice, so that neither the end of a stanza nor an end-stopped line from within a stanza coincides with the end of a page. There are instances, however, where the desired result has not been possible. In these cases, a note specifies whether the end-stopped line also signifies a stanza break.

In addition to David Carpenter's pointedly focused essay as introduction, we have included as Afterwords essays by Bill Hotchkiss and Judith Shears, each of whom provides a blend of literary commentary and personal reminiscence—an approach particularly appropriate to the "return" motif of this, the final volume of William Everson's *Collected Poems*.

⧉

There are, of course, various acknowledgments that both Bill Hotchkiss and I happily and gratefully make. Judith Shears' extensive work in entering Everson's poetry into the computer and the availability of the disc for this volume was extremely valuable. Steve Sibley's continuation of this work proved quite helpful as well. Once again, John Carpenter, Robert Hawley, and George Fox have made it possible for review of Everson's personal copies of his published collections. Roger Myers, Manuscripts Librarian of the Special Collections at the University of Arizona Library, supplied copies of relevant correspondence and the corrected page proofs of *The Engendering Flood*. Maureen Carey of the library at UC Santa Cruz has been considerably responsive to various inquiries. Anthony Bliss, Curator of Manuscripts at the Bancroft Library (University of California, Berkeley), has continued to make my visits to the Bancroft pleasurable and productive. The general staff at the Bancroft remain courteous and efficient. In particular, Ms. Naomi Schultz and her assistant, Patrick Yemenidjian, were especially careful and proficient in providing the many photocopies I requested. Susan Snyder, Head, Access Services and Photo Duplication, was helpful in responding to various questions, as well as in handling the procurement of photographs. Mary Morganti, Manuscripts Processing Supervisor, considerately arranged for archival material to be made available prior to my arrival. Once again, Ms. Lisa de Larios' meticulous cataloguing of the Everson Papers was indispensable. I must also mention that John Martin of Black Sparrow Press has been reassuringly dependable in carrying out his commitment to publish—and to do so handsomely—the three volumes comprising *The Crooked Lines of God*. Michele Filshie, Assistant to the Publisher, proved to be a congenial and efficient intermediary in the project.

As always, Bill Hotchkiss has been the invaluable co-editor and, beyond that role, has continued to contribute his expertise in providing the computer-generated photo-ready copy for printing.

—Allan Campo
Toledo, Ohio

INTRODUCTION:
SHE THAT LOOKETH FORTH
AS THE MORNING
David Carpenter

> She is the Mother of Life, Mistress of Death,
> Before her feet the tiger coughs and dies,
> And the bony elephant gives up the boast
> Of those vast passions that once filmed his eyes.

(Brother Antoninus, *Veritable Years*, 98 ed., 323)

What you hold in your hands, excepting the critical and textual apparatus, is the last volume of *The Crooked Lines of God: A Life Trilogy* as William Everson envisioned it, as he envisioned and shaped his life's work, as he envisioned and retrospectively shaped the poetic portrait of his life. Everson desired—and needed—to behold an identifiable pattern to his existence, this especially important in his last decade or so, and thus he embraced the concept of the monomyth, the three archetypal stages of the hero's quest. Everson has explained how he envisioned the pattern of his life, retrospectively delineated and arrived at, a pattern given shape to reactively, and thus we have the trilogy, as he came to see it: *The Residual Years, The Veritable Years* and *The Integral Years*.

Some readers will find the poet's retrospective and aesthetically tidy demarcating of his life and poetry handy, convenient; and why not, for the three stages of the monomyth are identifiable in the trilogy as envisioned by Everson. They do seem to be valid when held up against the broad strokes, the most salient movements of the poet's life as he has arranged them in his numerous volumes of poetry. A problem exists for the reader who desires to study Everson's psychological and artistic development, however, insofar as Everson frequently arranged the poems of a given collection according to his over-arching vision of the collection, not according to the dates of composition. *The Masks of Drought*, for example, opens with "Storm-Surge" (composed 24 December 1971), the earliest of the poems in the volume, but two poems later is "Runoff" (composed 1 March 1976), the poem directly following this is "Blackbird Sundown" (composed 2 August 1972), and so on. While the two sections of "Moongate" were composed last (4 August 1979 and 8 August 1979, respectively), the poem is presented as the thirteenth of nineteen poems in the volume, with the last poem in the volume—"Spikehorn"—composed 1 October 1977.

While Everson tells us in his "Preface" to this volume that he conceived of his life "as evolving under the dynamic nuclear formula, thesis-antithesis-synthesis, with my work following suit," he further admits he discovered the pattern retrospectively: "it emerged from the actual working-out of my life, and was born, after the fact, in the consciousness of inspired revelation." Noting that, prior to the publication of *The Masks of Drought*, "several readers [had] expressed concern that no synthesis was apparent" in his poetry (i.e., the vitally important third part of the dialectical triad was missing from his poetry and thus, presumably, from his life), Everson then tells us that with the publication of *The Masks of Drought* "these misgivings were more or less put to rest. With this book readers spoke of the quality of resolution, the vibration of wholeness, and even went so far as to proclaim it my best book and a true synthesis. I can't express the import of elation and relief these expressions occasioned for me."

Given Everson's lifelong struggles with the internal and external manifestations of his psyche's shadow-side and feminine principle; given the increasing debilitations he was suffering from Parkinson's Disease—as well as the tensions in his life his sexual impotence was causing him—before, during, and after he composed the poems of *The Masks of Drought*; given his lifelong pursuit to realize wholeness of Self, to realize the complete integration of the masculine with the feminine sides of his psyche, the complete integration of the spirit with the flesh; and given that he had determined the last volume of his life's trilogy would be the poetic expression and artistic embodiment of such integration, thus titled *The Integral Years*, it is no surprise he says in the "Preface" that "it devolves on *Masks* to assume the brunt of apotheosis."

Everson knew well that integration, synthesis, wholeness, apotheosis resulted from progressive movement toward the goal, and the arrangement of poems in a given volume could communicate progression—thematically, artistically, sexually, psychologically, spiritually. Indeed, arranged in the right order, according to the over-arching vision, the entire volume could convey a progression toward synthesis or apotheosis that the individual poems, read in the order of composition (especially important when studying Everson's psychological development), may not convey. Thus in "Moongate," the poem composed last of those in *Masks*, the poet envisions himself pursuing the "fox" of his vocation tirelessly, experiences once again his first wife falling away from him as he continues his pursuit, the first marriage subordinated to that pursuit, and yet an unknown feminine figure takes her place but follows him who follows the fox; she doesn't see what it is the poet pursues, but she follows nevertheless. Importantly, the poet stands between the male fox and the feminine principle, and it is a stretch to suggest such a tableau represents a "true synthesis." Indeed, Everson was mindful of how dearly his pursuit of vocation had cost him on the domestic front.

However one chooses to approach Everson's poetry, what becomes hugely apparent as one reads the trilogy is this: there has never been and is not now any poet, in any language, who has celebrated the power of the feminine as much, as complexly or as unabashedly, as William Everson. The celebration, furthermore, transcends time and personalities, as readers who are not limited by the restrictive thinking of so-called "political correctness" will come to see. The poetic celebration is not without tension or struggle, of course; one sensed struggle was inevitable early on in the poet's career when, in "In the Fictive Wish," Everson expressed his intensely determined desire to find "the woman within" himself in a "woman without." Indeed, he was on the lookout for her after betrayal had ended his first marriage, but he found more in Mary Fabilli than a woman willing to be malleably fashioned into the objective correlative of his "woman within"; he found through her a redefinition of his feminine side, as well as a formal religion.

No one who has studied carefully Everson's fascination with, attachment to, and love of the feminine should see irony in the fact that the poet was led by a woman into the monastic life of Brother Antoninus and then propelled out for the love of another woman. Even as Antoninus, the poet's celebration of the feminine principle continued; in fact, the celebration became most extreme, most tortured and most internalized, as we see in "Annul in Me My Manhood," wherein he pleads with God to make him "woman-sexed" if that is what it would take for God to enter his being and fill the emptiness he was suffering, and if "by that total transformation / I might know Thee more" (*VY* 113). No, it was not ironic when Everson / Antoninus realized vows of celibacy weren't right for him, fell in love with Rose Tannlund and then with Susanna Rickson, the latter to become his third wife.

What does seem sadly ironic is that one of Everson's final poems should be "Danse Macabre," wherein he recounts a recent dream in which he sees himself as he was in his "Waldport years," but then he— as he is forty years later—is confronted by the feminine principle of the dream: she's "hooded" but her face, he sees when she lifts it before him, is "a gaping skull, / Not bones dry from the tomb. / Rather, bluish white, glistening, tatters of flesh / Still clinging her jaws—butcher's bones / Housewives lug home for dog-gnaw"(171).

One must wonder if Everson knew Sherwood Anderson's "Death in the Woods," a story about just such a housewife, just such a type, whose sole purpose was to feed animal life. Even after her death in the woods, in the snow, her breasts exposed after her dogs rip her upper garments off her, she feeds animal life when a group of men and two boys gather around her frozen body, turn her over and stare at her breasts. In her bag had been just such "butcher's bones," which she carried home for her dogs.

In any case, after his life-long poetic celebration of the feminine, it seems as I said sadly ironic that Everson's unconscious would present him with the butchered face of the woman within: "She will not be put off," he tells us. Her unavoidable presence—regardless of what face she confronted him with over the years, what face he projected onto her— Antoninus discovered, as Everson had before the monastic years. Her power in his life would not be put off; she demanded his attention, demanded he celebrate her in his striving toward the knowledge and realization of the integral years he came to envision as comprising the last volume of his trilogy. Regardless of what face he envisioned the feminine essence with, he tells us in "Danse Macabre" that "I pull her to me"(172). Although the poems he wrote over a period of six decades exemplify time and again the truth of that utterance, this particular poem closes with Everson's apparent acknowledgment of and deference to an important fact: i.e., from the unsettling dream that presented him with the animatic but butchered face of the woman within, he tells us:

> I jerk awake.
> I am clasping the recumbent body of my wife.
> She is fast asleep, faced from me,
> And I press against her.
>
> Sensing arousal
> She stirs her hips, languidly, still deeply asleep,
> Too lost in the wonder of her own myth
> To waken to mine. (172)

The acknowledged fact, of course, is that the woman without has a life, a personal myth and quest independent of his, independent of his previously announced intention to conjoin—or, through projection, to fuse psychologically—the woman within and the woman without. No, Susanna's identity remained undeniably her own. She lay "faced from me," Everson notes, the prevalent face of the poem thus left belonging to the woman within.

PREFACE:
William Everson

This publication of *The Integral Years* brings to fulfillment the tri-form dialectic which I have long accepted as the defining principle governing my life-work saga, *The Crooked Lines of God*. That is to say, I have conceived of my life as evolving under the dynamic nuclear formula, thesis-antithesis-synthesis, with my work following suit. However, this time-worn dialectic did not, for me, originate in philosophical speculation. Rather, it emerged from the actual working-out of my life, and was born, after the fact, in the consciousness of an inspired revelation.

Of course, I was aware of the formula's prominence in the theories of both Hegel and Marx, whose energy made it famous. But it was the break-in-plane in normative consciousness that made it stick for me. My encounter with the awesome pantheism of Robinson Jeffers in 1934 when I was twenty-two broke the febrile agnosticism of my adolescence, and launched me out on the earth-bound thesis of *The Residual Years: Poems 1934-1948*, taking me through my first marriage and World War II. This period led after the war to my second marriage and terminated in my conversion to Catholicism and subsequent entry into the Dominican Order as Brother Antoninus, resulting in the God-fraught antithesis of *The Veritable Years: Poems 1949-1966*, a break-in-plane if there ever was one. Then came the final convolution, with my leaving the monastic life in 1969 to consummate my third marriage, instigating the composition of *The Integral Years: Poems 1966-1986* for synthesis.

When, therefore, in the prelims of *The Veritable Years*, I first made mention of the dialectic triad as the governing principle of my *Crooked Lines* saga, the first two sections of *The Integral Years* had been separately published, and several readers expressed concern that no synthesis was apparent, assuming that my break with the monastic life left me too preoccupied with guilt and remorse to rise to it. I myself had no doubt. *Tendril in the Mesh* (1973) was clearly a break-in-plane from *The Rose of Solitude*. It took erotic sensuality within a religious dimension to a new level, and *Man-Fate* carried my long-standing debate with the goodness of God into a new meld with Nature, setting me up for what was to follow.

But with *The Masks of Drought* these misgivings were more or less put to rest. With this book readers spoke of the quality of resolution, the vibration of wholeness, and even went so far as to proclaim it my best book and a true synthesis. I can't express the import of elation and relief these expressions occasioned for me. When I adopted the dialectic triad I had no premonition of its cumulative power. I thought of the three books as standing on an equal footing, with perhaps *The Veritable Years* getting the nod as the most exalted. But the reader response led me to reappraise the whole situation and I saw that apotheosis lies not in finality but in consummation, in synthesis. And it came to me with a shudder, the blindness of it all: the import of all those hours, all those years, the countless nights, the inordinate days, pushing poems into existence, word by word, with no map, no plan, no blueprint, not knowing what in fact was intended. I had begun *Masks of Drought* simply as another confessional sequence following *Man-Fate*, by which I charted my way through the changes in my life. There was no sense of impending climax. But regardless of this, since no blueprint exists for the whole of *The Crooked Lines of God*, this means it devolves on *Masks* to assume the brunt of apotheosis.

A staggering thought. For insofar as the work falls short of totality, the whole opus is diminished, leaving it for me to grimly conclude: the unconscious mind had better know what it's doing because the conscious one certainly does not. This should be no news to a life-long Dionysiac, but he had learned to depend upon his intuition for clearer signals as to what it was up to. But seriously, if on reflection, *Masks of Drought* indeed proves to be the moment of apotheosis for this life-saga (assurance at least that it was not contrived, but [that] the parts of the whole in their creative quietude found a measureless equipoise) then the same forces that precipitated its engendering will confirm its fitness in the wake of its consummation.

This leaves us with but one area to be discussed, if not explained. I mean the three "Poems of Occasion" to be found in this collection: "The City Does Not Die," "Melt Down the Guns," and "Blame It on the Jet Stream." I wrote a Foreword to the latter poem's first limited Lime Kiln Press edition, discussing the problem of writing "Occasional Poetry," and the reader is invited to peruse it where it serves as the Afterword to this volume.

Here the difficulty has to do with the poems overbearing their context: the book reads better without them. Overtly didactic, they draw on the splendid, if stilted, conventions of their ancient office. Unabashedly hortatory, they were written to be read aloud, declaimed on a public occasion, and fraught with urgent messages. In view of these prerequisites I cheerfully concede that the pieces are, judged by Modernist criteria, elaborately overwritten. People who have seen me through my period of Catholic religiosity and welcomed me back to the world of women and nature, argue for the suppression of these thunder-mugs from the Everson canon, as impedimental to its cause. They flout every tenet of the Modernist credo: didactic, hortatory, ostentatious, turgid.

On the other hand, these poems possess their own *raison d'etre*. They occurred in the normal working out of this poet's creative life and are plainly representative of it, ingrediential to the calling of a bard. In this final phase they serve the uses of synthesis by accommodating the element of public speech into my contribution. These are not my best poems, they are not even my best occasional poems. Clearly, my elegy to Jeffers is that. But neither do they compromise my aesthetic integrity. By genre they hold an ancient and honored place in the literary achievement of the race, and their witness will not be gainsaid.

—William Everson
October 19, 1991

THE INTEGRAL YEARS

1966-1994

BOOK ONE:

TENDRIL
IN THE MESH

(1966-1968)

TENDRIL IN THE MESH

to Susanna

PROLOGUE: The Terrible Torch

So the sea stands up to the shore, banging his chains,
Like a criminal beating his head on the slats of his cage,
Morosely shucking the onerous staves of his rage. And his custom
Of eyeing his plight, with malevolent fondness, never is done.
For he waits out the span of his sentence, but is undismayed;
He stands and expects, he attends
The rising up, the crest, the eventual slump of the sun.

For he bears in his groin his most precious jewel, the sacred fire
        of his crime,
Who pursued, like the beam of a laser, its solemn command,
Across the shires, red charts of his soul, the wrinkled map of his hand.
        And his heart,
Ridiculous, by someone denied, of a country preferment, never quits,
But clutches its need, like a duck. Somewhere his stain
Discolors the bride of defilement, whom rapine requested, under the form
        of his need,
A ventral oath. But parched without peace, a swollen defeat, the cunning
        sleep of the slain.

Pluto, regnant occultist, lord of the lorns of lost space, the serene
        distances fringing the skirts of the night,
Gleaming back from his visor the farthest, most tentative beam of the light,
Whom Kore constrained, with her hesitant breast, above his drooping
        narcissist plant,
To twine in her arms his loud male thong, his truncheon desire,
        and the flex and thrill of his chant.

She was bud. Daughter of Zeus, the Father, whose need Pluto was,
Of the incestuous darkness the daughter provokes in the sire,
When she comes of the blood; when a menstrual spurt, astart, pulses
        out of her loin,
And she quivers her sleeks, and exclaims, and her mother
Nods and denies, and watches her wander, bait for the god,

Believing it well; though she frowns, she smiles and sighs.

So pitiful Pluto, occultist betrayed, by the quince
Of a maid ensorcelled, daughter of god, of himself unable, succumbed
　　and was drawn,
From the cool of monastic deeps, the slats of his cage, where he beat
　　his brains,
Where he knelt in prayer, and shook the chains of his vows,
And clawed his breast in a rage. Persephone smiles,
The pomegranate seed in her pouch, her jewel of rape, and the stain
Of his lust on her lip. She measures his term. Cringing,
He sleeps on unappeased, in the hush of the solemnly slain.

Now sigh the plight of all sires, who groan in their sleep,
When their daughter, divested, glides by in a dream,
Alight with a mauve desire, as of spring,
When barley is born to the year. O sing
Of all sires, whose passion, Plutonic, gnarls in the heart
In the immemorial fashion
Of fathers, and groan of the unspeakable thing.

But fight through to the forcing. And, gasping, pull back to see
In the dream if the hymen is crisped on the violent cod like a ring
Of her lips, torn flower, salt-clung
Spoil of her triumph. But the aghast heart
Foretells in terror the shrink, the shy inexorable cower
Of the repulsed flesh. But an increase of need.
Oh my God the terrible torch of her power!

　　I

And it creams: from under her elbow a suffix of light, a sheen
　　of kept being,
What the gleam from along her arm prefigures of quest.
I sense over slopes a rondure of presence invoked.
In the small of the girl, where hips greet the waist,
A redolence lurks in the crease, a rift of repose.

And I take in a long loop of arm everything seascapes prefigure of dusk:
Sycamore-sweeps, the tableaux of massed chaparral, a rouse of rowans.
Let sea-licked winds wrap the inch of their roots with evening

There to compose what the chewn leaves of the tan oak pucker up
    on the tongue;
And there, like a wand, wonderment's long awakening, strong shaftings
    of light.

No, never. Not one shall survive. When two such as we are outlaunched
    on desire, neither one comes back.
We have staked out our bodies on mesas of glimmering vetch.
We have mapped territorial claims on plateaus ripe for inclusion.
Sentinels spring up alarmed: the guardians of places remote are alerted
    to cover our foray.

Scalptakers, yes. And have waited out eons of stealth to stalk our quarry.
Now our needs converge; we join in a scuffle of perns.
The nets and the spears of beaters off there in the dark enflank us.
When the cry of the hunter broke over the flesh we fled them afar.
We enmeshed our bodies in thickets, entoiled in the brush.

I am old as the prairies and wise as the seams of worn granite,
    but she is new burgeoned.
New as the minted tin, as sleek as the calmness of ivory engravers
    have tooled for emblems.
A girl like the glide of an eel, like the flex of a serpent startled.
But I catch her in throes of pulsation; we are wantoned in groves.

Crotch and thigh; she is reft. Let me break white flesh asunder
    to cock this woman.
In the glimmer of night a wedge of fern configures her croft.
Maidenhair snuggles the cleft. Its shadow conceals and defines.
When I dip my lips to drink of that spring I throat the torrent of life.

For passion subsumes: what is focused is fixed, denotes its spang
    of vector.
A long supple swell of belly prescinds from extinction.
When I reach above for the breasts my arm is a laser unleashed.
I have knifed through dooms that spelt long since the death
    of man's spirit.

I have fastened my heart on the stitch of your voice, little wince of delight
    in the thicket,
Where the slim trout flick like a glint of tin in the pesky shallows.
Salacity keels; our itch of an ardent desire consumes and engorges

my being.
I cannot look on your face; but my fingers start toward pockets of peace
    that lurk in your armpits.

Wild stallions of shuddering need squeal jumps of joy at your whistle.
I feel them snort in my ribs, they snuff for foods long bilked in their plea
    for existence.
Now they snook and are all transfigured in sudden aerial manœuvres.
They skip like gnats in the shafts, made mad of your moan.

Give me your nipples to lip and your ribs to caress,
Take down from your shoulders the silks that have baffled the sun.
But retain as your own the cordage of menacing loves,
Those fingers of others before me that seethed and passioned,
Those hungers you held in the crimp of your flesh,
    confounding possession.

For I sense the pungence of death alert in your loins, little woman:
All men in the past who have lain on the wand of your body.
Your belly is seeded with sperm, the slick of lovers cinctures your waist
    like the wake of snails.
I cannot expunge from your flesh what they wrought,
    or annul their passion.

But do not withhold from my gaze what from everyone else
    you concealed:
The remotest part of your heart that you kept immured like a jewel.
When I touch it to see in your eyes the sheerest expansion of terror,
To taste on your stretched out tongue as you die the tensile nerve
    of its anguish,
I know I have fastened the nail, I have quicked your core of existence.

For I am the actual. Telluric forces are groined in my being.
Uranian urgencies coil of their strengths in my soul's narrow passes.
Out of my sinews deep starts of hunger yield mixed epiphanies:
The snake that sleeps in the stones and comes forth out of winter;
The great cat of the mountain that stalks for fawns
    in the darkening barrows.

I am the grizzly that grapples his mate in his hug of sheerest survival,
The salmon that jells his milt on the clutch his woman has sown

in the gravel.
I am the river that breaks its back and pitches into the bay;
The osprey that jackknifes sidewise in surf to talon his quarry,

And I am the sea, its music, its instinct and whisper.
I encurl your rocks with my spill and embrace your shoulders.
In my estuary arms I entwine and enfold your thighs, I sleek
     your buttocks.
On my girth you toss like a chip to the crest of crude torrents.

When the great ships put out of port across my presence
Their seahorns chant me, sing mournful tones of presaging loss.

No ridge but the bone crest of power in the continent's nape.
A glaze of light is riddling the sheen of the wheat of Tehama.
Have the winds of Point Reyes, festooned with spindrift, declared
     anything other?
Do they glare for the spoil of the sun? Do they ache for the couches
     of night?

No bridge avails but the stretched out flesh of its coupling hunger.
Between the split of your thighs I plant spurts of voracious pleasure.
Not a hair of the nock that a woman widens anent the cob resists
     of a love.
On the nodes of transparent worlds we collapse, we pant and expire.

In all darks is my joy defined, that plaza, those nubian porches,
There my whole tongue turns in the col of your beating body.
In my hands of a man the sense is awake to mold idols of flesh for victims.
Plunged to the wrists I feel passion spurt through the instincts meshed
     in your nerves,
The peaks of clitoral quickness jetting spunk in a viscid issue.

You come back to be coaxed: I have caught you between the cheeks
     and will never be stinted.
Entwined in your thirst I tangle hair, the riatas of your desire.
In order to crest I snake angles of coupled completeness.
A flinch of fire, something struck from the meshes of passion,
     clusters my neck.*

---

* Stanza break.

Do not think to be stronger than death; to die is to drink desire.
To die is to take at the pitch of madness one fabled stroke of disinterest.
I have felt on those fields the light passion decreed, rived
    on sheer rapture.
When you moan and expire shrewd arrows of truth, shot through shields
    of zinc, pierce my belly.

Now I ken where suns have gone down when they quitted our country.
It is not as if they had nothing to gain in defaulting.
Rather with us for cause they seek stratas, new zones of extinction.
They annihilate zeros, total steeps to expunge; like us, they erase
    their condition.

Now my fingers conclude. They have founded whole sweeps
    of existence,
Have soaked up splendor in jets, have fed to the final.
No trace remains of what was; across the line of my life
Your breast pounds and proves; the sound of your heart extols
    its ancient surrender.

II

Man of God. Tall man, man of oath. Mad man of ignorant causes.
Like the mast of a ship, like the weathered spar of a schooner.
Long shank of a man, whose hair is all whetted with frost, and a nick
    of silver.
What inch of enactment cinctured your loins and is freed?
I can feel in my knees the scruff of time's thrust as you take me.

Finger of God! A stipple of terror shudders my skin when you touch me!
Who are you? In your eyes is the passion of John the Baptist
    and the folly of Christ!
Do not drop me! I have never been known of man, really,
    before you possessed me!
By all men, of any, who have bruised and straightened my body,
The marks of their hands are erased of your lips. I never knew them!

Now teach me your deeps! Prophet and utterer of godly
    imponderable oaths, great prayers of anguish.
Guru of my bed, who have taught me koans of revealment.
Adept of niches and slots, my woman's being convulses in truth

for your entry!
When your hands work marvels I fear I will die, will faint in your swells
    of compression.

Let rivers that run to the sea be my attestation.
You took me on Tamalpais, in the leaf, under Steep Ravine redwoods.
The bark of trees was broken to tear and divest me.
On the brow of the hill that brinks its base you thrusted me up
    to your God.

Beast and Christian! What manner of dog do you worship for Christ
    that you must rend and devour!
I have felt in my womb the index of Him you call God.
Do you wasten life that my flesh and my bone should be wholly
    consumed of your spirit?
What is His face if the eyes you blaze are the tusks of carnivores?

I have no defenses against your truth and desire none.
Make me a Christian, then do what you want with this dross,
For a strange pale fury that cannot be natural consumes me.
I blink back tears of relief to feel in your hands the awe of Him you adore.
Is your vow of a monk meant to serve for the seal of your lust?

For your lust of a monk is a hunger of all God's seekers.
In my nerve's raw marrow I feel Him teach me His witness.
Let me go! But do not desert what you chose to instruct.
If I cannot reckon what unstrings my knees what worth is survival?

Let me go! No, but breach my belly with godly unspeakable anguish!
This split of thighs you desire is more than my means.
Your face is flensed with an awesome devouring passion.
In the flukes of contortion I fear what I see as I need it.
My body is written with poems your fingers enscrolled on my flesh.

Let no woman survive me, old man, mad man of the mountain,
Wily old buck of the benches and bull elk of somnolent mesas.
Monk of the seashore and friar of granite enclosures,
The mad holy man who spread my legs for entry.
On the sill of a cloistered withdrawal my flesh is empaled on your spirit!*

---

* Stanza and section break.

III

And the storm swings in from the sea with a smashing of floats.
There are hulks on the rocks where wrecks broke splintering up
    under waves.
A kindling-making wind is tearing out scrub on the jaw of the hill,
And the encompassed bay where fishermen loafed is found a cauldron
    of spume.

Let it blow! Now a wild rejoicing of heart springs up in answer!
After summer's stultification what more can penetrate deadness?
The nerves that have slept for so long in the simmering flesh,
    complacent with languor,
Awaken to swing their stutter of fright at the crash of billows.

And those casual loves are swept out. Only a troth as stark as the tooth,
Elemental and sheer as the hurricane's whetstone incisor;
Only a love as clenched as the jaw of the cougar,
When the passion-responders grope for each other under the pelt
    of the storm.

They will find in the rain what can match the spatter of hail on a house.
They will know where to slake when the trees break free of what heaps
    at their knees.

And they moan. Couched on beach-grass under shelter of drift
They hug each other. They watch with the zeal of love
    the hurricane's howl.
With one eye bent to the weather they see the light on the head
    at Point Reyes
Hum like an axehead held to the stone, the sparks a spurt
    shooting leeward.

Now crawl to me shivering with love and dripping with rain,
Crawl into my arms and smother my mouth with wet kisses.
Like a little green frog slit the cleft of your thighs athwart me.
The rain on your face is the seed of the stallion strewn as it spits blue fire.

For the lightning forks like one naked the seething thud of the sea.
And swells like a woman's in birth when she heaves up her belly.
She has braced her heels on the land; her beaches are benched
    to that passion,

And her crotch is the hollow, sunk low under wind-heap waves,
    when its back breaks over.

She is fouled of bad weather but never of love, this woman.
In her blood the groan and travail of a birth is being fashioned.
Her spilth like the gasp of stallions clings round her ankles.
And her vulva tilts thwart the wind's wide lip when he whistles his force
    through her body.

Now crawl to me under this driftwood hutch and cower upon me.
Warm the stitch of rain in the drench of passion and forget
    to be frightened.
But build in your womb's young realm the germ of your mother the sea.
For to be found in this labor sunk under a shelf she was nothing loath
    of her mating.

Oh splendor of storm and breathing! O woman! O voice of desire!
Tall power of terminal heights where the rain-whitened peaks glisten wet!
But the heave of slow-falling sleep will follow outpouring
    in winter's wake.
This too is your meed when passion is flashed for blood
    in the typhoon's crater.

Now sleep in my arms, little newt, little mite of the water,
Little wind-beaten frog, pale delicate limper alone on sea-pulled pebbles.
Go to sleep and awaken in spring when your blood requickens.
And bear back to man in your flesh the subtle sign of him
    who marked you for God!

IV

Daughter of earth and child of the wave be appeased,
Who have granted fulfillment and fed the flesh in the spirit.
A murmur of memory, a feint of infrequent espousals,
And the tug of repose the heart hovers and tilts toward dawn.

Somewhere your body relinquishes creeds of defiance.
I have tasted salt salience, and savored its fragrance,
    have crested repose. [*]

---

[*] No stanza break.

Now appeasement crouches and wends its way through my being.
I sense fulfillment not breached of strings and torches.

Kore! Daughter of dawn! Persephone! Maiden of twilight!
Sucked down into Pluto's unsearchable night for your husband.
I see you depart, bearing the pomegranate seed in your groin.
In the node of your flesh you drip my flake of bestowal.

What will you do, back on earth, when you find your mother?
Will the trace of dark lips fade out of your flesh forever?
I have knocked your instep with rapture, I have wounded your flank.
Like the little fish in the dredger's boat you bear the teeth of the gaff.

O daughter of God! When the sons of man covet your passion,
Do not forget who placed on your brow his scarab
        of sovereign possession.
In the service of holy desire bear truth for escutcheon.
And when you return to the roost of night wear the mane of the sun!

        EPILOGUE: Hymn to the Cosmic Christ

Dark God of Eros, Christ of the buried brood,
Stone-channeled beast of ecstasy and fire,
The angelic wisdom in the serpentine desire,
Fang hidden in the flesh's velvet hood
Riddling with delight its visionary good.

Dark God of Eros, Christ of the inching beam,
Groping toward midnight in a flinch of birth,
The mystic properties of womb and earth:
Conceived in semblance of a fiercer dream,
Scorning the instances of things that merely seem.

Torch of the sensual tinder, cry of mind,
A thirst for surcease and a pang of joy,
The power coiled beneath the spirit's cloy,
A current buckling through the sunken mind,
A dark descent inventive of a god gone blind.

The rash of childhood and the purl of youth
Batten on phantoms that once gulled the soul,

Nor contravened the glibness in the role.
But the goad of God pursues, the relentless tooth
Thrills through the bone the objurgation of its truth.

Often the senses trace that simmering sound,
As one, ear pressed to earth, detects the tone
Midway between a whisper and a moan,
That madness makes when its true mode is found,
And all its incremental chaos runs to ground.

Hoarse in the seam of granite groans the oak,
Cold in the vein of basalt whines the seed,
Indemnify the instinct in the need.
The force that stuttered till the stone awoke
Compounds its fluent power, shudders the sudden stroke.

Dark Eros of the soul, Christ of the startled flesh,
Drill through my veins and strengthen me to feed
On the red rapture of thy tongueless need.
Evince in me the tendril in the mesh,
The faultless nerve that quickens paradise afresh.

Call to me Christ, sound in my twittering blood,
Nor suffer me to scamp what I should know
Of the being's unsubduable will to grow.
Do thou invest the passion in the flood
And keep inviolate what thou created good!

回 回

BOOK TWO:

THE SECULAR CITY

(1969, 1973)

THE CITY DOES NOT DIE

At the Dawn of the Aquarian Age

> *Dedicated to Joseph Alioto, Mayor of San Francisco,*
> *and Read Out by the Poet, at the Dawn Ceremonies*
> *Commemorating the San Francisco Earthquake,*
> *The Civic Center, April 18, 1969.*

Tense night: the taut air
Hung on the houses. From the oaks the screech-owls
Gasped and quavered in the stifling dark.
When the tomcats, in the April madness of mating,
Cried out their fierce climaxes, their screams
Tore through the silence like a wrenched violin.
All night long in the fire stations the great horses
Stamped and snorted, whinnying out of a blind
Apprehension, neighing and champing,
Rearing in the close stalls. On arid beds
Men and women threw off their night clothes
And flung themselves together, furiously,
Emitting from the convulsive loins and the strained torsos
The fierce impacted discharge of nature.
All over the city that sultry dawn
The oppressive tenseness gripped and tightened.
Moment by moment the elements, cramped in titanic impasse,
Relentlessly contracted: the inexorable
Dictum of the wedge.

          For deep in the earth the long rift,
The slip and shuff of vast geological epochs,
Fractures the coast. Like a cracked bell
It hangs athwart the hemispheric verge,
Fluxed with transition. Whatever the stroke,
Whether the trampling somber-thudded Pacific,
Or the oppressively pendent bosom of the air,
Each exacts of that ancient injury
The resonance of pain. Then the vaster tide,
The throb from outer space,
Sends through the whole mould of its metal
The clangor of the spheres. Twice,
Perhaps thrice in a century, these forces converge,

Shape for crescendo. When the great eccentric
Moves toward its maximum, the high clapper poises.
Then the coast hunches like a harelipped giant
Under the scorning gaze of his master.
Seizing the bellrope he readies his charnel syllable
And stoops to toll.

                         For the heavens too,
That amazed morning, hung like a bell.
From Uranus the Hammerer peaked at midheaven
To the solvence of Neptune swimming under the deep nadir,
Every planet in the sky was strung down the east,
Cupped in titanic interlock. Then the moon, overtaking them,
Plunged forward, a ruthless resounding stroke.
The solar energy, stored in the moon's belly,
Projected itself through the nerves of the system,
And the wrenched bell rang.

                         And deep in the earth
The fractured jaws of basalt and granite
Ached in response; they gnashed and gritted.
Like the teeth of the giant in nightmare,
When he dreams, near daybreak, suffering again
The images of his ancient guilt and his starved desire,
They ground together. If rock could know pain, if earth
Had the nerves of a stallion and the sex of a woman in love,
This passion could pour, interfuse,
Vibrate up the levels of being, transmute into life.
But the terrible break in the stone jaws, tectonic,
Like a compound fracture in the giant bone,
Could only, under the seismic stroke, mangle and tear.
Goaded, the earth-giant, seizing his bell-rope,
Howled his mortal anguish, and hauled down.

And the city reels. On Russian Hill the most proud mansions
Convulse in a narcissistic righteousness
Before they succumb. Their columnar limbs,
In an unreal marmoreal ecstasy,
Buckle, then slump. Like noblewomen
Flung down under the knees of marauders,

They stoop for violation and, enduring it, die.

While below them, infamous and unlovely,
The Barbary Coast, secret adept of lechery and murder,
Feels through the soles of her dancing slippers
That weird vibration. Made suddenly aware
She shivers: then the fact screams home,
The long arpeggio of terror
Rips her throat. Her sallow body
Cringes like a whore when her pimp fists her,
And she hits the street.

                         But surrounding them,
Rooted in the subsoil of envy and disdain,
The immense insouciant populace
Starts wide awake, bolt upright in bed,
Like a householder touched by a thief's hand.
Then everything they own comes down round their heads.
Spilled out on the floor they sprawl into the streets,
Hardly knowing how, and wait for the worst.

And the worst comes. In a trice, in an instant,
In the long wail of a brittle minute
It is over and done. Men and women
Crawl out of the rubble to face flame. What earthquake spares
Dynamite will topple. Fire eats all.

       ▣

Now, today, the same day later by sixty-three years,
To the hour and the minute, under the threat of dire prediction,
We gather together, here on the broad steps of this hall,
Witnessing our faith in our city and ourselves.
We are not disquiet. Below us earth sleeps;
The cracked-bone giant dreams easily now,
Untroubled by nightmare. Out there on the Bay
The April mist walks the slow waters.
Under the stone slabs of the streets

The deep streams nourish the sea.

And the heavens, too, are serene. Far out in space
The planets, grouped in a beautiful isosceles,
Temper the time. No quadrature threatens,
Not even an opposition bisects the Wheel.
The moon, freed from syzygy, is off and away.
There is no more symmetrical configuration
In the gamut of heaven.

                              I too have studied the stars,
And in some measure live by them. Whoever is alert
Knows he walks in the web of a vast relatedness.
Whether it be hills and houses or planets and people,
All things keep concourse. Existence
Presupposes polarity: it is polarity that governs all.
Night and Day, the Microcosm and the Macrocosm, the Self
        and the Other,
All the opposites converge and relate, move on,
Redisposing themselves eternally, commingling and separating,
To again converge. There is one place of peace, and only one:
To live at the heart of things, at the still center,
The eye of the hurricane. To look in the answering
Eye of the cosmos, and contain the opposites.

I too have studied the stars, and I do not fear them.
I am born under Pluto, how then should I fear Pluto?
If Pluto has power the power of Pluto is mine.

And if I am born with Uranus violent in the Fifth,
The mansion of the creative heart,
Then the force of Uranus is my inner measure,
And this poem is his praise.

                              Therefore do I say:
Any astrologer who uses the prestige of his ancient art
To confuse the people, who panics them with omens
And alarms them with predictions,
Filling fear in their hearts, the tock of blind terror;
Who freezes them with prophecy, rendering them
Painfully incapable of choice,
Who uproots their lives and sends them

Stumbling out of the State, mannequins of the doom they flee,
Such a one, such a man, is not worthy the name
Of his ancient calling.

Such are the things we have seen in these days.

In Jerusalem, the city of God,
There was no venality held in abhorrence
Like the mischief of the false prophet.
For the higher the calling the greater the trust,
And since Biblical times
The calling of prophet is the highest calling.

But we have seen in these days that calling profaned.
We have seen it given over to vanity and folly.

All the vision in the world,
Without conscience,
Is sheer illusion.
And all the awareness in the world,
Without humility,
Is a deceit and a pretense.

Therefore it was well known in Holy Jerusalem
That there was no mischief
Like unto the mischief wrought by the false prophet.

But today they are honored. Out of the very
Mouths of their foolishness, they are honored.
They multiply lies and are believed;
They spew forth visions and are begged for more visions.

Such are the things we have seen in these days.

But if the stars alarm they also reassure.
And if they presage pain they also presage peace.
And which of these is the greater?

Which is easier to say:
"Woe! Woe! Flee the doomed city!"*

---

* No stanza break.

Or: "Peace be with you.
The evil of the day is sufficient thereof"?

Let us hold rather with Emerson:
"No questions are unanswerable. We must trust
The perfection of creation so far as to believe
That whatever curiosity the order of things has awakened in our minds
The order of things can satisfy.... Let us interrogate
The great apparition that shines so peacefully around us."

Oh, and the dawn comes up in its moment of signal rebirth.
That reawakening, so pure and spontaneous, goes on within our flesh.
We are its hieroglyphs, icons of its awareness.
Let us interrogate, then, the great apparition
That shines so peacefully around us,
And be sure that its message,
All it is trying to teach,
Is purely one of creative release
From the grip of travail.

And if our city be once again shaken
We will bury our dead, mutely,
In tears, slaking the darkness of death,
The grief of all going.

But we will reach to the roots,
And out of this rock
Resurrect the deep spirit.
We will lift these lintels up out of grit.
We have done it before.

We will make a new marvel,
Refashion these forms,
Wrest from raw rubble more salient shapes.
The world will wonder,
Thinking our zeal more singular
Than the smashed forms of our pride.

And having done it we will look,
And ourselves behold, and ourselves wonder,
Having no more regrets,
Who have learned again

(Having learned it well of the first falling)
That the brute convulsions of nature
Are the pure opportunities of man.

And if our city slides under the sea,
As their claim decrees, as their hope precludes,
If our city sinks and is gone,
We will build a better, over there on the east-lurking shore,
Where a prouder peninsula, shaped of the indwelling waters,
Will hump like a shoaled whale, make a mightier harbor,
A port to tender the fleets of the world.
We will build anew and more boldly,
Take Mount Diablo for Twin Peaks,
Take the Straits of Carquinez, a more Golden Gate,
Watch our old familiar sea-lions
Swim their foam-figured sarabandes
Over the sunken quays of Stockton,
And reckon the home-returning salmon,
Pouring in forever from the withers of the sea,
As they streak the salt tide from Red Bluff to the Tehachapi—
And when we will have named it, that rippling
Mist-conditioned bay-beside-the-sierra,
When we will have tamed it,
Lacing its girth with forty-mile bridges,
We will finish that founding.
We will plant the brilliance of Berkeley
In the lap of the Mother Lode.

And if indeed we die, as they claim we are to,
At least we will die in the place where we were happy.
For to die in the place of one's happiness
Is the last blessing of life.

And here we are happy.

Therefore do I salute the dawn,
This sixty-third day of ominous disaster,
As the pale morning light,
Groping distantly out of the east,
Sifts on the sidewalks of San Francisco.

And I will walk where the lovers walk in the city,

And take their hands, and over the tables
Eat the fabulous food of this town,
Drink Napa wine, and salute my love.

And wherever I must go
In the way that life takes me,
Will come back again,
Through the teeth of all doubt,
To the city of my delight.

For it is here that I have lain with my loves
And found my God.

Here where the saint called Francis,
Prophet of joy, looks over his own,
And smiles a quickening recompense
For the instant of our rebirth.

And gives us his peace.

Here where the dawn gropes distantly
On the whiteness of the city.
And darkness drops in the sea.

MELT DOWN THE GUNS

To Beniamino Bufano, whose sculpture
"Saint Francis of the Guns," cast of metal
from firearms turned in by the citizens
of San Francisco in answer to their Mayor's appeal,
was dedicated at an Ecumenical Mass celebrated
on the steps of the City Hall, June 6, 1969.

Melt down the guns. Our need of them is over,
They make the carrion that was our brother,
Render the corpse that is our most impassioned lover.

We know them well enough now, what they mean,
Dark persuaders of the mordant spleen,
Wakeful and unweary. For them the vultures preen.

Melt down the guns. Because there is time still
To place our ruthlessness beyond our will,
Deny our hatred its capacity to kill.

Who troubles now to scorn the impious talk
With which our pilgrim churchmen schooled their flock:
"The gun, God-given, is holier than the tomahawk."

But still the ethos of that grim frontier
Precipitates its savage presence here,
Shaping our anger from its incremental fear.

Deathless as myth, infatuate and sweet,
Provocative as gunsmoke and more fleet,
It undulates about the entranced assassin's feet.

Lee Harvey Oswald, Sirhan, James Earl Ray,
Each lived it in his own obsessive way,
Confirmed its brutalizing pathos for our day.

Deep in our blood the gaunt gunslinger walks
Between bleak storefronts or past blistered rocks,
Gripped by the moment of untruth in which he stalks.

Time's renegade still haunts our fitful sleep,

Remorseless as the tears we cannot weep,
And stokes this dreadful dream, omnivorous and deep.

Wading a wind of tumult and desire,
The torsion of our elemental ire,
He crouches, turns to draw, aims low, and coolly fires.

Breaking the chamber of his smoking gun
He thumbs the blunted bullets one by one,
And stares incognizantly down at what is done.

He is ourself. Deep in Death Row we wait,
Fondling our phallic dream of innocence and hate:
The bed, the murdered love, the smoking thirty-eight.

Melt down the guns. Theirs is no truth to trust.
That power they hold is subject to our lust;
Their naked force subserves our fury for the dust.

Who can assume he knows himself so well?
Crazed by some mania we cannot foretell,
Each one of us may whirl, pull trigger, blast to hell.

All men are culpable. A massive hate,
A rage too red, too scalding to abate,
Whips the rapacious heart upon its plunging fate.

One nerve twitched by some dark secretive gland
Yields to the feeblest mind, the fondest hand,
The elemental power to kill, possess, command.

Melt down the guns. Take from our side the means,
Ere that obsessive malice intervenes
Between our reason and the goodness it esteems.

◻

Foregathered here we plead the nobler part,
Implicit in the sculptor's crucial heart,

The transmutation of our violence in art.

Can such a hope, improbable and faint,
Denature this rank metal of its taint,
Subsume our passion in the image of the Saint?

Melt down the guns. God's silence is the seed.
The Spirit bates its agonizing need
Till Christ, uncrucified, no longer kneels to bleed.

◧ ◨

BLAME IT ON THE JET STREAM

Ode: The First Commencement, June 17, 1973,
Kresge College, The University of California at Santa Cruz.

Remember it as the wildest winter.
Never in the memory of the oldest man,
Nor yet in the recorded history of these hills,
Has water run, has rain so fallen,
As the long rain ran in the winter of Seventy-three.

It began in October. Then hard frosts bit,
Blighting late crops. But November saw storms, fierce,
    pelting down trees,
And by Christmas, in the rain's renewal, the great salmon run
Battled its immemorial way up the creeks. Yet February
Kept everything in flood, rain falling hour by hour, day on day,
So that the steelhead pack hung back at sea,
No spawning beds left in those scarred creeks,
No sandbar shallows nor gravel flats to lay down their roe—
All angry, boiling, storm-shot water, the run-off of monsoons.

In the nights you heard stricken redwoods
Topple athwart the gouged-out creeks,
Fall sprawled and disheveled under the rain,
The columnar nudity of slain tritons.
You heard, too, the rockslides plough down the mountains,
The saturated canyon walls letting go their grip:
Boulders, hung high, balanced you'd think since the nub of time,
And set to hang forever—but not this year.
This is the year of their getaway. Inching forward and down
Through the long weeks of wetness, firm earth
Transforming to mud, till utterly without warning
All collapses, rock-chunk half the size of a house
Takes everything before it: tan-oak, madrone, the wide-rooted laurel.
Lying abed in the thick of the nights
You heard the clash—rock on rock like a fracturing of bones,
The splintering shins of giants. Or driving the pitch-black darkness
You brake desperately—your car hangs over a yawning gulf
That very afternoon you traversed as firm road.
Getting shakily out you stand by the car

Gazing into space, seeing your headlights probing blank night.
Far down below the sullen creek growls on,
Washing through blackness. Rain streaming your face
You hear segments of granite knocking together.
They chip and splinter. Bit by bit the ankles of mountains
Flake to the sea.

               Sometimes far rockslides
Block back creeks. When the freshet hushes
Know water is checked, trouble coming.
Where rapids roared hangs an ominous silence.
Five hours later all breaks over. The wall of water,
Bursting down course, takes fences, phone-poles, bridges, homesites.
Roofs of cabins and the beams of barns
Ride out to sea with a crazy sedateness.
The sea gobbles them. They break up in surf.
Wreckage litters the beach. Far into summer
Lovers will lie by driftwood embers,
The sills of smashed homes, vestiges of disaster
Warming their flesh. But in the storm-glut
No beach-fire and no rest. Wet to the bone
Lovers shiver through sodden grass,
Searching out any dry place to bed down.
The swollen mouths of creeks
Stick angry tongues through lips of cut stone.
All the rivers of the Santa Cruz coast:
The Pajaro, Soquel, Rodeo Gulch, the San Lorenzo,
Yellow Bank, the San Vicente, Big Creek and Scott Creek,
The Waddell—awash and pounding in the spill of centuries.

A season of excesses. "Blame it on the jet stream,"
Grinned the weatherman, "the high east-running current of air
Circling the globe." Veering south this year
It drenched California, left dry the Northwest.
When spring broke at last
The hills flushed green with a mass of new growth,
Every seed, lying dormant for decades,
Quickened into life by the saturating rain,
Aching up to the sun—foxtail, fiddleneck,
Wild oat, dock, plantain and thistle: every blade that bends

Thirsting for light.

                Now the sun rides high: summer
Looms on the land, all the flaunting, green-growing grasses
Suddenly burned brown, the shimmering slopes scorched pale yellow.
It is the solstice of the year, the very summit.
Within this week the sun crests and starts down.
And it is yours. It is your moment.
The storms of this birth have shuddered and passed away.
Something for you is peaking now.
The cycle of your learning has soared to zenith, and your sun
Glides on to new spaces.

                Go out now and climb.
Fight through to another solstice, the ridgepole of your life.
Go out now into the eventual experience,
The future for which you have passionately striven,
And soon now must become the past,
The shimmering distance of the farther future
Fleeting before it, to be sealed
Where all ultimate things are immured.

                Go up to the skyline.
Go with the pulse of that joy, the pang of your sorrow.
Go with the cool clarification of thought, the mind's baptism.
Go in the recklessness of your burgeoning blood,
Children even now alert in your loins, aching for birth—
Man and woman, already destined though not yet known, mate for mate.
Re-enter the womb of time, the belly of the future.
Go find what your fathers have sought and not found.
Go to the immolation of self, to the terrible testing, the annealing of fire.
Go on to the pain, the long psychic anguish all consciousness is.
Go in the involution of desire—the ecstasy of the flesh and the rapture
    of the spirit.
Go on to the insecurity, the never-really-knowing,
    the never-really-quite-believing.
Go on to the lovelessness, the emptiness all spent experience
    inexorably exacts:
The provocations and the betrayals, the crude seductions
    and the cheap denials.
Go into the open, the empty space where no help is,
    nor no friend survives,

And nothing avails you but your faith.

Go on into God.

But whatever you do, never fail the great premises:
Do not fail hope or hope will fail you.
Do not fail courage or courage will fail you.
Do not fail love or love will fail you.

But know that though you fail all things—
Fail hope, fail courage, fail desire, fail love—
And having failed all things seen all things fail you—
Know that truth, the irreducible truth, never will fail you.

For truth is the actual God,
And Fate His slow methodology.

All in the long day's running and the hot year's ascension.
All in the turbulence of desire and the rage of achievement.
All in the tremulousness of night and the stars' grave serenity.

You have asked me: what is meant by this strange Rite of Passage?
What does it signify? What does it promise?

And I say to you: up to this point
Each generation lives for itself,
Hovering between the sensuous and the ideal.
Sustained in a kind of trance-like embrace
The unity of its youth wholly involves it,
Renders it singularly impervious to the onslaught of time.

But beyond this point,
Each generation lives for the next.
Something possesses it,
Breaks its revery of self and compels it to serve.
Suddenly released, its separate individuals scatter into life,
Counting themselves as nothing
To secure for the future
What the present lacks.

And in your heart of hearts
Seek out the delicate prism of consciousness

You were each meant to serve.

Seek it through learning:
The inculcation of knowledge
Against the reductive brutality of fact.

Seek it through science:
The specification of phenomena
Rescued from the blur of contingency.

Seek it through law:
The organization of value
In the implementation of collective choice.

Seek it through art:
The projection of the possible
In the exigence of aesthetic form.

But however it is sought—
Through science, through learning, through law, through art—
No matter what the way or however the means,
Consciousness is the crux.

Unless man knows, and believes;
Unless man perceives, and acknowledges;
Unless man realizes, and assents:
The science, the learning, the law, the art
Pass like clouds, are gone beyond redemption.

For consciousness is the mind's awareness,
And perception is the spirit's gaze.
The presence of neither can be verified statistically,
Nor can the incidence of success measure their degree.

Look to success, if you will, for the spur to aspiration,
But never look to it for the spur to perception.
That, more likely, you will find in the guts of disenchantment.

Nothing deceives us like that which we crave,
And nothing chastens like that which we despise.

For the American, success and failure are polar opposites:

There is no middle ground.
He is crucified between his blessing and his curse.

William James, that dissector of our ills, deplored "the moral flabbiness,
Born of the exclusive worship of the Bitch-Goddess Success...
Our national disease."

And Melville before him, wrestling with the same penchant:
"Failure is the true test of greatness.
Unless a man somewhere fails, that man cannot be great...."

What to make of this paradox?
This obversion of our deepest values
By our deepest minds?

It is the contradiction that has riddled us.
A glittering success, carried to the point of perversion,
Has been our nemesis. Watergate
Is our Waterloo.

Somehow we must find the point of elevation,
Lift ourselves out of the intensity of involvement
Blinding us to fate.

Somehow we must cast ourselves upon a higher principle,
Transcend the compulsion, achieve
Deliverance from the bleak obsession goading us on.

For the long course of things is really out of our hands.
Destiny, the methodology of God, has us in keeping,
And the wisdom of religion never fails to remind
That what befell us as curse completes us as blessing.

Therefore I say to you:
Blame it on the jet stream!
The fateful overriding processes that shape the human scope.

Blame it on the jet stream!

The long litany of calamity and woe
Afflicting man's spirit, badgered between
Compulsion within and coercion without,

The tumult of desire and the nerve's raw dread
Contesting for supremacy.

Blame it on the jet stream!

"The wind that bloweth where it listeth,
And thou hearest the sound thereof,
But canst not tell whence it cometh and whither it goeth;
So is everyone that is born of the Spirit."

Blame it on the jet stream!

But retain as your own the inner awareness,
The sacred consciousness to reckon what comes,
Be it of good or be it of evil,
And through an act of perfect comprehension
Make it shine pure.

Only then can your blame become praise.

For that blame is holy, is the very threshold of praise,
Your profound attestation, verifying whatever ensues—
Dropping from above, upwelling from below,
Rising in the East, descending with the West,
Burning on the South, binding at the North—whatever ensues
Reveals the dark face of God.

Then, out of your soul's deep source, its still center,
Thirsting to know, gazing about you
In wonder and awe at the passage of life—
After the exhaustion of appetite in the purgation of pain;
After illusion on illusion have succeeded each other in the long scenario
        of self-deceit;
After success has fouled your face and failure licked it clean—

                                                        Then,
Throwing all to the winds, gather up the witness of those wounds
And quench your thirst in your God!

BOOK THREE:

CDAN-FATE

(1969-1972)

1: RITE OF PASSAGE

EBB AT EVENING

Tide-turn: and the surf
Swept back from the shore,
Crouched shuddering on its flat mat,
Unable to rise.

When the tide
Hunkers low like this on squat hams
Everything bates breath.

It is the solstice, the hip of the year
Bent double, the body of earth
Clenched for passage, time's
Ancient art, the deep
Rite of renewal.

In the evening ebb, as the sun
Wallows under a skirt of cloud and flares low,
Many people come forth to traverse the beach,
Seeking shells, stones, strange fragments of drift,
Seed of the lost fecundity
Borne back to their lives.

Now the sun is gone.

But the cloud
Defers, sidling offshore. For a moment
The beach, in the oblique
Bifurcation of dusk, confronts the west,
Immense and abstract, a massive slab.

The neap tide turns.

And the dark
Drops.

And the sea,
An awakening woman,

Simultaneously rising and turning, impulse
Groined in the ripple of immense repose,
The sea
Stands up in her bed and stares.

MAN-FATE

Susanna: girl and bride,
You sleep in the adjoining room,
And I sense the sea, at solstice,
Tide-turn, pivot and close in.

This turning of my life,
Like the long withdrawing wave,
Checks, wheels, steps forward.

And what was sucking fast underfoot,
The rustle of sea-pulled pebbles,
Swings back and resurges.

The fate of man
Turns on the body of woman.
She takes the long advance
And the long recession.
By what she is
She defines them.

In the dusk,
In the adjacent room,
I hear your body
Stir in its berth.

The moan you make
Is a murmur of seabirds.
It marks the turning of the day.

The tide turns.
The season turns.
The year turns.

And life
Curls on the node of its solemn disclosure,
And gropes renewal.

SEED

Some seed in me,
Some troublous birth,
Like an awkward awakening,
Stirs into life.

Terrible and instinctive
It touches my guts.

I fear and resist it,
Crouch down on my norms, a man's
Patent assurances.

I do not know its nature.
I have no term for it.
I cannot see its shape.

But there, inscrutable,
Just underground,
Is the long-avoided latency.

Like the mushrooms in the oakwood,
Where the high-sloped mountain
Benches the sea,

When the faint rains of November
Damp down the duff,
Wakening their spores—

Like them,
Gross, thick and compelling,
What I fear and desire
Pokes up its head.

◙ ◙

THE GAUGE

Time is the gauger of all things,
And the solver of all things.

Wrapped in its breast
The nature of consequence
Peaks and divulges.

Only in consequence
Is implication verified.

Only in time
Is implication, consequence,
Actualized.

In my span of existence
I touch with new hands
Its wake of passage.

Out of its belly,
Time's opulent womb,
The nature of the actual
Quickens, is born.

Susanna, I hear your body
Turn in the dusk; the great
Languor of life
Broods on the shadowy lids of your eyes,
Where you sigh,
Where you sleep.

Howler of gulfs and sunken undredgeable deeps,
Time flows, curls over your body, as a wave
Cups stone on the bench of this sea,
And restores me, the God-blunted man,
To my measure.

SOCKET OF CONSEQUENCE

On Stinson Beach, long spit of sand scything the sea,
A clutter of beach homes and summer cottages
Sprawls beneath the wind's pelt.
A few shore pines and cypresses protect from the gales
The love nests, the hippy pads and the homosexual lairs.
And we, among them and of them,
A fugitive monk and an unwed mother,
Making love in the solstice weather,
Thread time's needle eye,
Clasp in a welter of conclusive rapture.
Blow out of the Pacific,
The vast waters beyond the Farallones,
O wind of the solstice and the knuckle of the year!
Within your arms I embrace the twin facts of love and death:
Death of the past, the love
Of future and the life, one rapture that abides.
Under us the perdurable sand,
That shifts and washes and remains forever,
Gift of the sea, gift of the wind's
Somber indirection, and the vane of time,
Changing, changing on its hub,
Spelling out of the socket of consequence
Its terror and its truth.

▣ ▣

IN THE FULNESS OF TIME*

What is it to be God's elect? It is to be denied in youth
the wishes of youth, so as with great pains to get them
fulfilled in old age.

—Kierkegaård

The child cries out. Getting up in the dark
You nurse softly, with infinite
Evocative tenderness, and quietly return.
Through half-slitted eyes I watch from the bed,
Awaiting the nudge of your flexed body
Settling by my side.

              In the doorway you pause.
Looking strangely back you linger,
Caught there, trembling between the crib of the child
And the bed of the man.

              You are nude. As you gaze
Your girl's body tilts on its axis of repose,
The lithe waist, the taut belly and the narrow thighs;
But above them those drooped, apple-ripe, youthfully maternal breasts
Alive in the night.

              What can name the mystery,
The blood-grace that hovers you?
A power tore me out of the shut monastic mold
At the peak of life and then, almost indifferently,
Threw down my pride.

              I gaze on you covertly, half-feigning sleep,
Impotent, the male intruder, stumbled on some archaic
Female rite, stunned by the power that seized him there,
But unable to claim it.

              Suddenly you stir.
Like a questing otter, almost sensing my sight,

---

*First draft, January, 1970; the poem was put aside until August, 1974, too late for inclusion
in *Man-Fate*.

You turn, hesitate, then noiselessly
Glide back to bed.

                         What was seen?

I ask it now
Only to probe the incidence
Compressed within.

From the depths of dream,
At a child's cry,
We woke to vision:

                         Yours, but not to know.
                         Mine, but not to keep.

　回 回

THE GASH

To covet and resist for years, and then
To succumb, is a fearsome thing. All you craved and denied
At last possesses you. You give yourself
Wholly to its power; and its presence,
Invading your soul, stupefies
With its solace and its terror.

There is nothing so humbling as acceptance.

I sense the mushrooms in the night,
Tearing their way up through loose soil,
Brutal as all birth.

               And I bend my head,
And cup my mouth on the gash of everything I craved,
And am ravished with joy.

    ▣ ▣

GALE AT DAWN

Landwind: a gale at dawn scooping down from the hills.
It pours west to the water, hits the foam
Like a counterattack repulsing a beach landing.

But the brute surf stalks in, stupendous breakers
Born out at sea, inexorably arriving.

The landwind, honing them, combs back their furls,
And the low winter light, shining flatly through,
Wreathes the powerful, doomed shoulders,
Gives each lion wave its rainbow mane,
Hackled with gold.

                    But the wind,
Like a holy terror, rips back those brows.
Plunged in the hollow of each ponderous breast
It explodes into fire.

O wind and water! Like a gale at dawn
Man hits the wave of woman. She arches her throat
For the stab of his lips. Over the wallowing blood
His sudden face divides her life; his terrible gift
Wreathes her with flame.

                    At dusk,
All falls still. The air, curiously spent,
Hangs inert.

            We savor salt.

                        In the immense quietude,
Under the nimbus of sunset, we find by the water
The surf-quenched scoter, the depth-disheveled grebe.

回 回

11: A TIME TO MOURN

A TIME TO MOURN

A time to weep, and a time to laugh.
A time to mourn, and a time to dance.

—Ecclesiastes

A time to mourn.

For to suffer the loss of a way of life
Is as hard a hurt
As the loss of the closest friend.

A time to grieve.

For when the fates
Exact, drive home their denial,
A great hole is left in the breast,
A gap and a gulf,
Where all that was once most meaningful
Is ripped away.

Grieve, then, and not grudge the grieving.
Mourn without shame.
For what life asserts
The self must swallow.
On its own dark curd
The soul must suck.

Though a man in his going
Be filled with delight,
The leap of liberation—
His hurt of avowal,
Of broken allegiance,
Is not to be scanted.

Truly, the loss of a primal way of life
Is like the going of a great love.

One carries it within,
A festering sorrow,

An unfillable lack.

And the delicate
Feeder-roots of the soul,
Denied their sustenance,
Starve and shrink back.

So the sea falls, falls.
The tides return.
The long apostleship of the surf,
Revolving over and over,
Shapes its harsh indenture.

Obscuring as much as it clarifies,
It fills its function,
Effects what it denotes.

And once again, in the ineffable
Gulf of alienation,
On Stinson Beach I ponder fate.

I grope the impacted nucleus,
The paradox of love and denial,
My taproot of guilt.

And the fresh wind,
Obliquely out of the south,
A breath of charge and renewal,
Cross-angles my brow.

I lift up my face.
On the far horizon
One flake of sail
Skitters and dips.

Then my sight drops.
When my gaze levels,
Steep surf accosts it.

▣

Offshore, swimming leisurely south,
A pride of sea lions
Glimpses me first.

Instantly alert
They lift their shoulders
Stiffly from the surge,
Gazing intently landward, fixing me
Where I stand, the one
Conspicuous object on the beach.

Curious and suspicious
They float warily with the drift,
Hieratic and immobile as tritons,
Lords of the sovereign sea.

Their august presence
Accuses me. At one with their element,
Knowing no remorse, they are what they are.

I am what I am not.

And the span of my attention
Snaps back, coddles my grief.
I envy them, with a wild throttling yearn,
Their serene composure, their calm
Simplicity of being.

◨

In the monastic life
Celibacy is the catalyst of fire,
The signature of the ultimate.

It is the cross upon which the monk
Crucifies his intuition
In the spasm of God's grace: desire
Memorialized in the rapture of the spirit.

Out of the clench of the flesh, its energies
Transform instinct into awareness,

The octave of comprehension.

In the seal of its assurance
A man invokes encounter, the impenetrable
Gaze of God.

Who knows it
Knows the power of banked fire,
Outlasting the thirst of life,
A sentient flare.

6

Westward the surf falls,
Somberly and without cessation,
On the pulse-stroke of man's blood,
Revamping under our feet
The fundamental berm, this beach, our narrow
Shelf of existence.

The sea lions are gone. In their place,
Beyond the white line of the breakers,
Drifts a gaggle of surfers, oblique on their boards,
Facing seaward.

From the shore
One sees but the tilted torsos,
Tense shoulders, the alert heads.
They look to the far
Wrinkling of the sea, surmising increment:
Which influx of the swell, impending,
Will coalesce into consequentiality,
Engender thrust, and, reaching forward,
Stoop towering in, all ultimate
Augmentation?

This, in their mind's eye,
Is the vision of beatitude:
The great wave of their wonder.

Like the paired sea lions,

Equally alert, equally sustained,
They float immobile, awaiting their instant.
But where the sea lions, water creatures,
Looked in to the shore,
These drifters, essentially land animals,
Gaze narrowly out to sea.

So do the divisible natures of life
Look to otherness for significance.
And just so does the heart,
An organ of the blood, look to the spirit.
Only then can it find its singular definition,
Its rare essential meaning.

A strange breed, surfers of the salt.
Neither landsmen nor sailors,
Neither flyers nor divers,
They inhabit the obscure interval,
The zone of force and chaos,
(Force of the swell, chaos of the cracking wave)
That obtains between the primary entities,
The worlds of earth and water.

Awaiting the momentary surge, the eluctable thrust,
Each will turn tail, seize
Groundswell in its strong inception, climb
The shark-shape board, pick
Power from the heave, to come shearing in,
Utterly at ease under the arched
Immensity of the wave.

Then, in the final deft manœuvre,
When the breaker is quelled, its force
Spent, its momentum
Gone—then,
Redisposing body weight on the tipped feet,
The surfer deflects, blades sideways,
Climbs the inside of the wave's depleted convexity,
Pauses balanced along the purling subdued crest,
And, the long surf's power abandoned to the shore,
Drops lightly down, crests the tilting board,

And prows it back to sea.

I watch them,
And I watch the wave,
The unity of force and response,
The ease of conjoined purposes.

A time to mourn.
A time to savor hurt.
A time to turn the mind's blade
Back on the heart,
The pierce of self-recognition.

And let the living gaze
Gouge to the guts.

⬓

The monastic life as well
Absorbs the surge-point of the real,
The interlude of force and chaos
Between God and the soul.
(Groundswell of events,
Chaos of the cracking world.)
And like the surfer,
Silently intent and electrically alert,
The monk, too, watches the shape of things,
The riptide of events,
For the ingathering flux.
Mounting it, he seizes power, the world's
Hidden transtemporal force,
The wave of the future.
This he takes, takes it at the pitch,
The steep insurge of investing time,
Climbs, crests;
Then, spent of his instancy,
He yields to the deep depletion,
And comes gliding in.*

———————————————————

* Stanza break.

One of the great ways of life.
One of the primal vocations.
He who accepts it and betrays it
Spalls his integrity,
Insults his God.

And the sea affirms it,
Tells it as so, as true.

Utterly without equivocation
It speaks of certitude and denial.

Ever-changing, it has never forsworn its role.
Invincibly active, it has never ceased
Balancing the margin of victory
Between what abides and what alters. It allows
Every recourse, every omnidiversion,
Except the betrayal of essence.
And what essence is
Constitutes the nature,
Denotes the real.

A monk is a monk is a monk is a....

Given his commitment,
Whatever else proffers,
Be it never so evocative,
Is unthinkable, a thing
Not to be countenanced.

            ▣

Over my head a shadowy intrusion,
A ripple of gulls, ringbills,
Larus delawarensis, float lightly in the air.
They ride the ripples
As the sea lions balance the groundswell,
As the surfers teeter the wave.

One by one they glide over me,
Veering right and left as they go forward,

Each tilting the black-tipped beak of its insignia,
Its categorical distinction,
As if consciously authenticating its identity,
The manifest sign of presence:
That which confirms it.

It is what it is.

No, the habit does not make the monk,
No more than the ringed bill makes the gull.
But as positive distinctions
Each sign is intrinsic.
Each signifies an actuality,
True marks of the self.

Suddenly I see myself as nondescript,
Rootless and unbelonging, a fugitive identity:
Monk without monastery,
A friar without vows.

And the sea falls, falls.
The vast world of water
Lips the shore.
Southward, where the cliffs kneel,
It gnaws the rock bone of its mutable contention,
Growling and mouthing its sputum of intent.

And I nod to it, bending into it,
Half piqued with its sullen recalcitrance,
Unable to isolate, nor effectively categorize,
Save in the pit of my own subjectivity,
My rancor with my self.

A time to mourn and not contend.
A time to grieve and not be ashamed.
A time to moan, and accept consolation.

For the sea consoles.
In his time of need let that consolation
Be no man's scorn.

◨

Suddenly by beach-grass fringing the dunes
A flitter bats my eye. Black shape,
Skewed presence, a bandy-legged crow
Hops awkwardly, peering for fish heads,
Gills, fins, the scooped-out hulls of crustaceans,
Anything under the sun.

He caws me, derisive and unflappable.
Here on the beach, a creature utterly out of his element
But equally unrepentant,
Ineptly competing with gulls, sanderlings,
Phalaropes and willets, the diligent
Researchers of the shore,
For the surf's refuse, the offscouring sea,
He perks and skitters.
I skim a rock at him; he takes off, squawking.
Teetering on a twig he beaks the troughing wind
And scolds me. He blusters my head with his curse.

Whoever forsakes his element
Is ludicrous and, in his perverse
Exacerbation, damns his own eyes.

Or so I surmise.

◨

Man has free will, no denying that; but freedom's
Accessibility to the soul
Is gauged on the apex of individual consciousness
Achieved in the man—a consciousness
All the fluent force of heredity,
Compressed in the resistant frame of environment,
Has basically contrived.

                    A consciousness
Subsumed in the ever-evolving awareness of the breed,
Wherein the great interior archetypes
Work their awesome way,

Grope toward clarification,
Painfully contesting dominion
In the hegemony of the soul,
The precise point in the blood's evolution
A man represents.

Man has free will, certainly.
But a will subsumed in the brute
Stubbornness of the earth, a stubbornness
Fluid but inflexible, the short seasons
Shaping him. Who can measure the hemispheric stress,
The stone-paced impress of geologic flux?
Or what the rock-beds of continents
Do to man's soul?

                        And islands?
Dappling the wine-dark sea
They redispose the elements,
Shaping anew our insular fates,
The singular destinies of all who inhabit them,
To make of old races
The tongues of new breeds.

I have soared, and seen beneath me
The flat plain of the Mississippi,
Apparently the absolute of levelness, but actually
All watershed, from the snow-pitched Rockies
To the Allegheny scarp,
Vaster than the aching eyes, contesting distance,
Can ever encompass. And have seen in its trough
The River itself, snake-nested,
Torpid in twilight, thick serpentine silver,
Uncoiling down the stretched
Alluvial plain, clean to the Gulf,
To bury its throat, all unslaked thirst,
Deep in the uterine sea. On its curl
Whole cities deploy, and new peoples
Body forth substance in its sinuous girth.
My own mother shaped to its impress,
A child of those prairies,
And my father, in the Twin Cities astride it,
Endured transformation

From the stark Norwegian temper,
To the straight American cast. The very
Latitudes of the globe, so evocative in the mind,
Modify inheritance. Our eaten food
Determines our flesh. The trajectory
Of growth and decline as the sun charts it
Etches the red jag of its glyph
On the graph of our soul,
And when it relinquishes us into our fate
Our names change.

　　　　⊡

Man has free will, assuredly.
But the will of the world
Is subsumed in the will of the cyclic cosmos,
Where the planets, like floats on a maelstrom,
Mark the recurrence of galactic flux,
Each a creation of the complex of energies
Sustaining the universe: "The conversion
Of energy into mass." But the energy there
Before the mass, each star, each
Planet, a crest, a peaking
Of the operative complex,
Where the converging energy-fields transect,
As the presence of man, the individual human being, denotes
A corresponding peak of the same focus,
So that the energies peaking in the one
Conform to the energies peaking in the other,
The root energies, as it were, endowed there,
The planet nothing in itself, a sign,
As the man is a sign,
To be interpreted, yes, but attributed, never;
To be read, yes, but reverenced
Not at all.

　　　　For man's free will,
Like the cold will of earth,
Like the hot will of the cosmos,
Is subsumed in the inscrutable,
The savagely oblique will of God,

Shone through the great orchestration of the All,
His actuality of pure existence
Throbbing throughout the galactic spawn.
The solar system fluxes its force
Down through the ambient climate of earth
To the brute soul of evolving man,
Blind, split by temptation and crippled by sloth,
To touch the archetypes asleep there,
Each latent symbolic core,
Ordain his fierce evolution,
The growth through pain and contradiction
To the point of unbearable consciousness,
The ego anguished between contesting powers,
The archetypal configuration within
And the planetary configuration without,
And all ordained. In the will of God
Subsumes the will of cosmos and earth.
In the will of God
Subsumes the pitiful will of man.

A time to mourn. A time to drink
Deep of the life-purge.
A time to slake pain
In the instance of acceptance.
To acknowledge and repent.

     ▣

Last night, under the sudden
Solstice dusk, I left for a moment the crackling hearth.
I walked through sere beach grass
Gazing at stars.
Wrapped in the muffled night chill of earth
I stared at great Saturn,
A cold core glinting the East.
Gazing out of the burgeoning archetype
His place there denotes, I watched him, watched
Till the sinking rim shook him free,
As birth, the wild unfolding womb,

Frees what we are into what we will be.

For in the year of my birth
Saturn stood early in Gemini,
Sign of Communication, the first decan. On that instant
He swung through the Ninth House,
Not for nothing called the House of Religion.
Nor is it all for nothing
I was born to the vocation of religious poet.

And the planets that morning
Strung up the East like an express train,
From Uranus in the Fifth, the House of Creativity,
To culminating Saturn, the hard diamond of the cutting edge
Ploughing the sky. The horoscope
Charts the sequence. The open trine
Embraces the West, spans the sinking Descendant,
A configuration, in the literature of gestalt astrology,
Sometimes called the Locomotive Type.
As such it denotes a congenital force,
"A self-driving individuality, an executive
Eccentricity that is not queerness or unbalance
But rather is power." As leading planet,
Saturn decrees the point-focus of symbolic force.
For me, in the deeps of the endowed imagination,
Father and God are one. And they are terrible.

When I deny such presences,
When I controvert such determinants,
I violate my soul.

          ▣

And I do deny them.

For in the First House, the House of Life,
Venus and Mars, conjunct on the same degree,
Clasp in a spasm of convulsive rapture.
Like Antony and Cleopatra
They exult in each other's arms,
Throwing whole empires away.

In Libra, Venus is paramount.
Mars, in his fall there, wallows into her womb,
Pouring his resplendent phallic strength
Between the grope of her clutching thighs.
All his sublimely militant energy,
Made to serve God as the sword serves the spirit,
Subverted from rooting out error
To rooting in the bed.

Like Samson shorn of his radiant locks,
Mars in Libra can prosper and excel
Only in the service of Venus.

                              She rules him!

She rules him!

                    Let Saturn the Father
Intone from the pulpit his somber decrees,
But the power of procreation,
Flaming from the House of Life,
Defies proscription.

For eighteen years as a Dominican monk
Saturn, which rules my soul, reigned in my life.
Then Uranus, smasher of limits, moved into Libra,
The hammer of the thunderer jarred the scales,
Skewed the balance. In the arms of Mars,
With Uranus for goad,
Venus laughs at law.
High in the Ninth,
The House of Religion,
Mighty Saturn bows.

And the monk, gone crazy,
Flies his cell,
Forsakes his holy vows.

It is the disconsolate
Irony of life. And not even rare.*

---

* Stanza break.

These are the episodes
Our tabloids daily flaunt: MAGISTRATE
FLIPS WITH B GIRL! STRIPPER
TAGS PROF! Should the monk, then,
In high disdain, account himself
Superior to these? Poor human facts
The world well knows, its genial code allows?
But if not, if he holds himself no higher,
Why, then, his vows?

And the sea falls,
Falls. Its sigh, the long whisper of mortality,
The syllable of consummation,
Pensive with understanding.

A time to mourn.
To drink deep of the sorrow of the life purge.
To slake the pain in the instance of avowal.
To acknowledge and repent.

回

I lift up my head.
The surfers are gone with the sea lions.
The gulls and the crow are no more.
Only the sea obtains,
Champing and gesticulating,
Throwing up the substance of its implication,
The reckoning spume,
Bestowing the salt of its wisdom
On the beaches of man's world.
Immemorially responsive,
Supremely acknowledging and participating,
The sea, in its endlessness, consoles.

When the selves within a man,
Like the sources in the cosmos,
Contest together,
What word denotes betrayal?

It is the heart that knows,

And it is the heart which whispers:

"God gives man freedom:
The power to do what he ought."

I chose.
Because I betrayed my vows,
I betrayed myself.

Because I betrayed myself
I have betrayed my God.

And the heart howks it up,
The old immemorial utterance,
The keyword of repentance:

"My fault, my fault, my most grievous fault!"

And the sea, like a mother,
Broods and reflects,
Within her vast attentive ear
My words, like offshore leaves,
Whirl out and sink down.
They settle in the surf.

And the surf responds,
Rippling and flowing,
The eternal flux,
The sublime benediction,
The whisper of silence.

Under the whisper
The stillness of the heart;
Under the crash of events,
Breaking, breaking—

But the heart,
Sounded on silence,

In quietude subsumes.[*]

---

[*] Stanza break.

And absolution?

O my God! What have I forsaken?

Old sea, old mother,
Grant me surcease!

Lave my wounds
And lift me home!

III: THE NARROWS

STORM AT LOW TIDE

A storm at low tide is like the dark night of the soul.
All the surface surge comes shattering in,
Impelled by a sixty-mile-an-hour gale
And something violent far out to sea
Menacing more. But the outgoing suck
Is relentless, and will not yield.
Caught between wind and moon
The water stands up to the beach going every which way
But perpendicularly contained in the inexorable tension,
A quivering wall poised to plunge,
And frighteningly twitching its skin like a demented horse,
Only to topple and collapse as if something utterly trivial had tripped it,
Scattering its myriad particles and fragments
In the ultimate exasperation of purposeless dispersion.
I walk along the tortured ribbon of foam that traces the violent nadir,
Reflecting how I too was torn so, knowing this rage of resistance,
This exasperate, desperate madness, this inexpressible
Chaotic lust.

THE NARROWS OF BIRTH

Christmas night: the solstice storm
Muttering in retreat, threatening rain,
Cypress witlessly clawing the roof,
Its vague hand scrawling the obscure
Prophecy of reprisal. Across the dunes
Wind rakes the hollow-breasted sea,
Coughing and expectorating like a consumptive invalid,
A feverish old woman racked in senility's
Festering decrepitude, morbidly ailing.

I awake from a dream of ritual slaying: beachfire
Back from the surf; hunched in an angle of logs and driftwood
Crouches the clan. Among them,
Free and unsuspecting, a youth lounges,
Perfectly relaxed, a man
Stalwart, high-minded and virile,
In the deceptive way the dream
Inveterately falsifies reality,
Approximating the ideal.

To me, in the freezing awareness of apprehension,
It becomes increasingly apparent
He is not guest but victim.
Yet my very prescience, which denotes my involvement,
Renders me powerless. For I have entered into complicity,
A kind of unspoken pact, with these people, seeking something
They have which I need, which I once knew and lost,
And have come to recover in my own quest;
And because of this need, this involvement,
Have forfeited my freedom.

And suddenly, with great clarity of vision,
I see them for what they are,
The castrate sons and the runt daughters,
Maimed progeny of the Mother,
From whose destiny I myself, long ago, had somehow escaped,
And have returned now, improvidently,
To verify my lack. They hobble about their appointed tasks,

Preparing the terrible rites of immolation.
They seem to be concocting some revolting brew,
The narcotic that renders the victim senseless,
Of which the elements, I am aware, are parlous:
Milk and dung, blood and semen, menses and afterbirth,
The mordant ingredients of parturition.
These, I see, stand for the universal postulates of generation:
Twin compulsions of Desire and Death:
The inexorable forces which every major religion
Has pitted itself to overcome; and from which
The vows of every monk
Are structured toward deliverance.

And I sense, from the depths of this recognition,
The utter ineffectuality of everything I am—my own monk's vows
Jettisoned in a spasm of precipitate repudiation,
Leaving me weaponless, hands utterly empty,
To grope my way back to these somnambulists,
These ominous dark sources,
In the reassessment of my life.

Across the fire I face the matriarch,
My ancient ancestress, the fountainhead of my blood,
Saying, "I have come back, Mother,"
And I bow my head as a penitent
Bows for absolution; or as the prodigal,
Having squandered his heritage,
Lowers his neck to signify his wrong.
But in the old mother of glittering eyes
Is neither absolution nor forgiveness.
Her gaze searches me narrowly,
Unrelenting, utterly unimpressed
By anything I might say,
Waiting for proof. She will be appeased now
Only by deeds—by words
Never.

        I waver in the firelight,
Uncertainly, unable to know
What it is I am to do, unable to reassert
Who I am, or say what brought me here,
What motive or what reasons avail

In this weirdly familiar place.

The plotting goes on.
I see the body of the youth,
Beautifully muscled, like Michelangelo's
Immortal slave, the raised shirt
Banded about the nipples,
And all the magnificent body
Slumped in its unmistakably erotic swoon.

The castration begins.

I wake to the dawn, bolt upright,
With the retreating storm
Muttering in the eaves, uncertain
And vague and foreboding.
I feel beside me in the strange bed
The body of my young wife.
She is breathing deeply in sleep,
The clear pulse of her being
Mustering within it all the life-force
Against my fear. In the next room
Her nine months' son cries out, softly,
Under the wince of my pervasive torment,
An anguish which haunts the house,
My pain and my guilt.
In the stretched silence
I touch her again, the flank of woman,
Modulant with the subsumed
Rapture of life. And everything I have come for
Clutches my throat,
Warring in the narrows of this birth.

THE CHALLENGE

Then what do I seek?
Truly, I know not.

Destiny,
The oblique force of my being,
Evicted me from a measured life,
The austere life of perfection.

It thrusted me
Back into the convulsive and uterine world,
Where the animal cry
Bellows at the gate,
Where the engine and the beast
Groan in travail.

In this my certitude,
My sole conviction,
Is that my nature does not lie,
That destiny and nature are one.

Clearly my soul's trial,
Its naked ordeal,
Lies in this acceptance:
The reconciliation of what I believe
With the fact of what I am.

This is the wound that tears me apart.
Neither peace of spirit
Nor serenity of psyche,
Till that gap closes.

Why, then, do I fight it?
What is the fester, the seething sore
Refusing to heal?

Pride? That the lofty
Pinnacle of aspiration,

At the eleventh hour of life,
Slipped from my grasp?

Or a morose preoccupation with image,
The disconsolate craving for the high religious profile
The habit of the monk gratuitously confers?

Or mere stubbornness,
A mulish refusal to accept the obvious,
The fact that I failed?

All these and more.
They name the fester;
They do not constitute the wound.

Something seethes beneath them,
More mysterious,
More keen and more blind.

Something lives on that the heart can't help,
Something below the proud flesh of that bruise:
A hunger for God and nothing but God
This world cannot fill.

Neither wife nor child nor fame nor fortune.

The brute thirst for the absolute,
The apotheosis of desire
In the guts of God.

                    What?
The reconciliation of what I believe
And what I am?

                    Rather
Desire slaked in its raw Source.
Intelligence stunned in its Prey.

        ▣

For in the monastery

What I believed and what I am
Truly *were* one—

Up to a point!

But beyond that point
Something rebelled.

(Not in my spirit:
No real reservation
Troubled my spirit.)

But something more visceral.
Something I can only call
The subsistent self,
The basis of my being.

As a monk
I sought to immolate this subsistent self
In the interest of transcendence
And for years it availed.

But after a time
That basic being climbed down from its cross,
Embracing its need,
Thirstily,
And refused to return.

No matter how I implored.
No matter how I threatened and cajoled.
No matter how I appealed to the supreme imperatives,
The fiery strictures—

(No matter! No matter!)

It would not go back.
It refused to return.

But rather, when the woman came,
It followed her out,
Back to the wild convolutions,
The mouthing and the tonguing,

The bitterness and the dross.

Leaving the spirit stunned.
Leaving the mind sick.
Leaving the psyche sullen.

Until, realizing at last
Nothing more could change now,
Nothing save itself alone,
The mind gave over.

In the anguished need for unification
The malleable mind
Relinquished and succumbed.

And now *it* endures crucifixion,
It endures torment and incertitude.

For the spirit's belief,
The soul's conviction,
Lie back in the cell.

　　　　　◨

Somewhere there exists
The crystal prism,
The clear point of reconciliation,
This I know.

To find it is my challenge.

But its shape remains closed,
Closed against the surging myth of futurity,
In the legend of the past—

The dark, blood-ooze origin of things,
The spurt of birth. And that, after all,
Is the gasp of completion.

Let then my basic being,

That savageness of soul,
Project the guerdon of its need.

Then my cross-stretched mind
Will grope deliverance
This flesh cannot abide.

THE SCOUT

Passing a leathercraft shop in Mill Valley I see
Yellow buckskin, long undulant fringes,
Lazy-stitch beadwork of the Plains tribes,
Strong, tawny wear of the old frontier.

Buckskin right now is a youthful fad, but not
This grade of the authentic. And turning inside,
On the moment's crystalline decisiveness,
I allow myself to be fitted. The cost:
A hundred dollars down, a hundred
Dollars on delivery. I pay
Without a quiver. Returned home,
I muse by the fire, smoking,
The first of a few slow nights' reflection
Before the garb is my own.

                        For the implications
Are revolutionary. Tonight, back in the monastery,
My black and white habit is worn by another.
But now, in the shimmering imagination,
I assume the regalia of the Old West:
Beads, buckskin and bearclaws, the extravagant
Fantastic image. Yet for all the grandiose
Self-projection, which time must erase to confirm,
I know I have come to a steep divide,
A fork in the crooked trail of my life;
That I have truly chosen; will bear that choice;
Wear it about my being, as I learned to bear it,
As I learned to wear it over long years,
In the habit of a monk.

                        For a way opens up
Taking me instinctively back,
Back beyond the first frontier, beyond the advent
Of agriculture or the civilized dream,
Back to the Stone Age myth and the ethos of blood.
These rare integuments are its powerful insignia,
A way of ordering what, to the imagination,
Is truly there but rationally denied, and hence

Vague, without substance, lacking essential symbolic force—
Back beyond the confirming vineyard of my youth,
That took me out of my father's world, setting me free—
Back to the archaic mysteries,
The fertility of the soil, the magic of animals,
The power-vision in solitude, the terrifying
Initiation and rebirth, the love
And ecstasy of the dance, modalities
Governing the deeps of instinct,
The seat of consciousness itself,
Where the poet, as shaman to his time,
Ritualizes for the race—all, all subsumed
In the skin of the bison and the antler of the elk,
And borne on the being. Just so
The habit of the monk, received in solemn investiture,
Confirms its tangible ethos, feeds
Participation to the flesh, yields
The meaning it denotes.

                    Or so in my musing.
But suddenly a mounted figure rises in my mind,
Abruptly accosting. The single
Eagle feather of the scout marks him Protector,
Watcher of the Spirit, Guardian of the Sacred Mysteries,
Keeper of the Pass.

                    I raise my hand,
Palm forward, the immemorial gesture of peace.
But wheeling his pony he disappears.
I am left apprehensive, touched by a strange foreboding,
Vaguely disturbed.

                    Gazing into the flame-lick
I catch for the first time the vibration of menace.
I smell danger at the divide.

🔲 🔲

BLACK HILLS

Riding a horse up a narrow gorge I pick
Traces of an old trail. In my dream
All is weed-grown, brush-choked, my clothes
Tear on quick spines, and here and there
Thorns have scratched blood. Suddenly in the abrupt dusk
My horse spooks and whinnies, refusing to go on.
I dismount and drag forward, exasperated, the bridle
Straining in my left fist as I shoulder through,
Press on and in to a lost clearing.
Then I see, obliquely up-slope, skewed in stark branches,
The ancient tree-burials of the Indians.
This is the place. I have reached at last
My dark quest's end.

     For it was here,
At the close of the final bloodily-doomed campaign,
A band of exhausted Sioux, burying their dead,
Endured ambush. United States cavalry,
Charging down-slope at dawn, leveled
The ritual-keeping remnant. Braves, squaws,
Even the cradleboard papoose—all alike
Riddled under the skirl of lead
From the snout carbines. Scalped, mutilated,
The sex of the women hacked out with Bowie knives,
Jabbed over saddlehorns, to be worn
Swaggering back to the stockade saloons,
Derisive pubic scalps, obscene trophies
Of a decimated people, a scalped land.

     Left here the bodies
Made whitened skeletons under the tree-hung graves.
Then blizzard and grizzly scattered about the little clearing
The buzzard-picked bones. With the next spring thaw
Dispersed remnants of other bands found their way here,
Collected the littered remains, grouping them into awkward bundles,
Pathetic attempts to reshape the dead,
And hoisted them skyward, joining the earlier
High tree-burials the Plains Indians use on the vast prairies
When the earth is frozen, and now, strange transplants,

Adapted here in the shortness of time
To the dark mountains, the dense firs.

The dust of battle is all washed away with the years.
But the sky-hung mummies still survive the snows.
I see their tattered shrouds
Flutter in the night-wakened wind
That prowls down the canyon.

But my terrified horse balks unmanageably.
Contorted at the clearing's edge he plunges and shrieks.
Thinking it no more than the spectral graves
Terrorizing the acute nostrils and the fearful animal sight,
I tether him short and grope forward alone.
But suddenly the intangible presence tormenting him
Transfixes me. Nailed to the spot
Terror like an electric vibration rivets my being.
Confused, immobilized, fighting to retain consciousness,
I sense the ominous locus, the magnetic spot
From which all that threatens
Issues toward me.

It pours from a spill of shattered boulders
Just beneath the sky-swung graves.
Here the last braves took refuge,
Fought till every arrow was gone,
Fought till the white man's
Pitifully malappropriate firearms
Fell silent in their hands,
Fought with knives arced and the tomahawks
Screaming like insane eagles,
Hacking and whirling over the melee
When the cavalrymen charged in,
Blasting, kicking, gouging,
The pistols spitting till the last riddled body
Jerked limp and flopped dead.

Gazing toward the cluster of rocks
I gather into focus the incredible emanation,
The torrent of hatred pouring into me.
It is as archaic and irreducible as weightless stone,
A kind of psychic lava,

Pouring across the narrow space
And the cavity of the years.

And it is male.
The savage violence.
The primal pride.

For this have I come.

And seeking to master it, to neutralize
The hate, confirm desire, convert
Power to purpose in the hope that brought me here,
I project in my imagination the sublime
Patriarchal image I reverenced as a boy,
The composite visage of all the great chiefs,
Their names and singularities: Roman Nose, Black Kettle,
Red Cloud, Crazy Horse, Gall, Sitting Bull....
Confronting the torrent of malediction
I wring that image from my buried past,
And give it life.

        But the vision fades.
The white man's guilt, founded in my heart,
Warps between, a massive, misshapen block.
I see only the piebald ponies,
Retreating, their tails
Flattened before the blizzard of time,
Humpbacked under the weight of the years,
A splendor despoiled, a ravished pride.

"Father!" My desperate cry
Echoes through the gloom,
"Come back to us! Return to our lives!"
My words ring through the dusk,
And a wind springs up, rattling the leaves.
"I have come to close the wound,
Heal the gash that cuts us from you,
And hence from the earth!"
I pause, listening intently,
Aware of the unanswering gloom, the dusk
Muffled and intense.
"I have come to bury the hatchet,

That we who must live
May live in peace!"

Something moves there in response,
Of this I feel sure,
But no light remains to let it be seen.
Only, from the heap of rocks,
Like an answering hail of arrows,
The torrent of hate.

I sink to my knees shouting:
"Give me your blessing!"
There is rain in the air now
And no time to lose.
I expose my lacerated hands,
The ancient sign that suffering proves one true.
Leaning into the blast of repudiation
I sway desperately, a lost scout
Swaying on the frozen prairie,
In the killing cold.

Aware only of the unrelenting force
Pouring over and around and through me
I lift my head as the night closes down
And shout the one thing left,
The old, hopeless, human attestation:
"I love you!"

The force of malediction
Increases to something almost physical.
And indeed the actual wind,
Pouring down the canyon,
Rises to a roar, bearing a volley of torn leaves,
Twigs, loose bark, flung gravel.

And suddenly the rain begins.

Crouched in the weeds
I summon up again the vision of the chiefs,
Call them back into consciousness:
The painted shields and the war ponies,
The painted bodies and eyes,

Buffalo hats, the lynx-skin headdresses,
An eagle feather dangling for every slain foe;
Rippling war-bonnets trailing to the heels,
The jewel-work of beads and the delicate
Fancy-stitch of porcupine quills, arrow quivers
Furred with the magic skin of the otter—
For an instant I possess it again,
The fabulous, unspeakable vision,
Primitive and elegant,
The unquenchable glory of primal man.

Then it fades. A sudden
Spasm of hysteria doubles me up.
I relapse into uncontrollable sobbing.
"I love you," I scream. "Can't you hear me?
God damn it, I love you!"

                🔲

I wake up shouting. I am in my own bed,
Rigid beside my young wife.
It is hours before dawn.
I rise wordlessly, without making a light.
Shaken and trembling, I grope my way to the adjoining room.
On the grate a few coals
Gleam in the fireplace,
Remnants of last evening's blaze,
Dying in ash. A flood of moonlight
Pours through the window. Standing naked in the dark
I let the feeble warmth of the embers
Caress my cold shins.
I gaze shudderingly into the darkness,
Still plunged in the awful atmospherics of the dream.
Moonlight glows on an improvised mandala
I have fashioned out of my mute desire
And hung in the room:
Two gigantic eagle claws
Fixed above the black and white
Pony-tail braid-ends of the Flathead tribe,
Pinned on a Navajo saddle blanket

And nailed to the wall.
The claws clutch upward. I placed them so,
Following the ghostly eagle's death-flight,
Which left life behind and flew at the sun, its father,
Flew till the great unreal talons
Took peace for prey,
Exultantly, their death beyond death,
Stooped upward, and struck
Peace like a white fawn
In a dell of fire.

              I believe it. And believing as well
That what we wear and how we wear it
Bodies forth our hope, the deep implication of our underlying need,
I turn to the adjacent wall where, flanking the eagle-claw mandala,
My great buckskin coat hangs in the moonlight.
I have placed it high on the wall,
As my religious habit, hung high on the door of the monastic cell,
Stood sentinel there
Against the intrusion of the world.
New and untried, like a novice's tunic,
The close-fringed coat yet typifies a faith, the image
Of all I seek to recover in the urgency of quest.

But now, in the aftermath of the dream,
The bravery of buckskin jeers me derisively.
Even as I gaze the Navajo saddle blanket
Glows with the pallor of death,
Some tattered burial wrapping
Salvaged from my dream.

Out on the dunes
The sea falls conclusively,
A muffled, explosive gasp,
Final as doom.

              But opening the door
The drench of moonlight embraces me,
A sudden inundation of suffused radiance.
It is the beautiful, unsullied present,

Eternally renewed, eternally reborn.
And it envelops me, and blesses me.
I look up into its immensity and its love,
Its past-dispelling love.
And standing there in the doorway,
All Indian at last,
I lift up my arms and pray.

　　　▣

But it is too much—
Too heartbreakingly much.
Shivering, I turn back to bed.
The ghost of what was,
All that never again can be,
Bodiless and fleshless,
Gleams in the eagle claws,
A spectral presence as I pass by.

Suddenly I jump like a man stabbed.
Under my feet something cracks sickeningly and collapses.
It is only a plastic toy,
The dropped plaything of my wife's infant child.
But reaching down I feel blood on my thumb,
Where the bones of all the buffalo
Gashed my heel.

　　　▣ ▣

THE DUNES

I dream once more: a vision
Sharp, brief and conclusive.

Shipwrecked on a desolate coast
I crouch on the beach,
Miles of interminable dunes behind me,
And watch the rolling, endlessly revolving sea,
That falls incessantly on the rustling sand.
Fog swaddles all. Like a gaunt
Sea-pelican come here to die
I stare before me, hollow-eyed,
Unable to cope with the cold
Sunlessness of the air,
Oppressed by the sand, the stifling
Heavy-hanging fog, the sullen
And indifferent sea.

      Suddenly from the dunes
Thrills the twitter of a bird.
It pierces the fog like an electric stinger.
It is the call of a woman.
Urgent, imperative, insistent,
It energizes my blood.

And lifting my head
I see that everything has changed.
The world of the possible
Tingles about me, crisp and vivid,
Compelled into being by the sheer
Imperation of a song.

      Getting to my feet
I follow stiffly where it leads,
Unmindful of fatigue, the call

Echoing as it withdraws, haunting
The beachhead, beckoning
Through vales of the distant
Strangely inviting dunes.

DARK WATERS

Chipmunk: slash with quick teeth
These rawhide ropes.

Little fox, sleek cat of the thicket,
Puma, ringtail in the quaking bush,
Mink in the meadow.

Otter-woman:
Drive devils out of my blood.
Scare off fear.

I have made a long run.
I have swum dark waters.

I have followed you through hanging traps.
I have risked it all.

O cut my thongs.

At the fork of your flesh
Our two trails come together.

At your body's bench
I take meat.

◨ ◧

NOTE:In the published *Man-Fate* (New Directions, 1974), Everson added a "Note" to account for the sources of certain elements in the poems, as follows: "The lines of verse by Robinson Jeffers quoted in the Preface [not included in the present volume] are from 'Love the Wild Swan,' and the ghostly eagle's death flight, from *Cawdor* by the same poet, has been incorporated into 'Black Hills.' The vision of the chiefs in that poem is adapted from William Brandon's *The American Heritage Book of Indians*; the astrological quotation in 'A Time to Mourn' is from *The Guide to Horoscope Interpretation* by Marc Edmund Jones; and the archaic mysteries in 'The Scout' are from a statement by Gary Snyder."

III

Some birth in me
Like a terrible awakening
Is stirring back to life.

                        resist
I fear and ~~love~~ it
Crushing down on my nans of assurance

I do not know its nature
I have no name for it.
                      shape
I cannot see its ~~face~~.

        there, implacable,
But within me,
Like the mushrooms in the oakwoods
where the mountain bares the seed,

When the long rains of December have
   unlend their spores

It lifts up its head.

Brutal, cruel, compelling   thick, gross, c/o
Completes its birth.
Compels

Some awful birth
Like a terrible awakening
Is stirring back to life.

                    instincting
Terrible and intricate
It clothes my vitals.

Like them,
gross,   c/o
it lifts up its head.

"Seed," first draft, December 22, 1969.
Courtesy of The Bancroft Library, UC Berkeley.

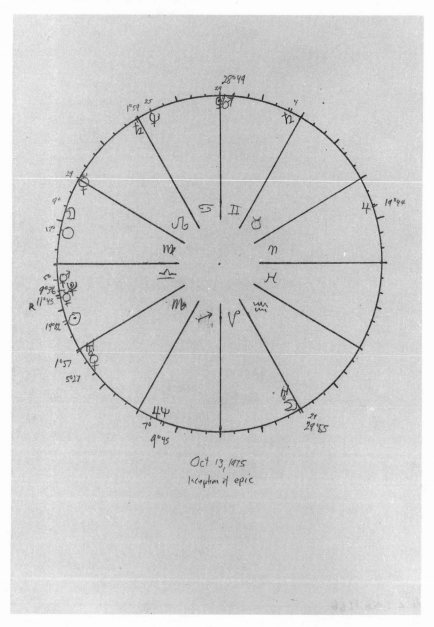

Astrological Chart Prepared by Everson for "Inception of epic
[i.e., Dust Shall Be the Serpent's Food], Oct. 13, 1975."
Courtesy of The Bancroft Library, UC Berkeley.

First draft of "Hallucinations," April 14, 1994.
Courtesy of The Bancroft Library, UC Berkeley.

Final Reading as Brother Antoninus, UC Davis, December 7, 1969.
Courtesy of The Bancroft Library, UC Berkeley.
Photo: E. David Show.

William Everson, Susanna Rickson Everson and Jude. Day of
Wedding, December 13, 1969.
Courtesy of The Bancroft Library, UC Berkeley.
Photo: Allen Say.

William Everson, Spring 1970.
Courtesy of The Bancroft Library, UC Berkeley.
Photo: E. David Show.

William Everson, East Lansing, MI, 1980.
Photo: Robert Turney.

William Everson, Kingfisher Flat, CA, 1985.
Photo: Robert Turney.

William Everson's home at Kingfisher Flat, CA, 1985.
Photo: Robert Turney.

William Everson at 80, Kingfisher Flat, CA, July 27, 1993.
Courtesy of Allan Campo.
Photo: John Prince.

BOOK FOUR:

THE GLYPH
OF GOD

(1971-1985)

I: THE MASKS OF DROUGHT

STORM-SURGE

Christmas Eve, night of nights, and Big Creek
Is on the move. At the equinox
Tempting rains toyed with us, teasing, and offshore at sea,
Beyond the slant sandbar blocking the rivermouth,
The great grey salmon skulked in the trough, dreaming the long
Genetic dream, plasmatic slumber of the unfulfilled,
Awaiting the moment of the forth-showing,
The river-tongue in the sea's vulva,
The strength in the slot.

           First incremental showers
Flushed dead vegetation, cathartic,
Purging the veins of the cleft mountain.
Then a month of drought reimposed itself,
The turbid summer's condign sterility
Drying the glades, sucking the flow back into the hills,
As if the mountain begrudged what it gave, called back its gifts,
Summoning them home, the high largess
Repentant of its grace.

           Advent broke dry,
December harsh on the hills, no sign of cloud
On the steely horizon. But solstice
Brought respite: a northwest flurry
Shook the last limbs bare, the drum of hailstones
Rattling the shingles under riddled cloud.
Then wind swung south and nimbus struck,
One thousand-mile storm enveloping the coast,
Forty-eight hours of vertical rain, water falling
Like the splurge of God, the squandering of heaven—
As if forever on the mountains and the draws,
As if forever on the river-forks and creeks,
As if forever on the vast watershed, its sheer
Declivities, its seaward-pitching slides,
Thirst-shrunken slopes of the parched ridges.

And I lean in the dark, the harsh
Pulsation of night, Big Creek
Gorged in torrent, hearing its logs

Hit those boulders, chute that flood,
Batter their weight to the sandbar
And the sea, ripping a channel
Out to the future, the space beyond time,
On the eve of the coming, when Christ,
The principle in the purpose,
Splits the womb in his shudder of birth.

GOSHAWK

A rush of wings: the sound of sheer
Knife-thrusts, or the hatchet-stroke
Of thrown blades. Then the sharp
Slap, high up, a hurtling shape
Hitting thick branches. The great goshawk,
Knocked out of the sky, awkwardly teeters,
Clutching at twigs. But our canyon redtails,
His fierce tormentors, close in on him,
Snarling like cats. The stunned intruder
Takes off, uncertainly gliding. His pursuers,
Like vengeful priests, follow him out. Abruptly
The canyon is quiet. The morning sunlight
Calmly descends. The clean day
Soars on.

       What portent?

                Over the horizon
Some dark approacher forecasting his presence?
Or a movement out there from the larger life,
The nation, or the world? Or maybe
My own dark thought, a sudden impulsion of spirit
Momently intruding, to be harried forth,
Unable to challenge set purpose?
Or something more somberly glutted?
Some reflex of the life-force
Inconsonant with the whole,
And hence obtrusive, and unavailing?

Any or all. One waits to know.

But something was meant. In the visionary dream
A movement from beyond of the cosmic whole
Was registered here. In the wing-clash and the snarling beaks
A counter-force challenged the fixed field. But to no avail.
Met and overcome it was swept from consequence,
Evicted, thrown shuddering out.

▣ ▣

RUNOFF

Four wet winters and now the dry.
All the long season a sterile frost
Grips the mountain, the coast like flanged metal
Bent thwart the sea. Above:
Stripped trees, taut-twisted branches
Catch stark white light. Below:
Shriveled creekbeds, raw to the air, run naked roots,
Obscenely groined through flaking rock,
The scat of torrents.

Then early last evening
A thin drizzle, gaining toward dusk. Before dark dropped
The low-hanging cloud slit its belly and the rain plunged.
All night long the thirsty slopes drank straight-falling water,
Soaking it up, filling those tilted, deep-shelving seams,
Blue veins of the mountain, zig-zag crevices of fractured shale.
When dawn flared and the rain held
The runoff began.

We rise with the light,
Sally down to the stream to touch fresh water
For a kind of blessing. We find instead a river of ink.
All the hoard of tributary creeks, those catchers of leaf-drift—
The strip of alder and the slough of fir,
Acrid shuff of the leathery tan-oak; and laurel,
The redolent, littering leaves of the laurel—
All that autumn-spun opulence
Frost drove down and ruthlessly squandered
Four moons back, to rot where it fell,
Now crawls to the sea, a liquid bile.

You look up at last in a wondering way
And exclaim softly, "Why, the mountain is menstruating!"
Something in your voice, a tremor there,
Tells of the natural womanly pulse, the deep sensing,
Its sympathetic pang, its soft vibration.

Looking, I see indeed it is true:
Leaves like dead cells

Long held back in the frigid womb
Begin now to flow—under the rain
A deep cleansing, this rite of renewal.

For me it is runoff but my heart purges.

Touching you and creek-throb in the same impulse
I am healed of frost:
Woman and water in the blood-flow.

回 回

BLACKBIRD SUNDOWN

High Ridge Ranch: back of the barn
A live-oak thicket, and redwing blackbirds
In the late afternoon. They cluster on fence posts,
Twig stems, barbed wire, telephone lines,
Any proximate perch. Their brilliant epaulets
Gleam in the fading light,
Vivid scarlet on glistening black.
Intensely alive they frolic and strut,
Chatter the twanging blackbird tongue,
Jubilant in the bird-loud evening.

A sudden hush. In the suspension of sound
Silence drops to stunned terror.
Then all explodes, every bird for itself,
Up, down, out and away.

                    For over the ridge,
Her shoulders of flight massively outstretched,
Her hunched body tense with hunger, gravid with need,
The Great Horned Owl glides implacably in,
Wide staring eyes fixed on her prey.

Instantly every bird recovers. Springing back to the defense
They converge on her, a racket of protest, a squall of imprecation.

Undeterred, she spans the yard, plunges into the oak thicket.
Behind her swarm the defenders, the stiletto beaks
Stabbing and yanking, a flurry of snatched feathers
Ragging her sides.

                    In a trice she emerges,
A half-dead fledgling gripped in each fist,
Her malignant face swinging right and left
As she scans the yard, glaring down her confronters.

Again the redwings close on her, railing and scolding,
Their punishing beaks a fury of reprisal.

She shrugs them aside, contemptuously,

And pauses a moment—ugly, umbrageous, triumphant.
Then she takes off, her dread profile
Humped in departure. Insolently unhurried
She clears the corral, skims the fence, and is gone.

And with her going the dusk drops. Where a moment before
Late light glimmered, now darkness
Swoops on the land.

                    The redwings
Circle and descend, seeking their roosts,
Pulling their shattered world back together,
Settling into the oak thicket, drifting toward sleep.

Out in the woods the she-owl's mate
Hoots once, hoots twice, his soft tattoo
Muffling the hush. She does not reply.
Her silence is the answer of the hearkening dead,
Listening for life, when life is no more.
Over the ridge the darkness shuts like a wing;
The earth-chill tightens; the claw moon
Talons the west.

回 回

JAY BREED

All the young summer the jay breed prospered.
The new brood, fledged early and growing apace,
Took over the canyon, a stellar triumph.
Bright, black-crested, sporting the razor-sharp profile,
They probed every cranny. Whatever accosted
Must pass inspection else suffer abuse.
Scolding, truculent, cunning, vindictive,
They strutted about the canyon, and we endured them.
Downstream by the meadow our creekside neighbors
Shot them with guns, then hung the skewed bodies in the apple trees
To scare off robbers. Here, under the towering
Canopy of redwoods, we let them live
And suffer their gall.

          And indeed their very abrasion
Bespeaks them: after the gloomy tree-sodden winter
That jaybird bravura fills a definite need.

I have, in fact, gone so far in complicity
As to scatter crumbs on an old stump to lure them in,
Swooping, blue iridescent streaks,
Angling through slant shafts of the sun
Between columned redwoods, their raucous bravado
My guiltful delight.

          But the cats
Are not amused. Skulking the yard they endure that umbrage
Nastily. Dive-bombed from behind
They crouch flat-eared and bare their fangs.
Often they scan the sky, the trees, the hedging thickets,
Possessed of a throttled rage, a passion
Apparently hopeless, given the jays'
Treetop immunity, but nursed nonetheless,
Corrosive desire clenched to the heart
Against the long-deferred accounting, the Great Day
Of feline retribution.

          Meantime,
The jays cursed back, and streaked in,

Jeering.

      Then early afternoon,
The hour lazy and bland, a stripling jay
Dropped down from the trees to pick off a cricket.
At ease in the grass, confident of his long legs
For quick takeoff, he speared his game
With nice precision. Furled in his beak
The hapless insect wriggled and strove.
Intrigued, the jay let it squirm,
Then flipped it aside, pounced, stabbed twice,
Artfully toying.

      But all unnoticed
In the wide summer day the black tom
Got his wits together. Aslink under the hibachi stand
He inched stealthily forward, tail twitching.
Suddenly the jay sensed him: one electric spring of those long legs
And he lit out, the cricket still furling his beak.
Too late. Too late. Lightning unleashed, the black tom caught him
Full stretch in the rush, a foot off the ground and going away.
One terrified squawk sent the cricket spinning,
And bird and cat hit the grass together, a feathery tussle:
The end, the mad scrambling end and the clutched truimph,
Abrupt close of the long life-gamble.

      Not yet. Not yet.

Pressed under the paws the jay's head struggled out,
Screeching piteously. The jay breed responded.
Converging from thicket and scrub,
From the tall stands of redwood and the streamside alders,
They closed in. The long flight-angles
Planed down, not jockeying now for scattered crumbs
But swooping for life, the only life they know:
The perdurable breed.

      Wheeling above the crouched pair
They danced like blue devils.
The black tom grinned up at them,
His neck craned, his white teeth
Gleaming behind stretched lips,

His eyes yellow fire. Under his feet
The caught prey implored, piteously, the long lament,
The life-going.

                    That hullabaloo
Brought the cat tribe in from the listening woods.
First little Squeak, least of the litter,
Who snatched the prey from her brother's paws
Distracted by jaybirds. But she, too, dawdled,
She, too, toyed with that pleading life,
Till her bigger sister, greedy minx,
Snatched it away, and with one clench of her jaw
Crushed the black-crested head.
Instantly all fell still, the fierce clamor hushed,
The yard deeply silent. From twig and branch the jays looked down,
Stunned, shaken. Then the parent bird
Gave the sharp *tut-tut*, abrupt signal of termination,
And they all took off.

                    The cats
Ignored what they caught, left the futile remains,
Small wing-flurry of the spent cyclone,
Scattered in the grass. As for me,
Something within was held suspended,
The extravagant episode suddenly quenched
Like a drench of ether splashed on my heart.
I picked up the disheveled, resplendent wings,
And stretched them to let the light fall through,
Translucent blue in the wild feathers. Then the arrogant tail
That had flirted with death and not won.
And for final gesture the elegant claw
Crooked at the sky.

                    I took the numinous trophies
Inside the house to dry on a ledge. Well-placed,
Their iridescent message glows in the room,
To reveal from beyond the screen of Nature
The life of God.

                    But what was the vibration
That trailed through the rooms as I bore them in,

And clings yet to my hands, like mountain misery?
A speck of blood flecked my fingernail.
Tasting, I imagined it salt.

                    But the moment was no more.

Outside, in the languid day, the black tom
Slunk beneath the hibachi stand and took up his post.
A touch of swagger, transmitted out of the fetch of the jay,
Invested his movements with auspicious pomp.
Oh, what animal cunning licked the feline lips,
Appeasement clean as a wing-bone whistle?
Reality reduced to a feather in the grass,
A plume in the fern?

                    Whatever death is
The jaybird learned it. But the black tom
Demurs, coiled in contradiction, the infinite
Satisfaction of life. Crouched on sheathed paws
He watches. His yellow eyes, blank as the sun,
Ceaselessly scan the jayless sky,
And not blink.

STEELHEAD

Incipient summer, scorch of the sun,
And the great steelhead shows up in our creek.
He lies in a pool, the shallow basin of a thin rock weir,
Impassively waiting. Ten days go by
And still he lingers. His presence
Is inscrutable. No one around here
Recalls such a thing: steelhead
Landlocked in summer.

                                For the tag-end of April
Sees the last of them. Unlike all salmon,
Rising in winter to die at the spawn,
Steelhead commonly wrig back to sea,
Reclimbing the river-path year after year:
Continuous the trek, the journey joined;
Indomitable the will, the life-thrust.

But this? This aberration?
What is its meaning, and why here?
Deeper hideouts, below and above,
Where salmon and steelhead alike at the spawn
Await their time—those same deep holes
Are perfect places to bide out the drought
Were such his purpose. But no. Dangerously exposed,
In window-pane water he lies alone,
And waits. Inexplicably waits.

Dreaming last night I stiffly arose,
Groped my way down through scarred slopes
To a shallow pool. I knew it for his.
The moon, gibbous, lacked light to see by,
But sensing him there I made vaguely out,
Alone on the bottom like a sunken stick—
No, like a God-stoned monk prostrate in his cell—
That enigmatic shape, sleeplessly intent.
Daunted, I left him alone in that hapless place
And crept back to bed.

                                To go down in the dawn,

Seeking him out as in my dream,
Holding him there in my mind's eye,
Still pointed upstream, smelling the high
Headwaters, while all about him
The dance of life sweeps rapturously on—

Giddy with delight the moths fly double.
In a spasm of joy the mayflies breed.
Above on the bank our Labrador bitch,
Massively in heat, hears her elkhound lover
Yelp on the hill and will not heel;
While under the weir the phlegmatic crayfish,
Gnome of these waters, ponderously grapples his viscid consort,
All fever aslake....

          Only myself,
Stooping to fathom his meaning here,
Know the tightening nerves....

              What his time portends
I dare not guess. But much or little,
Brief or prolonged, in this recondite presence
I am favored in my life—honored in my being,
Illumined in my fate. As hieratic gesture
He sounds the death-pang of abnegation,
Witness to the world.

          Segregate,
Wrenched out of context, bearing the suppressed
Restlessness of all disjunction, subsumed
In the abstract dimension this bloodlife abhors—
Out of time, out of season,
Out of place and out of purpose—
Ineluctable pariah, he burns in my dream
And calls me from sleep.

          Who am hardly surprised
To find by the water his scattered remains

Where the raccoons flung him: tore gill from fin,
Devoured the life-sustaining flesh, and left in clay
The faint skeletal imprint—as fossil
Etched in stone spans time like myth—
The glyph of God.

⧉ ⧉

CUTTING THE FIREBREAK

Mowing the east field under the ridge
I wade the wind. The bent-rib scythe found rusting in the barn
Swings in the sun; the ancient blade of my wife's great-grandfather,
Drawn from the dust of seventy years, riots in the grass.

"They don't make 'em like this old gull anymore!" cackled the smith,
Hunched above his spectral grindstone,
Shouting across the howl of iron and the fleer of sparks.
He paused, spat on the blade, wiping off rust. In the sudden silence
The wedding band he wore on his finger chimed fine steel.
Cocking his head like a listening bird he snatched up a file
        and rapped again.
"Hear that hum in her spine, that tone when she shivers?"
He barked harsh laughter. "Old timers
Got a name for it." Turning, he cut the power,
Stepped down from the bench. *They call it*
The moan of death!"

                    And that hunger
Vibrates up the crooked stock as the grass reels.
I feel it hum in my arms; stroke on stroke
It sings in my shoulders; my collarbone
Rings to the pulse of it, the ravenous steel;
And I swing with it, made one with it,
Wheeling among the standing fern, goat-footed,
Trampling tall bracken, ruthless, the radiant flowers:
Iris, wild orchid, leopard lily—
The flush and shimmering splendor of life!

And then the honing: whetstone and steel
Kiss each other, they crave it so.
They lick their lips greedily together,
Like reckless lovers, or as the whore mouths the man.
I have to pull them apart.

                    The mad scythe
Hisses in the vetch, a snake denied, moans in the yarrow.
Whumph! Whumph! Oh, the grunt of lovers biting each other,

Stroke on stroke coupling through hell. It makes the sex
Growl in my groin to call them down, wild iris, lily,
The moan and the shudder. All the women in my life
Sprawled in the weeds—drunk in death.

◧ ◧

RATTLESNAKE AUGUST

A rainless winter; week on week sun edging the hills,
And the frost's grey grip.

Summer broke dry,
A tightness of heat clenched the sterile coast, a fierce parching.
No fog fended the light; a threat of fire
Stung the rustling air. By midsummer's moon
Leaves littered raw earth.

Then late one dusk
Our Labrador bitch slogged home half lame,
Bleeding a little under the jaw, but we thought nothing of it:
Likely stuck on a thorn.

Morning found her prostrate,
The head hugely swollen, the throat hemorrhaging blood.
"Snakebite," said the vet, "and she's too far gone.
Tonight she will die."

We stared at each other.
Rattlesnakes in Big Creek canyon? Unheard of.
But the vet shook his head. "This God damned drought
Forces them down from their mountain dens
To creek water. We've known places this year
No snake's ever been seen in before,
And we're not done yet."

Now, with night dropping,
We sit in the hot unnatural silence,
Awaiting the friendly scratch at the door
We know will not come. This loss is a wound,
Tearing the sensitive fabric of our life, and it aches in us.
We think of the snake out there in the dark,
Lurking, the vibration of evil,
Coiling under the roots of trees,

Alive beneath stones, listening.

I see tears blind your eyes.
Tonight, I know, you will tear my snake-totem
Down from the wall, and burn it, bitterly,
Your lips moving, your eyes blue ice.

I do not begrudge it: your way is best.

For two themes contend here: the loss and the menace,
Double pang of the twisted heart.
We braced for disaster, a vast conflagration,
A holocaust borne on an eastern draft sweeping down to the sea,
Burning homesites and bridges, driving the coastal population
Out onto the roads.

                    It has yet to happen.
Rather, this subtle insinuation,
Gliding secretly into the warm nest
To spit venom.

            Because sunspots
Distantly flare on the fountain of fire
Must something displace, hit at man's life,
Take his friend and companion?
Whatever he loves, be taken, must go?

I leave the table, step out under stars,
Smelling dryness in the air. And death,
The presence of death.

                Lurker in the dark,
Where are you?

              Harried by heat,
Possessed of a taut desperation, the serpentine itch,
Driven down from some cool commodious hole higher up,

He descends, seeking water, water,
Raw slake for his thirst.

For he, too, loves life. He, too,
Craves comfort, smells it cunningly
Out. And when Fate accosts—
Licks his lip and stabs back.

CHAINSAW

Three alders, shimmering
Graceful presences,
Swaying below the creek-bank,
Halfway down.

They will make welcome wood
Come winter.

I bring the blade,
Wiping it,
Handling it gingerly.

Scythes and axes I understand,
But the chainsaw?
What governs it?

The mechanistic fury.
The annihilate god.

I hear him moaning there,
Drawing the lovely alders down,
Calling them.

I feel the hunger of death
Pulse in his loins,
Tremble in his thews.

I smell his breath.

回

Settling the squat
Metallic beast on the ground
I grip the starter,
Spin once, spin twice.

With a deafening blast
The engine grabs,
Coughs, grabs again,

Then settles into it,
A rapacious snore.

Holding it forth in tense hands
I approach the trees,
Footing my way through vine-tangle,
Cautiously stepping.

As I move, the lethal snout
Roves ahead,
Snuffling for prey.

I place the blade,
Toothing the woman-smooth bark,
The naked skin.

My trigger finger crooks
And the chain leaps forward,
Chews white flesh.

Sawdust pours at my feet,
Spurts from the jagged gash like gore,
Like flowing blood.

Cutting in close
I lean on the steel,
The blade whining.

The tree starts over,
Then hangs there,
Hovering on its axis,
Death in its veins.

An ominous rushing of wind overhead,
A splintering shriek.

I scramble aside,
Watching it topple.
With a shattering crash
It hits, the heaviness

Flattening the air.

Fulcrumed across the granite lip
It twists crazily,
Butt flopping skyward.

I stand there staring,
The hushed saw whispering in my hands,
Asking, asking.

Next, number two.
Sheared through the trunk
It drops without a hitch:
A pushover.

Confident now I turn to the third.
The shrill saw whines,
Steel teeth tearing.

I bear down on it,
Forcing it, the blade
Snarling.

At last it goes over.

But as it crashes across,
Skinning the others,
The butt whips wide,
Spins toward me.

Startled, I jump back,
One half-step back into—
Nothing.

Saving myself,
I lunge forward,
A bid for balance,

But the blade stoops.

Suddenly I feel a terrible
Insinuative plucking at my knee,
A picking at my flesh.

It is the chain,
The chipping incisors,
The nipping teeth.

Just over my leg the lewd thing hovers,
Floating there, all its passion
Suspended in check,
Eager to pounce.

Appalled, I heave the beast up,
Falling back,
The blade rearing.

I hurl it aside and go down.

It lands on granite,
The chain spewing sparks,
The engine chattering.

Flat on my back
I struggle up and crawl over.
I cut the switch.

Then I look down.

॒

In a crystalline terror
I see the nick of shark-teeth
Etched across my knee:

The dreadful angle
On the blue denim,

The white-plucked thread.

Stunned, I pull up my jeans,
Looking for blood,
The target area.

Bald kneecap.
Naked thigh.

Not a scratch.

A gasp of relief
Delivers me.
Then a dizzying faintness,
Something clutching my throat.

Shaken, I get to my feet,
Leave the beast where it lies,
And hobble home.

Pouring myself a stiff one
I belt it down raw.

The slug hits like a fist.

In the still afternoon
I hear the shivering glass
Chip my teeth.

    ▣

All evening long,
Musing alone,
The family away,
The house empty,

I sip my whiskey,
And feel for it,
The lopped leg:

Groping for something no longer there,

Something gone.

All evening long and the long next day
I hobble about on my pitiful stump.

Something is finished,
Something cleanly done.

Sprawled on the creek-bank
The trees lie untouched;
I have no appetite for the saw.

I might have died there under those alders,
Bled to death before help came.

But that is not in the mind.

What is there is an absence,
A simple loss,
The lack of a leg.

Perfectly sound I hobble about,
Not the ghost of a member
Swung from my hip.

Not even a peg.

　　　▣

And I think of the three graves,
Silent under hanging moss,
Up Scott Creek canyon.

Three clearly marked graves,
All pioneer women,
Peaceful in the sun.

But among them,

According to legend,
A man's leg is buried,

Torn off long ago by a sow grizzly
Protecting her cubs,
Then solemnly interred
In the quaint pioneer fashion.

Dust and ashes
The maimed member reposes.
But in my mind's eye
It glows in the ground,
Inseminating the female presences,
Instinct with seed.

Like Osiris, his phallos
Potent in death,
Or song-struck Orpheus,
Fragmented under the female fury,
The singing flesh.

And, musing, I let my fingers
Grope down, feeling,
Fumbling,

            Seeking
For what is no longer there.

Only the absence.
Only the emptiness,
The blank truncation.

The folly of the three alders.
The terrible stump.

THE VISITATION

Midsummer hush: warm light, inert windless air
Smoothing for sundown. We linger at table, sip wine,
Idly talking, the casual things of the day's dimension,
Our thought settling toward dusk.

Suddenly, in the vast
Calm of the canyon, an ominous crack, a break and snapping.
We look up alarmed. Something in the sound
Wrings our senses, flings us to our feet,
Slamming back chairs.

Then the crackling
Begins to rip, something going down out there
Tearing its guts out in an awful fall,
The air slashed by the shrieked agony of a form
Hauled down out of life, the shrill
Maniacal whine of fibers at last letting go,
The whoosh of a great weight falling, twisting as it drops,
Plunging toward chaos.

And then the crash,
The clobbering smash of that force as it hits,
The boom sweeping over like dynamite blast.
We gaze at each other, thunderstruck,
Utterly aghast—what in God's name!—
The terrible question in each other's eyes,
What skeletons toppling out of what
Unacknowledged closets, nakedly asprawl—

And then the aftermath,
Shock and counter-shock, agonized limbs
Snapping and thrashing, severance in the air,
Gash, splinter, rupture and slump. We hear lesser shapes
Taken down with it, hideously atwist, topple across.
We burst out the door, echoes pounding around us,
And dash down the road toward the wallowing sound,
Incredulous, stumbling and staring bewilderedly about.

For everything is changed. In the smash of disaster

Nothing looks the same, in fact is unseen—
The most familiar objects, house, trees, rocks, path,
All somehow displaced by the intrusion of violence,
The wrenched dimension thrown over them all.

A hundred and fifty yards downstream
A wall of dust, like burnt gunpowder,
Yellow and angry, is boiling toward us.
Then, before it arrives, some last hanging branch,
Scraped off and hung up in the weight of passage,
Sickeningly lets go, an abrupt finale.
The crack as it hits is a man's
Decapitated head dropped over a cliff:
We hear it thud and lie still.
Then a terrible silence floods back and engulfs us.
We wade through dust to that stunned place,
Expecting there we hardly know what.

A giant tree lies aslant the cut,
The narrowest part of the steep gorge,
Spanning creek and roadbed, a total block.
There it had stood, a great dead fir,
Daily passed by year in and year out,
But never seen, unnoticed in the dense foliage
Above and beyond us, where the road snaked by
Along the lightly-flowing creek
Through dense alder and laurel clumps,
Among strewn boulders.

                              Suddenly emerging, out of the long
Anonymity of its dream in the massed forest,
Expending its whole potential of life-force
In the apotheosis of its collapse, it staggers,
It descends.

              You have in your mind
The vision of this form, secretly sprung from a blown seed
Three centuries ago, quietly growing unobserved,
Gaining tremendous girth and height,
Sucking sunlight above and water below,
Then slowly dying, to stand in death
Many decades more, until at last,

Having weathered the howling hurricanes
That whip up the gorge, finally, in the utter
Calm of an August evening, suddenly letting go,
Pitching out of its ancient potential,
To shatter the canyon with its hideous scream,
Smash down the cliff,
Drop sharply across the shimmering creek,
Naked and fractured and stark,
A kind of final assertion of self,
The dropped trunk and branches
Blocking the trail. Nothing can pass now
Till chainsaw and peavey arrive and divide,
Section the torso, pull apart the limbs,
The crossed, sprawled members,
The fractured bones, and the crushed
Samson-like form of the prone giant.

Not Samson. A female thing, the high fork
Clearly denoting the vulva-crotch
Loggers call schoolmarms—
She lies sprawled and wanton in death,
Like a big-boned woman in a highway smash,
Half flung free, her twisted torso,
Laced with blood and lingerie,
Collapsed in the ditch.
Yokels arrive to stare dumbly down,
Brought dazedly out from their shattered supper,
But dare not touch....

                    Nor do we now.
We gaze and marvel. We stand in stunned silence.
We grope for words, twisting our anxious
Fingers together, talking low,
Letting our thoughts run on and on, aimlessly,
Till the drag of dark
Pulls over, leaving between us
The shape of vast immensities, and above our heads
The stars' blunt dismissal.

KINGFISHER FLAT

A rustle of whispering wind over leaves,
Then the stillness closes: no creek-music,
No slurred water-sound. The starved stream
Edges its way through dead stones,
Noiseless in the night.

                I feel your body
Restless beside me. Your breathing checks
And then resumes, as in a moment of dream
The glimpsed image, mutely desired but scarcely believed,
Fades and revives.

              In the long drought
Impotence clutched on the veins of passion
Encircles our bed, a serpent of stone.
I sense the dearth in you also,
The bane that is somehow mine to impose
But yours to endure—cohibition of the blood,
Flaw of nature or defect of the soul—
Dry turning of leaves, cessation of desire,
Estrangement gripped in the roots of the hair,
And around the loins, like a fine wire,
The cincture of nerves.

              I think of the Fisher King,
All his domain parched in a sterile fixation of purpose,
Clenched on the core of the burning question
Gone unasked.

              Out in the dark
The recumbent body of earth sleeps on,
Silent as dust, incognizant. Many a moon,
Many a withering month will she weary
Ere the black knight of storm whirls out of the West,
Churns from the turbulent fosse of the sea,
Assaults the shore, breaches the continental slope
And takes her, his torrential force
Stripping the iron zone of chastity
Down from her thighs, drenching belly and breasts,

All the pores of her famished body
Agape—

        Oh, wife and companion!
The ancient taboo hangs over us;
A long suspension tightens its grip
On the seed of my passion and the flower of your hope.
Masks of drought deceive us. An inexorable forbearance
Falsifies the face of things, and makes inflexible
The flow of this life, the movement of this love.
What prohibitive code stiffens the countenance,
Constricts the heart? What fear constrains it?
And whose the blame?

          Enough.
There is no need now, nor ever was,
For the ghastly rote of self-accusation
Scrupulosity enjoins. To find a new mate
Were nothing difficult for one so young, so lovely.

But something other, more inscrutably present,
Obtains here, possessing us, cohesive in spirit,
Divisive in the flesh—the lordly phallos
Never again to joust in the festive lists of love,
Quench its ardour in the uterine fens,
Assuage your cry?

        Myth and dream
Merge in a consanguinity of kind,
Fuse the soul's wild wish and the hunger of the race
On the body's pang.

        But something forbears.
Like Merlin and Niniane, bound in a fatefulness
That set them aside, wisdom and delight
Crucified in bed, polarized on the stretched extreme
That made them one, we twist our grievous fingers together
And stare in the dark.

        I hear quaking grass
Shiver under the windowsill, and out along the road
The ripe mallow and the wild oat

Rustle in the wind. Deeper than the strict
Interdiction of denial or the serpentine coiling of time,
Woman and earth lie sunk in sleep, unsatisfied.
Each holds that bruise to her heart like a stone
And aches for rain.

BRIDE OF THE BEAR

We camp by a stream among rugged stumps
In logged-over country. No tree shelters our bed.
In the year-long drought gripping the Sierras
There is no snow, and the night is warm.
After our fog-haunted coast the air at this height
Seems weightless, without substance, almost clairvoyant.
Luminous stars, low overhead, look into our lives.
At ground level the campfire
Dapples the stumps, throws fitful shadows,
Guttering the dark.

                    We drink late wine.
Arriving at dusk we had pitched camp quickly,
Eaten nervous supper. For a ranger going out
Warned of bear sign, and a wrangler behind him
Showed packs ripped open, bacon gorged. Seeing it
We prudently stashed our food in the jeep,
Gathered firewood, branch and root,
And built up the blaze. Fumbling through our gear
My hand touched in passing the great bearskin
Carried in from the coast, belated wedding gift
Brought along to delight you, a savage pelt to throw down by the fire,
Barbaric trophy in a mountain lair—but here,
In the actual presence, in bear country,
Furtively concealed: discreet hibernation
In the cave of the car.

                    When the blaze dies down
I step out of its circle to fetch more wood
Against the presences of night. Standing in the dark
I look wondering up at those luminous orbs,
Hovering like moths just out of reach, preternaturally intense.
I sense around me the ghosts of slain trees,
Nude giants, slaughtered under the axe,
Pitching down from the slopes, the prone torsos
Hauled out with engines. Listening, I hear the famished creek
Drain west, a gurgle in a gravel throat,

Gasping.

             Back by the fire
You have fallen asleep, dazed with wine,
Curled by bright embers on living fern.
I lace a clutch of twigs on the coals
And in the spurt of flame see gooseflesh
Stipple your arm. Under the mellowing influence of wine
My nerves loosen, and I dismiss caution.
I fetch from the jeep the great bearskin
And draw it across you, then fondly step back to admire my care.
But what have I wrought that my own hand shaped
Yet could not forestall? Oh, most inadvertently
I have folded you in the bear's huge embrace,
A hulking lover, the brute body enveloping you,
Massively yours.

             You snuggle happily under it, sighing a bit,
The moan of a fretful satisfaction breathed from your deeps.
Is it wine on your lips that reddens them,
Or something deeper, in the bear's hug,
There, below the heart, a more elemental zone
At the body's base?

             I cannot tell.
But whatever it is it wantons your mouth,
And your mouth mocks me: inviting and denying,
The enigma of desire. I think, So be it.
Thus have I made you
Bride of the bear.

             And thinking it,
The night chill shivers me, a sudden *frisson*,
The languor of wine possessing me.
I feel surge through my veins
The madcap days of our courtship,
Crazy monk and runaway girl,
Panting in discovery, goading each other on,

Wildly in love.

You stir in the bearskin.
Has memory touched you, two minds drenched in wine
Seeking each other through the cavern of sleep
Along the ancient line, the tendril of desire?

Drugged in dream you turn heavily. That nubile litheness
No longer is yours. But something better lives on in its place,
A mature abundance filling your flesh, the bloom of full life.

I, greybeard, nurse my drink and suck my pipe,
Watching the stars expire.

Now you turn,
Lifting your dream-drenched face to the light,
Still sunken in sleep, the wantonness
Splashed like wine on your parted lips.
Stiffly, raised on one elbow, you fumble at your blouse,
The heat under the animal pelt
Oppressing you. When your hand succeeds,
I see the naked globes of your breasts
Flash back the fire.

Bride of the bear.

Gazing up the dark I watch the stars
Cross the verge that shuts midnight from dawn
To walk down the west. Whatever happened to time?
When we pulled down our packs
The night lay before us. Now, in another hour,
Night is no more.

Somewhere out there
The ubiquitous beast, gorged on raw bacon,
Sleeps off his jag.

Raising your head
You look dazedly about, dimly comprehending,

Then sink back to sleep.

                              Around the campfire
The ghosts of slain trees look over us.
Out of the eastern peaks, traced now with light,
The dawn wind whispers. The starved stream
Gropes through the stumps.

回 回

MOONGATE

Las Gaviotas, Baja California

Something calls me from sleep.
I arise and go out, passing the bed
Where my brother and his wife,
Blanketed against the mild nightchill,
Lie side by side, at peace with themselves,
Serene in their world, the ineffable
Satisfaction of shared event,
The long-married.

                I recall how they met.
A young bachelor-foreman, out of sorts with himself,
He drifted about a vast city without direction,
Till an old craftsman on the job he managed
Admonished him:

                "Son, take my advice,
Don't live alone. Go to a small town,
Find the eldest daughter of a large family,
And marry her."

                So it happened.
Thirty-nine years they have been together;
Their children are grown, their grandchildren
Half grown. I think of my own fragmented life,
Torn in two, the lost loves, the passions,
And wonder what karmic hazard
Promised the permanence
But denied me the term.

                I open the door.
Standing on the threshold I gaze south and west,
Where the deep sky domes a wide bay,
Embracing the sea. The night is hushed,
The air winsome and smooth in balmy midsummer,
The vast sea dark, silent save for the abrupt thump,
An intermittent shuff of sudden wave,

Slapping the shore.

                    Glancing west,
I see the red moon low on the sea,
Sinking fast. A ribbon of cloud,
Sealing the horizon, divides like a curtain
Closing a stage of consciousness,
Preparing for exit.

                    The moon hovers a moment.
It is nascently gibbous, two days past the half
In the waxing cycle, slightly misshapen, a youthful wife
Seductively pregnant.

                    I have not got a child.

Suddenly I sense my brother behind me,
Gazing outward across my shoulder.
"The Chinese," he whispers, "call it moongate,"
His voice kept low not to waken his wife.
Uncomprehending, I shake my head.
"The wake," he insists. "Look,
The path the moon makes there on the water."
Then I see it, a shimmering track,
Smoking on the swart sea's surface,
Reddishly gold, inviting and denying,
The way death does when it glints its promise
And withholds its peace.

                    My brother
Turns back to bed. Above the house
A flight of terns going west,
Invisibly talking together in the night,
Passes beyond, their strange speech falling softly about me,
The unearthly guttural of an archaic tongue
Unknown to man.

                    And I think of Susanna,
Far to the north, deeply asleep in the redwood canyon,
Where the great horned owls
Chuckle together in thick-set darkness,

Hungry for quail.

                And I remember again
Those madcap days and that courtship,
When we lay all night on the beach at Point Reyes,
Hearing surf shape the dunes,
While our souls, entranced, trod the moongate together,
Back down the path to man's beginnings,
That was yet our future.

How could we know what death it presaged,
That singleness of self at last given over,
The birth of new being?

                The moon
Trembles a moment and then plunges in,
The suck of an utter surrendering,
Drawn to the depths of all beginnings,
The watery womb.

                There is left only the night,
Stretched point to point of the dark horizon,
The night and the sea.

                Bahía del Descanso,
Mexicans call it: "The Bay of Repose."

                                Inside,
I hear the sigh of my brother's wife, turning,
Questioning and murmuring,
As he slips in beside her,
Settling to sleep.

                Bahía del Descanso.
Something clutches my heart,
The sudden years of unrealization,
Where the moongate closed
And the nightbirds vanished.

A dream awaits me back in bed,
And I turn to take it up.
Hovering on sleep I hear the ragged mutter of surf

Chewing the shore. The dawn wind
Rattles the blinds.

II

My brother and I are standing together
On the banks of a river. It is the Kings,
(Called *Río de los Santos Reyes* by the Spanish)
Back in the country where we grew up,
Below Piedra (meaning *rock*) where the water
Pours from the mountains, flattens out on the plains.

It is springtime; grass is tall green,
And all about us the ubiquitous poppies
And wild purple lupine
Pull in the wind.

On the slope above
Remnants of the old sugarpine flume
Lumbermen built to float logs from the mountains,
Still span the gullies, skeletal remains,
Keeping tryst with time in these relic-less hills.

Not eighty years old, in so new a country
They yet embody the ineluctable past,
Residual traces of the ancient ones, the Pioneers, for us
As potent with meaning as Stonehenge,
And as evocative.

In the dream
My brother and I are high-school age
Or just past; but when I turn to speak
He is gone, following the river
Out onto the plains, off over the flatlands
To the cities of the world.

I myself
Turn back upstream, into the mountains.
They pile above me, ridge beyond ridge.
In the roots of my consciousness
They have always been there,
Aloof, majestic, their cloud-hung shoulders

And their imponderable brows,
Like congeries of ancestral fathers,
Gazing down on the distant breed they engendered,
And waiting, waiting....

                    Now Edwa is beside me,
My first love. The mountains are forgotten.
We go hand in hand, boy with girl
Through the magic springtime,
Rapturously in love.

                    As if
All we will ever have is each other,
All we will ever need is each other,
All we will ever know is each other.

                    As if
Nothing will ever exist but ourselves.

Suddenly, in peripheral vision,
I see the fox. He springs up before us,
Audaciously striking out to the left,
Looking back as he runs.

                    The intrusion
Dazzles me. Edwa does not see him,
But tearing my gaze from her eyes as I turn,
I follow the fox.

                    He leaps through the grass,
Dodging and twisting, half-crawling,
Then inexplicably showing himself,
Seductively beckoning, only to disappear again,
Running rapid as light.

                    Rust red,
Somehow flecked with blue, like fire,
And the flowing tail like a flame, he runs.
He beckons and runs.

                    Now Edwa is gone.
But still I press forward, urgently,

Following the fox, the illusive one,
Fleeing, beckoning.

                    Then I remember:
It is the great canyon of the Kings,
High in the mountains, the inaccessible
Headwaters, the abode of God.

To this I am drawn.

Now I hear someone running behind me.
Looking back I see her, the strange woman.
She is following, watchfully intent,
Not seeing the fox but sensing what I seek,
The mysterious bourn, the quest.

Returning to the trace
I press on up the river,
Following the fox.

When the dusk draws down
I look back at the woman.
As if by sign she moves up beside me.

What I follow she cannot see.
But what I see she follows.

And her eyes are shining, shining.

    ▣ ▣

BUCK FEVER

Drought-stricken hills. Somewhere ahead
Lay a waterhole, and the thought
Moistened his mouth. But there was no game,
And late in the day, the camp calling him back,
He relented: "To hell with it. One more swing
Round this blistered ridge and I'll give it up."

Then deer-scat in the trail, buck shit
By the size of it, and, sure enough, there in the dust,
One fabulous print....

                         "Son of a bitch!"

A rustle of leaves in the scrub oak,
A thump of hooves on dry earth
Stopped him in his tracks.
Eyes fixed on that muffled ripple of sound
His pulse skipped, then pounded on.
Something cautiously moved there, that much was sure.
Then the great crowned head, the twelve-point antlers
Rode slowly across his line of vision
Between two trees, but instantly gone,
And the footfall checked.

                    The buck, warily upwind,
Had not caught his scent. He crept forward two steps
But his foot scuffed twigs and the beast snorted.
Suddenly it minced into view, nimbly,
On tiptoe, ears up, nostrils flared,
The arched neck craning—and the eyes,
The liquid eyes in the spade-shaped face,
Staring.

          He stood transfixed.
"Oh God and Jesus," his heart whispered,

Then his brain sang: *This is it!*

But suddenly
A giant hand reached out of that presence and gripped him cold.
Something in the beast itself, motionless there,
Reached out of its magical shape and possessed him,
An invasion of awe.

His arms shuddered,
Hands fluttering rags. The rifle, cantilevered ahead,
Wobbled between them. As he strove to raise it
An eternity of helplessness sucked down his strength,
Wrung him limp.

Then, in a sudden convulsion,
His whole being revolted, cracked the somnambulism
Of desire that held him in thrall,
Shook him free.

Pitching rifle to shoulder
He got off a shot, the report smashing the silence.
The buck jumped sideways, a shocked nerve,
As if the sound alone had struck it broadside
And thrown it back.

Suddenly it broke,
Took one long incredible leap,
Spun away, cleared a fallen log,
And was off, a tawny streak.

With the back of his hand he kicked the lever,
Heard the fresh shell slam in the chamber.
Crash! His head jerked as if punched,
The gun muzzle whipping. He kicked shell after shell,
Crash! Crash! plugging the emptiness
Round the vanishing shape, a crazy staccato.
When the hammer snapped on blank steel
He dropped his arms, his retina
Retaining the futile spurt of gravel
His last shot picked on the shale slope
Above and behind the streaking shape

Before it was gone.

                    He stared, disbelieving.
There was the jagged hole in space that had held it.
There was the magical moment, and the rent silence
That let it go. There was the acrid reek of gunsmoke
Stinging his nostrils.

                    No more. Nothing more.

Looking about him, suddenly aware of the low fading light,
Everything burned pure: the squat trees,
The stiffly hunched hills, the bleak
Pitch of the sky.

                    And the remoteness, the wrenched
Remoteness of it all.

                    He sank down on a log,
But instantly climbed to his feet,
Seeking proof, the crucial verification,
The track of the buck.

                    When he found it,
The clear etch of its print in the thin dust
Was the sign of a wonder his infancy knew,
But thought could not reach.

                    There was no blood.

He stood there a moment,
Letting the fever fade from his hands,
Fade from his knees and his fluttering heart.

When his nerves steadied
He shoved three cartridges into his gun,
But it took four.

                    Where the empty shells
Lay scattered about the print of his boots

He stared dumbly.

There were four, all right.

> Picking them up
He tossed them pensively into the brush,
One by one, where none could be seen.

Then he went back.

> That night in his dream
A puma stalked a dappled fawn under bristlecone scrub
But missed its quarry.

> Next morning,
Sousing his face in mountain water,
Something he'd learned once long ago
Slid into his mind:

> *The fawn has no scent.*

He thought of the hollow space,
The weird light that held the buck
Before it vanished, and a childish wish
Crossed his mind:

> *A silver bullet.*
> *Fake out that magic.*
> *Kill that devil.*

> Stooping to drink
He glimpsed his own furred face in the ripple,
Those strange eyes in the deep.

THE SUMMER OF FIRE

"California is burning!" The voice of the newscaster,
Portentous and somber, tolls off a hundred spotfires
Strung up the State, from the South San Gabriels
To the Siskiyou chain.

Ten days back
Thunder rattled us out of the house at dawn
To scan the sky and watch dry lightning
Walk on the hills.

Why the Santa Cruzes
Never caught fire no one could guess.

But eastward,
Across the inland oven of the Central Valley,
The entire Sierra felt the whiplash fall,
And in the withered tinder of a two-year drought
Canyons threw smoke like the belch of chimneys
Tonguing the sky.

North of us
Mount Diablo wrapped itself in a crimson mantle
And claimed its name: a surging inferno.

To the south
Big Sur exploded: impacted brush,
Flattened by heavy snowfalls of the past, lay on the slopes,
Fifty tons to the acre round the Ventana Cones,
And the runaway burn tore rugged country
Like a raging bull.

This morning at dawn
The sun rose bloody through a pall of smoke
From sixty miles south. At noon
Our shadows, askew on the ground,
Cast an amber aura.

It gives a weird refraction,
Something unspeakable, covertly glowering behind one's back,

Edging into view when crisis looms.

                                    I waggle my weight,
Make the aural demon dance, thinking,

                              "So?
The white light around the body
Turns angry when denied?"

        ⬜

                              Angry and umbrageous.
City people shake their heads and thank their stars
But the local folk are sardonic: they've been through it before.
When a young State Forester knocks at the door
And hands us a list of printed regulations:
Clear every building down to mineral soil sixteen feet back,
We thank him grimly and reach for our rakes.

But the widow McCrary, from the porch of the house in which she was born
Seventy years past, glances at the list
And glares at the man:

                              "I resent this. Our people
Took care of this country before your department
Ever was dreamed of." The offending document
Flutters to the ground. "We don't have to be told what to do."

I stand in the dusk on Kingfisher Flat and think,
"How beautiful!"

                        Pride, itself fiery, incites defiance,
Rising out of the char of the past
To re-envision crisis—what came as affliction
Lives on in the mind as a kind of grace,
Restored to legitimacy in the distancing of time,
Made memorable through struggle.

                              And indeed
Out on the flat the twin giant redwoods

Carry the scars of ancient fire from centuries back,
Ennobling them, were that possible, with the dignity of pain.

Farther up the slope the blackened hollows of burnt-out stumps
Honor the primal war between them,
Vegetation and flame.

One is life and one is death,
Yet polarity binds them. Definition is the clue.
Only out of the screaming tension, each true to its own,
Comes clarification.

囘

Procreation and death.
The conflagration of sexuality
Whips through the taut congestion of nerves,
Like the van of fire in the canyon sluices,
Singeing and searing, scorching root and branch,
Tendril in the mesh, driving the beleaguered ego
Back and forth between the rages of excess.

A year of extremes. Creek-bottoms
Flake with the frosts of winter; flash floods shatter;
High ridges endure the fires of drought.
Season on season the great God of All Weathers
Grinds down the mountains, reducing the coast
Under the hands of those terrible abrasions,
While man, a pigmy, dances between them,
Dodging fire and water, reeling beneath the twin flagellations,
Shaking a puny fist at the sky, cursing and blaspheming,
Till old age chastens him to dignity at last.

And what of me? Has age brought peace?
Imposing a wry chastity

On the flammable mind?

To the contrary.
The pummel of suppressed exultance
Rages through me, crying:

"Burn! Burn!
All you dead grasses, fallen under the scythe,
Wild iris, leopard lily, sweep skyward in flame,
Meet fire in heaven with fire on earth!"

I look up above at the towering trees,
That took at the root the red demon
From time out of mind, monumentally impassive,
And I cry:

"Burn! Burn!
O chaste ones, magnificent presences,
Scream in the ecstasy of consummation,
Torch and expire!"

I gaze wildly about at the rim of the sky,
Craving a luridity of glare,
My eyes smarting, my nostrils
Flared.

Only the dark drops.

Inside the house my young wife
Fixes the supper, her lithe body
Moving between the table and the stove,
Sinuously alive.

I look at the sky
One final time. Over my head the first star
Glitters through haze, a liquid agate.

And I think: Whatever

Idiot catastrophe the heart craves,
This is the peace.

            Let autumn
Bring in its wake what it will or can,
The summer is supreme.

            Old earth
Hugs pure fire down deep at her heart,
And banks power.

SPOTFIRE

A single cap pistol,
Found on a shelf in a local market,
Left over from the Fourth.

Bought with his carefully hoarded coin
It hangs in his hand,
Cradled home through the heat.

Whipped from the hip,
Snapped fast, multiple explosions
Shatter the calm, break
The lazy afternoon.

He cocks and fires,
Cocks and fires,
The solitary sport of the only-begotten.

Round the corner of the house
He twists and slithers,
Fleeing bandits,
Then down across the creek
And up the other side.

Behind a fallen log
He flops on his belly,
Himself now the bandit, picks off
The converging posse.

Plunging back to the creek,
Bullets zinging about his head,
He makes his getaway,
Disappears down the road.

🔲

A half-hour later
I stand in the yard of Kingfisher Flat,
In the late light,
Barefooted, gazing leisurely about,

Smelling the air of approaching autumn,
The rare tang of fall,
Before drifting indoors
To mix the first drink.

Suddenly my eye, attracted upslope,
Catches color, a bright blaze,
Fire crackling up the skewed log.

"What the hell...."

I grab up a bucket, yelling to my wife.
She comes out the back, wondering,
Sees fire sharp on the hill
And her face blanches.

I race for the creek,
Aghast, bucket in hand.
There is hardly water,
But somehow I scoop it,
Half a pail at best,
And climb the steep slope,
Twisting and slipping,
My feet bleeding.

Where an eight-year-old kid
Scampered like a chipmunk
I can hardly crawl.

Just in time I reach it,
The climbing fire,
And the water dashes it down.

Sliding back to the creek
I hit hard. My wife,
Standing slipper-deep in muck,
Hands another bucket,
Full and slopping over,
And I start the crawl back.

Now the boy shows up out of nowhere,
Running scared, grabbing pails,

Tin cans, fruit jars,
Anything to hold water.
Suddenly beside me,
He sloshes burning punk.

        Three trips and it's out,
        The blaze quenched.

We stand in the creek, the three of us,
Panting, thoroughly frightened,
Looking up at the hill,
The tangled thicket,
Mountain brush, tall standing timber,
Looking up the long half-mile of hillside above us,
And thinking:

        Beyond it the range,
        The crackling heat of fire-prone September,
        And beyond that the State....

Incredulously staring, hardly daring to ponder
What a minute or two more
Must surely have meant.

(Who would have thought
The paper cap of a toy pistol
Could ignite the world?)

Breathing gratitude to God
For deliverance, the spared moment,
The sudden reprieve.

      ▣

Two days later the episode is fading,
But what is etched in my mind
Is the glob of fire in the late light,
Orange red, the flames licking up,
A burning core of intensity,
Like the essence of a giant fruit,
As if we were being shown,

Through a slit in the skin,
The fiery inside:
A hole in the surface
To another dimension—

                  As if suddenly
Through the film of the earth
A flame stuck out its tongue,
Licking greedily,
Exposing all the impacted fire
Compressed at its heart.

And I fix my sight on it, my eyeball
Glued to the glory-hole of a blast furnace,
Shaken by the intensity within,
The terror, a fury
Utterly belied by the inert scruff,
The thick vegetation
Masking the hill.

             It is crisis
Makes intensity intense,
Reality real.

            Place consequence in the scales
And watch the pans shiver.

Put fire and death,
Guilt and mortality
In the obsessive choice
And feel the nerves tighten.

I have seen my heart's fate
Shaped in the balance,
And known what I am.

But does *he*?

            His cap pistol
Is contraband till wet weather,

And he truly knows why.

> *But is knowing*
> *Enough? Is knowing*
> *Ever enough?*

I look up above at what might have been,
What fate just missed,
Black char climbing the sky,
Ten thousand acres of smouldering ash.

Somewhere, in the interstices of the self,
Like molten lava at the earth's core,
The principle of existence
Possesses its essence,
Primal, dangerous, unpredictable.
Out of our wayward impulses
It flashes and breaks free.

And I whisper:

> Lord, may what has been learned
Be learned in depth.

> For him.
For me.

◨ ◧

THE HIGH EMBRACE

They stand in the clearing of Kingfisher Flat,
Twin giants, *sequoia sempervirens*, the ever-vernal,
And take in the arms of their upper branches
The last light crossing the bench-ridge west,
Sinking toward dusk.

            Standing between them
I look up the double-columned space to the soaring crown,
Where those red-ribbed branches clasp each other in a high embrace.
For hundreds of years they have stood here, serenely apart,
Drinking clear creek water through their subtle capillary mode,
Feeling the flake of mountains sift chalkstone gravel about their boles,
Watching giant grizzlies scoop gravid salmon
        on the spawning bars below,
And tawny cougars stalk for fawns in their leaf-dappled shade.
They heard the kingfisher chirr his erratic intemperate cry,
While over their tops the slow-wheeling condors circled the sun,
Drifting south to their immemorial roosting-ledges
        in the Los Padres peaks.
And they felt the demon of fire lick its running tongue up
        their shaggy skin
And not flinched, scorched but unscarred in the long warfare,
The stress-tension shaping fuel to fire,
The life-flux of their kind.

            Tonight,
In the heat of drought, we will forsake our bed,
Shutting the house-presence out of our thought,
Taking our respite in the open air. We will muse late,
And lay ourselves down by fir-bark embers,
Under the cape of the twin redwoods, swept back in time
A thousand years when this coast nurtured its kind—
The great beasts, the towering trees, the bird-flight migrations,
The shy coastal tribes. And in the sea-troughs of sleep
Our dreams will mirror the world above
Where stars swim over, and shadow the bloodstream's sibilance,
All through the foliage of the flesh, its fern-like fronds.

Up there above me the last light

Filters in as through stained glass windows,
Diffuse, glowing in the lofts of the upper branches,
Radiant and soft. And the mystery of worship
Descends on me, out of those far fenestrations.
And the God-awe, wake-wonder, envelops me,
Between the monumental straightness of columns
Bearing the sky, illuminate zone, twin towers
Conjoined above, clasped in the high embrace,
The soaring arch.

                    And the face of my son
Dawns between the gigantic boles
As he runs to meet me. And I ask in my heart
The graciousness of God, that he may grow in their presence,
As the tan-oak grows, as the fir-tree and fern,
As the chipmunk and the jay shelter under their span.

And I invoke their mystery of survival,
That the lightning-shattering years,
And the raw surge of fire,
May skim but not scar him—
As they themselves are scathed but unscarred—
Through the skip years of his childhood
And the leap years of his youth.

Make over our heads, then, the high embrace,
Like a blessing, the numinous descent, faith-fall,
Out of the heights, the leaf-light canopy,
The lofts of God, induplicate,
A gift regiven, the boon bestowed.

　　◩ ◩

STONE FACE FALLS

Sheer naked rock. From the high cliff-cut
Straight falling water. Caught halfway down in a stone socket
It checks, boils over, then widens as it drops,
Snaking dreamily into the rockpool below.
Many months back it roared in flood;
Now, in the grip of drought, Big Creek the brawler,
Tamed and gentled, takes this pitch like a gliding dancer,
A shimmering sleeve against dark waterstains,
Storm-trek of the past.

                    We have come,
The two of us, in the white heat of noon,
To bathe at the fall-foot, a lambent pool
Under the salmon-stopping cliff.
We are struck by silence, the reduction of force,
Recalling those thunderous torrents of the past,
When the wild cataract drove everything before it,
Generating in its plunge a saturating gale,
Sopping a man a hundred feet below,
Drenched to the eyes in stinging spume.
But now, in the drought, the diaphanous film
Ripples down the rock, maidenly, a silken
Scarf, the veil of a bride, as virginal
And as lovely.

                    Over our heads the great stone face
Juts from the gorge, a chief's visage hewn in raw granite,
Staring north, gazing up the long south-trek of his people,
Ten thousand years from the Bering Strait.
And the mystery keeps, the indomitable spirit
Guarding the secret where the water pulses,
The source, the slowed rhythm at the timeless center,
The heartbeat of earth.

                    I lower my gaze.
You are standing under the waterfall, nude, your body
An ivory wand against the seamed granite.
It is gleaming there, wreathed in water,
Breasts erect. The woman belly

And the female thighs
Shine in a shimmering ripple of lace,
The circling stream.

     I move to meet you.

Suddenly a kingfisher swoops between.
In midflight he sees us, veers sharply,
Utters a sudden electrifying screech,
The ineluctable tension cruxed at the heart of things
Splitting his beak, the mystery
Out of which life springs and from which it passes.
Three times he circles, skirling his fierce
Importunate cry, then climbs the thermal,
The lazy updraft transcending the falls,
And disappears up the canyon.

You hold out your arms.

Dropping my clothes
I enter the pool,
Wade the ripple to where you stand.

It is the longest walk—
Out of the glacial
Past, through the pulsing present,
Into the clenched
Future—man to woman
Through time-dark waters.

     Far ahead,
Beyond the stone face of the falls,
The cry of the kingfisher
Pierces the noon.

  ◱ ◱

SPIKEHORN

The yearling buck, shot through the lungs,
Made it out of the brush and halfway to the stream
Before he fell. The illegal hunter
Never followed through. What dropped in the meadow
Died where it lay, unnoticed by any save two red bulls
Fenced in that field.

The following day
A great black bird rose up when we came,
Lurched clumsily off, the wings made for soaring
Baffled now in this hemmed enclosure,
This deep forest field.

Late that night
The coyotes found him. We heard from afar
The yelping chorus, clamoration of the feast,
High sung litany to the winnowing of time,
The brevity of life.

Early next morning
The great bird was back with a dozen others,
A vulturine horde. Ghouls out of hell
They perched on the carcass, angling each other out
At the plucking, obscenely gobbling
The riddle of gut.

Our abrupt arrival
Sent them hissing aloft to circle and alight,
Teetering and balancing on the tall fir tops,
Refusing to abrogate their ancient
Prerogative, their ancestral place
At the sharing of the kill.

Two days later
The sentinel bulls stood over the torn and scattered remains,
Bellowing, lugubriously lowing, solemnly lamenting
The passing away of all slotted-hoofed kind,
Mourning the death of their nimbler comrade,

Little cousin of the woods.

                We paused there,
Disbelieving, and spoke to them as best we could.
They stared back, uncomprehending, not to be consoled.
Chagrined, we trudged on.

                The following weeks
Left nothing much but a chewn shinbone and a scrap of hide.
No birds in the sky, no movement in the woods.
Nothing but the sparse pasture, the two red bulls
Placidly cropping the lank cover,
An emptiness in the air.

                Then the changing year
Brought a leaf-flurry. Equinoctial rains
Replenished the earth. In the body-print of the buck
The first green grass quickened the bronze.

                And we said:
                The cycle is complete,
                The episode is over.

But the silence that hung about that place
Was haunted, the presence of something anciently ordained,
Where we, unwitting acolytes, with the birds and the bulls
Enacted its rite: there in the immemorial clearing,
The great listening mountain above for witness,
The sacrificial host between the river and the woods.

🔲 🔲

II: RENEGADE CHRISTMAS

SIXTY FIVE

I stand in the center of a twilight field,
Distantly circled by dark woods,
But the woods hold no fear.

The meaning
Turns on an emptiness of space, of vague half-light,
The shadowless dusk beyond sundown.

My awareness
Is clear, the sense of subsistent identity
Distinct and whole. But there is nothing to apprehend,
Nothing save the circling space
And the weightless air.

What comes home
Is the total absence of force, the suspension of power,
Any capacity to *make*. Not paralysis,
Rather the dispersal of focus, as if the spirit
Retained unimpaired its powers of perception,
But the counter-thrust of brute causation,
Or the dramatic synthesis of form,
Have ineluctably passed.

I think:
This is the ghost-state—to behold reality
But no longer affect it. Soon comes the clinging
To what is no more, the ineffectual
Fumbling of shards of experience,
Like King Arthur's ghost,
Dabbling his hands in Dozmare pool,
Groping the memory of a fabulous sword
That once was his all.

I awake in chagrin,
Curled in a foetal suspension, afloat in time,
Hugging a sense of enigmatic loss.
A pulsation of pain, relinquishment
Of all the incisive forms I stood yet to create,
Drifts through me. Not the pang of death,

For death holds no terror. Rather,
The passing of rapacious joy, that appetitive
Sensuality and intellective thirst
Our slaking of which yields all we know
Of basal impulse: all we can keep
In heaven, or all we can hug
In hell: the signal
Instinct, the sovereign spirit,
The sceptral mind.

回 回

RENEGADE CHRISTMAS

Full moon at the solstice:
The head of the month and the heel of the year
Graze as they pass—incongruent syzygy.
The feminine principle prevails,
A reversal of roles. It behooves the wise
To walk warily.

                    But the night glides without mishap.
Under the moon the sheer exaltation of loveliness
Suffuses the world.

                 Then deep toward dawn
A gaggle of coyotes perched on the hill
Serenades moonset, a shivering ululation,
Suddenly to break and hang suspended,
The startled silence that swallows sound.

Out on the road our cross-breed elkhound
Roars in response, lawfully invoking the territorial imperative
Against the call of the wild.

                 The coyotes sing back,
Arcane variations on the primal theme,
An evolving line of canine invention
Casting its spell on the listening night.

Once again the elkhound's challenge
Splits the silence, but this time uncertainly.
Something has touched him, some insidious affinity,
Aslink in his genes, betrays itself,
A quavering falsetto that gathers as it grows,
Subverting the measure of human fealty
To the wolf-pack in the blood.

For a time they contend,
The relentless torsion of opposed loyalties
Contorting his voice,
From whine to moan to incipient yelp.
Then all succumbs, domestic devotion

Capitulates to instinct,
Rustily joining the virtuoso performance
High on the hill.

I climb from bed
And look wonderingly out. He sits in the yard,
Muzzle pointed skyward as if baying the moon.
Never have I heard such unspeakable perturbation
Wrung from the throat, an atavistic intrusion
Gusting the heart.

Up on the hill
The listening coyotes laugh themselves silly,
Jubilant at the tell-tale ambivalence
Tormenting the dog. Then he is gone.
The movement of brush
Marks his passage up the canyon slope,
As a surface ripple charts the zigzag course
Of a foraging carp.

The rout is complete.
In his mad dash uphill he sloughs
Ten thousand years of domestication
In search of his soul.

▣

He is gone for two days.
I remark to my wife, "It looks like the gods
Claim another victim."

She considers this,
Pursing her lips, then decides against it,
"He'll come home."

And so he does.
This evening near dusk a scratch at the door.
I am all alone, and when I let him in
He goes straight to his corner,

Not greeting me, and curls up in a ball,
Nose tucked to tail.

But when my wife returns
He rises at once and goes to her, tongue lolling,
Half closing his eyes in a way they have,
Seeking satisfaction.

She brings him his food,
And he wolfs it, ravenously, then flops in his corner,
Insensible with fatigue. Soon I hear him
Whine in his sleep, muscles twitching, every instinct alive
As he chases Coyote Woman through the moonlit glades,
Pursuing his dream.

I step out in the dark,
Look up at the stars in the crystalline night,
Brittle with frost. I think of Coyote Woman,
Snug in her den, the clot of the god
Alive in her vitals.

Tomorrow is Christmas Eve.
"Why, O God, do you do as you do?"
The question is moot: only the wonderment
Is real.

Back in the house
I poke at the fire. Beyond the bedroom door
My wife is asleep, no God-clot
Wakening her womb.

In the fire's last light
I say my prayers and tally my sins,
Such as they are, then make for bed.

Suddenly I hear Coyote Woman sing on the hill.

Curled in his corner
Elkhound raises his head,
Listening.

Coyote Woman

Cries again, the wild and careless
Inexhaustible joy
Of life resurgent.

                    Elkhound
Lowers his head between his paws
And takes up his dream.

        ▣ ▣

COUGAR

A sensed presence: turning our heads
We saw him at once, the great cat,
Not thirty yards off at the clearing's edge,
Tawny red in the late spring light,
As if years in the redwoods, the rose manzanita
And the russet madrone, had deepened his hue,
But of his own accord and set purpose
Entered the precinct of Kingfisher Flat,
Stepped out of the zone of protective coloration
To accost us, not as menace or threat
But as revelation, the glimpse of something
Long withheld that we needed to know,
Something given, purely for our own well-being:
A glimpse of the god.

                    And we gasped,
Gratified. The cat looked at us calmly,
To then turn back, but paused again,
Gazing over his tawny shoulder,
Holding us in that level look, the sinuous tail
Leisurely atwist, tentatively weighing
Whether or not to go or to stay.

                    That was the moment
The dog caught scent and sprang up bristling.
One explosive bark burst out of his lungs
And then he charged. Instantly the lion swung on his track,
Swung in the long cat-lithe lope,
But when the dog gained on him
Broke into the flat-out feline streak
And disappeared down the trail,
The dog in pursuit, purposely following,
But at a safe distance.

                    And I too, at a safe distance
Followed. I found his track in wet clay,
And then ran on. Ahead up the ridge
The dog broke into furious barking
And then fell still, to return untouched,

But slouching head down and well quit of it,
The event clearly over.

                         I went back to the track
For confirmation, the wide padded paw, the rounded toes
Unmarked by claws, the signature
Of the cat.

           Days passed by,
April merged into May,
May burned itself out in the swelter of June,
And summer pounced.

                        We never saw him again.
But the single print in the set clay
Retains its distinctness,
As tangible as the stunning presence
In the hushed afternoon, the solemn moment
When the veil was rent, the earthly music
Suddenly fell still, and the god,
Imperious, gathered us into those wakeful eyes,
And was gone.

           ◲ ◱

DANSE MACABRE

The place is public—a thronged station
Or perhaps the lobby of a large hotel.
Someone I know approaches, friend or acquaintance,
Dimly recalled but not clearly seen, his line of advance
Tangential to mine.

              Who?

I will know him later for my very self,
That heron-like hunch of my Waldport years, but now
Unrecognized. No face and no name,
Nor has he yet noticed me.

                        I step aside,
Averting my gaze, and quicken my pace.
It is this evasion that sets me directly on course
Toward a man and a woman sitting casually by.
Turning my head I make to deflect again,
But before I can follow, the woman, rising,
Steps into my path. She will not be put off.

I check my stride. As I do
She lifts up her head, hooded, the cowl
Framing her face.

                  No face—a gaping skull,
Not bones dry from the tomb.
Rather, bluish white, glistening, tatters of flesh
Still clinging her jaws—butcher's bones
Housewives lug home for dog-gnaw.

                              Taken aback
I half turn aside, but before I can dodge
She slips away, off toward the man,
Laughing, her face hidden now,
But her voice provocative.

                      Suddenly I seize her.
Under the cloak she is supple and firm,

Pulsing with life. I pull her to me,
Amorous, crush her in my arms
While she laughs and struggles.

                                        I jerk awake.
I am clasping the recumbent body of my wife.
She is fast asleep, faced from me,
And I press against her.

                        Sensing arousal
She stirs her hips, languidly, still deeply asleep,
Too lost in the wonder of her own myth
To waken to mine.

                        And I lie listening,
Harkening the changing rhythm of my life,
The hope in the horror of the yet-to-be:
What the dream denotes.

                        As the ringing bell
Sounds in its knell the certitude of deliverance
From the sorrow it extols, so the eternal,
Haunting the instances of mutilation,
Chimes the measure of the unconceived.

        ▣ ▣

REAPER

Winter's wake: week after week the sopping northwesters
Soaked the coast. When May, bedraggled, finally limped in,
The liberated sun sent the grass knee-high
And thick as cat's fur. Taking up the scythe put by last summer
I started to mow.

This morning, honing the blade,
A spasm shook me—the Parkinson's reflex.
Struggling for balance I stumbled, fell forward,
Dropping scythe and hone to free my hands and break my fall.
But the crooked stock counterbalanced the blade,
Cat-quick, flipping the long point up and back.
Steel struck my face as I fell on it,
Drove into my cheek along the jaw,
And stuck there. Down on my knees I struggled with it,
And when it broke free blood gushed from the gash,
Drenching my beard.

I staggered indoors,
Raining red on the floor, and yelled to my wife,
"Susanna! Come quick! I fell on my scythe!"
Who came wondering from the bedroom,
"Fell on your side?" then spotted the blood and ran to me.
Wrapping a towel round my lacerated jaw
She got me to the car and into town before I could grouse.
But when I badmouthed my lot the doctor would have none of it.
"Count your blessings, man. It was very close.
A little to the left and a bit lower down
Would have split your mouth or slit your throat.
Consider yourself in luck."

Back home, luckily unlucky,
I regard my image in the looking glass
And I say to myself: What a way to go!
The mad scythe, cutting the firebreak ten years back,
All the women in your life laid low with the flowers,
Now turns on you. Drunk in death
Would you hug them to your heart?
The world at large would receive your demise

With grave satisfaction, struck by its fitness,
Savoring the rough justice, the karmic violence
That never quits, those howling Erinyes
Pursuing vengeance down the rooftree of the world.

It is not so—not yet anyway. In the springtime dusk
I feel no fear, and I whisper,
"Death, you darling! Come quick if you love me!
Tease me not, brazen hussy! Think rather
We have pledged our troth in violent verse
And not flinched.

                    Today you kissed me
Almost on the mouth. I know by this
You have readied the place, prepared the bed,
Where breast to breast we will slake desire
Each of the other, and leave this life
Enjoined."

MEXICAN STANDOFF

Inner space: a rock cavern
By the look of it, and I stand alone,
Facing the center; air still and no sound,
But a lampless light fills the emptiness,
Tempers the darkness,
Dimly.

I stand in the dream's expectancy,
My presence a purpose I have yet to learn
But I wait to know.

The voice, when it comes,
Has no gender, being either or neither, yet is somehow
Not sexless, which subtly enforces
Its oblique import.

"It's up to you,"
The voice says evenly. "Remember,
What you use is yours; but what you don't use
Is mine."

Nothing more.
Nothing but the chill light
And the still air.

The implication
Is ominous. For eight years
I have endured it, the dread *paralysis agitans*,
Unable to take the mild calisthenics
Prescribed for its care. Some baleful blockage
Prevents it, some obdurate
Perversity of the will, that frustrates
Every energizing impulse, brings it to naught.
I am my own keeper; my own arch-enemy; my own denier.

And I see in my mind the insidious paralysis
Inch up my flesh, a neuropathic degeneration,
Tracing my limbs and the joints of my bones.
I think of my shrunken sex and my stone-cold seed

In its wrinkled sack, and I ponder the meaning of use,
What it entails.

*Usage: the act, way, or extent of using
or treating: treatment, use... .*

But definition is irksome,
And on the instant my heart retorts:
"I am a poet, for God's sake!
Use without passion is for the birds!"

And the thought
Sends me. I find myself chortling: "Atta girl!"
Saluting the old inveterate female heart which,
Like the primal lizard at the base of man's being,
Never defers.

Churning my blood
She doggedly croons her litany of life:
"Not use but ecstasy! Passion alone
Clues consummation!"

Suddenly awake
I heave myself up, stamp round the room
In a hobbling dance, lamely cavorting,
A cackling old man, babbling in aimless
Self-confabulation, crazy as a loon.

I cease abruptly.
Drawing myself to full height I confront the emptiness:
"You say," I demand, "that what I don't use
Is yours?" My voice cracks. "Then take it!
God damn it! Take it!"

Getting no reply
I smile benignly, blandly magnanimous, and whisper,

Darkly:

     "I wish you well of it."

          Silence.

              Cocking my head
Like a teetering jay, like a magpie on an elderberry stem—
Suddenly I am solicitous:

         "Are you sure
You can handle it?"

       Silence.

         Then, licking my lips,
I smile slyly:

     "What are you going to do with it?

Use it?"

   ◙ ◙

BOOK FIVE:

DUST SHALL BE THE SERPENT'S FOOD

(1975-1991)

The wolf and the lamb shall feed together;
The lion and the ox shall eat straw;
And dust shall be the serpent's food.

ISAIAS, LXV: 25 (*DOUAY*)

CANTO ONE:
IN MEDIAS RES

APRIL 7, 1945, SELMA, CALIFORNIA.

The bleak Masonic rite faltered to a close,
And the mourners filed out, impassively. The undertaker
Beckoned the family forward, brought round the coffin
For the final convocation, our last togetherness
Before the closing of the tomb.

                        Approaching my father's body
I felt cold constriction tighten my chest. Five years past,
Nearly five years now, in this same Masonic temple,
The family had convened, gathered round the body of our mother,
Stunned with the suddenness, shaken with loss.

I had stood dry-eyed, but when the lid was closed
Something snapped in my skull. In a choking
Rage, twisted by unreckonable guilt,
I pounded my fists on the coffin,
Sobbing: "Why! Why!" and slumped to my knees,
Jarring the bier.

            Lifting my face
I met the terrible gaze of my father,
Glaring across the lidded coffin—
Those Viking eyes, the awful accusation of Thor—
"You bastard! Profane the last sacred moment!
Spoil it! Go ahead! Ham it up!"

                        I sagged to one side,
But the eyes jerked me upright, scorning:
"From the moment you were born
You took her from me, and now, at the lip of the grave,
When everything she was slips away and my life with it,
You throw your misbegotten body between!"

I crawled to my feet, dizzily erect, and spun blindly,
Sobbing shut frustration, galling guilt.
My brother and sister, seizing my arms,

Hushed me, hoarsely whispering: "Bill! Bill!"
Fearfully urgent. And with them, my wife,
Imploring, beseeching, her voice
Taut as a wire.

                    I flung off their hands,
Stumbling blindly, erratic, fleeing them,
Gasping: "Leave me alone! Keep away, all of you!
Let me be!" But my father's eyes,
Back beyond the coffin, drilling from afar,
Nailed me to the wall, taunting: "Go ahead!
Rant! Ham it up! Play the heavy!"

And gathering up my will, a kind of throttling mastery,
I clenched back my sobs, swept tears from my eyes,
Choking: "Forgive me!" Then my sister, still aghast
But suddenly compassionate: "Bill, if you don't want to...
I mean, you don't have to go to the cemetery if...."
But I thrust past her: "No, I'm all right!
I want to! I have to be there!"

A long moment of awkwardness, an eternity
Of embarrassment gripped us, and we hung on it,
Inflexible, caught in a ghastly suspension—
Till suddenly the undertaker clapped his hands,
Seizing the moment to break the spell,
And the pallbearers filed in, mechanically,
Automatons of death, looking neither to right nor to left.
For something unspeakable hung in that room,
And they knew it, something not to be named,
Something indecent....

                    We moved out, then,
Behind the wheeling coffin, saw it
Enter the darkness of the door, the shadowy threshold,
Saw it tilt down the stairs, steeply, strain forward,
Checked by the staggering pallbearers, stumbling
Awkwardly on the steps, out in the drizzling December day.

Behind the family I followed them down,
And could not but notice the mourners below
Staring up at me, open mouthed,

Painfully aware of my death-side outburst,
My shocking scene....

                    Five long years....

And now, in this same Masonic temple,
I moved to my father's inscrutable coffin,
Sensing my brother and sister
Close in behind me, just in case—
But my wife not here, she far away,
Doing God knows what in San Francisco.
("God does know what," the fact flared in my mind,
"Crawling another man's bed, that's what!").

But ferociously shut down the searing thought,
Knuckles whitening in the fist's clench—
"But that's all right," I grimly concluded,
"This time no outburst, right? No hysterics.
Not this pig...."

                    At coffin-side
I gazed down a time at the set
Composed features, unseen these many months
Since conscription claimed me;
Looked at the death-set lips that had cursed me,
The calm folded hands that had never blessed me.
Then the short torso, so faultlessly attired,
Immaculately groomed in the mortician's art,
But shockingly stilted. And felt for the first time
The mordant pang that would soon become familiar,
The wince of pain that I let my father go
Unreconciled into the grave. And a tremor
Shook through me, but nothing like what happened before,
No, nothing like that....

                    The coffin lid closed,
And watching it settle, my gauche outburst
Shoved from my mind, I thought how everything
Had changed, changed utterly: five hapless years
All stripped away, everything gone—
Mother gone, wife gone, father gone, vineyard gone—

Brother and sister turning back to their lives,
Their separate existences—Gone!
And I to return to my northern incarceration,
To wait out the war with the stark objectors,
Who denied the State its injunction to kill,
And paid for denial with a slave's labor.

And I looked up, taking my sister's hand,
And the hand of my brother, ·
And then turned aside, smiling faintly,
And said simply, smiling and turning,
"Let's go!"

       And the coffin moved.

                Following it out
I watched it pass through the door, the shadowy threshold,
Burst into the searing sunlight beyond,
The strong light of April;
Saw it tilt down, the steep stairs taking it;
Saw the pallbearers staggering under the load,
Stumbling awkwardly on the steps,
While the massed mourners, deployed below,
Awaited its passage into the hearse.

Following it out, the straight-falling sunlight
Suddenly enveloped me, and through squinting eyes
I looked down the steps to the sea of faces,
My fellow townsmen and my boyhood friends,
Gathered in homage to the man who had led them,
Thirty years, first as bandmaster then as judge,
Thirty long years.... I paused uncertainly there,
Balancing on the top steps, half blinded
By the sun, and let my brother descend,
My sister following.

         As the hearse
Swallowed up the stone-cold coffin
I started down, then paused, feeling unreal, floating,

For a dizziness seized my sight.
And I gazed about me, gathered focus in my mind,
And saw to my left a green cupola, the Victorian mansion
Where Jess Morgan, that affable sportsman,
Had taken his life with his own deer rifle,
And his daughter Doris, my childhood sweetheart,
Had fled this town, never to return,
Nor ever to frolic together again,
Through the long summer days on the spacious lawns,
Swinging under the mulberry trees,
Never again our eyes to meet, our secrets to share....

And beyond the house lay High Street,
The civic concourse, and across the way
The Carnegie Library where, night after night,
From the time I could read,
I crouched in the stacks devouring books,
Bushels of books, till the spinster librarian
Closed it at nine....

                    And suddenly,
There on the tall steps, above the sea of faces,
Friends and townspeople, my mind
Swept out beyond the city limit
To the little cemetery, the plot where
Redolent in the earth, my mother lay buried; and beside her
The naked hole that would take down my father,
Darkly glowing, a subsumed luster,
Numinous with the haunting infusion of death....

And around them, dwarfing them, lay the mighty
Spread of the earth, field beyond field,
Like an inland sea, rolling,
Sweeping away to the shining mountains,
The majestic grandeur of the Pacific Slope.

And thinking of mountains, I remembered my father,
The white-crowned brow—high peaked ridges athwart the east,
Thunderheads forming in the fierce spring heat,

The long ranks of forest like desperate armies charging upslope
To the bitter timberline where the hordes fall back,
Repulsed by granite and eternal snow.

                              And suddenly I realized
I would never see it again, this world, not as I knew it.
For look, what was become of it?
Already it is changed—changed as the world within me
Had changed, as naked, as starkly unreal as my inner self;
That what swam about me, there on those steps,
Above the sea of faces and the sea of my world,
Was another dimension, another existence,
Not defined by the valley or the valley towns,
Nor the majestic realm of the Pacific Slope.

For beyond the Sierras lay a continent,
Crouched like a beast, a giant cougar
Tensing to spring, and out of that tension
The nation, its nerves coiling for the final drive,
The war sweeping toward apotheosis,
The mighty Nazi war machine
Beaten to its knees, breaking, fragmenting,
Thrown back on every front,
Europe convulsed in a tentacular paroxysm,
The powerful American sweep
Thrust deep in its vitals, boring remorselessly in;
And I, remote from it, watch and wait,
Suffering in the soul what it suffers in the flesh.

And reeling there on those tall steps
I put out my hands, as a man
Balances in a dream, giddily entranced.
And suddenly my sister started back up the stairs,
Calling "Bill! Bill!" And I realized I had turned,
Staggered, convulsively sobbing,
Tears streaming my face.
But before she could reach me
I gathered strength in a mighty effort,
And my head cleared. I straightened,

As a man straightens under a load,
And walked down the stairs, limping
But upright, straight now,
"Under my own power, by God,"
No hands sustaining me. And the faces
Of friends I no longer knew
Swam in my tear-blind eyes.

CANTO TWO:
SKALD

DECEMBER 22, 1870, BREVIK, NORWAY.

A legendary life: by the blood,
Norse, a bantam born to a race of giants,
He fell from the womb the last of twelve,
Taking his mother's life in his leap,
And bore thereafter the ineluctable sorrow,
The pall of matricide haunting his heart,
Stifling his soul, the insidious
Guilt of survival.

        Who, then, nurtured his life?
Not, for one, his dour father. That worthy fanatic
Was never around. Itinerant preacher,
Founder of his own evangelical splinter,
The Iversonians, he cast fire and brimstone
On the hummocks of Norway; yet his awesome ardor,
Not wholly quenched in apostolic zeal,
Found an opening in the mundane sector. A cobbler by trade,
He brought the art of vulcanization
To the Norwegian people; but its raw toxicity,
Ill understood, cut him down. The ardor died
Unslaked.

        Orphaned at twelve,
My father was taken by a well-to-do aunt
To the urban ambience of the capital city:
Now Oslo by name, but then Christiania,
An awkward, Dane-derived appellation.
There he languished, mutely unhappy,
But soon came a day when a giant ship
Hove to in the harbor, riding high in the slack,
Having lately discharged its whole bill of lading
From foreign shores; but would soon
Resettle to the waterline
When the horde of emigrants boarded.

        For these were the days

Of the great migrations, the cream of Norway's
Burgeoning populace skimmed off for the States,
A lemming-like tide of human hunger:
Wanderlust West, reliving the atavistic dream,
Leif the Lucky, the whale-haunted sea, and the lure
Of the Vinland tryst.

                     So the bustling emigrants
Surged through the streets, and he followed,
A sad-faced, tow-headed stray,
Unnoticed among them—farmers and workers,
Wives, children and mothers; infants
Slung in a shawl or hitched on the hip.
And he ran unremarked out along the wharf,
Darted up the funneling gangplank,
Out onto the deck—almost as if
He himself were choosing the shadow-way West
(America, the wonderful word on everyone's lips),
Almost as if he too heard the call—
Fare forward! Fare far! Almost as if
He too laid claim to a fabulous future
Uniquely his own.

                     And so, small for his age,
And unobtrusive, he mixed with the throng,
Roamed the boat absorbed with its fixtures,
Instinctively shunning the fetid steerage;
Descending at last to the monstrous gut,
The beast's great groin, pulsing heart
Of the savage leviathan, the mighty turbine.
Stopped in his tracks by that awesome organ
He found a nook, sank sighing down,
And so fell asleep.

                     Awake with a start
He dashed up the stairs and out onto the deck
To find it deserted, night falling fast and land gone;
Rushed to the stern where, all alone,
Looked longingly back at the widening wake
Creasing the Skagerrak, and the stormy petrel
Gleaned the sea-churn for the dark
Propeller-torn kill. Suddenly afraid

An immense forlornness swept over him.
He turned back to a bulkhead, sank down,
Great sobs shook through him, unstemmable.
Then a strong hand fell on his shoulder;
He looked fearfully up through brimming tears
To the genial face of the mate.

⬚

                              And a strange
Voyage they had of it. The great ship surged forward,
Shearing the deceptively flaccid sea. At summer solstice
A black storm broke, a howling tornado, its waterspout
Twisting and writhing, a monstrous phallus
Sucked down by the uterine sea. Driven off course,
Lay in doldrums with a broken rudder
Till rescue reached them—ignominiously towed
Into New York harbor by a scrawny little tug,
Triumphantly tooting.

                    Officially, of course,
He was slated to make the return passage home,
But early on caught emigrant fever and now
Jumped ship, went over the rail
Down a rope ladder to a fruit vendor's lighter
Tied alongside, hoping to hide under heaped produce.
Intercepted there, he dodged, sprang overboard,
And forthwith swam ashore.

                        And so, by the grace of God,
Entered America, an illegal alien,
Almost as if he too heard the call—
Fare forward! Fare far!—almost as if
He too laid claim to a fabulous future
Uniquely his own.

                    The third of July, 1883.
Spending the first night under the docks,
He who had never heard tell of a firecracker
Woke next morning to the thunder of the Fourth.
Terrified, speaking no English,

Stumbling about the turbulent streets,
With no money and only the clothes on his back
For keeps, he persisted and survived.

                              Survived?
It was the first decisive act of his life,
And the most crucial. Heretofore, he had been
Only life's pawn, passively witnessing, moving but as moved.
Now, with one importunate stroke he cut free,
Severed the ethnic umbilical cord
To Norway and the past.

                    After the first bewilderment
He caught the rhythm of the pulsing streets,
Found the company of his own kind,
The wild waifs who haunted the alleys,
Selling newspapers or shining shoes,
Pilfering, ganging up for mutual protection,
Perfecting a kind of pig-latin argot to faze the police,
Arcane confabulation in the cunning of the ruse.

          ▣

From this point on his odyssey darkens.
He spoke of wanderlust, riding the freights
To other cities, rarer climes,
In the drifter's gambit. He once surmised
By the age of sixteen he had seen it all:
North, South, East, West: every section of the country
Duly transected, briskly shown the back of his heels,
The trace of his tracks, and him unscathed;
But that's to be doubted.

                    For it wasn't that easy.
In the first place, the competition was killing.
From the Civil War to the turn of the century,
Hardly thirty-six years, forty million people
Poured into America. They matted like herring
In the East Coast cities, invaded the Northeast,
Overflowed the Midwest, to span the Mississippi

And streak for California.

                    In the second place,
"Riding the rods" was a dangerous game,
In an age still largely harnessed to the horse,
Not fully acclimated to the stunning intrusion
Of locomotive speed: the intolerable wheels,
Iron on iron in the demon's dance,
Obsessively pounding a stupor in the brain;
The implacable distances, beckoning, fleering,
Disappearing over the fleeing horizon,
Stretching the nerves to the screaming point
In the rack of the body; malnutrition,
Common denominator of the hobo lifestyle,
Wasting the frame; death by maiming
Or prolonged exposure a foregone conclusion,
Everyone knew it but none could know when,
In a social structure the bottom of the heap,
The pit, the noxious human dregs: degenerate tramps,
Vicious police, and the loathsome
Ubiquitous jails.

                Or so I believed.
And the litany of privations
Became my bane, a roster of risks
My sheltered beginnings could never match.
Rather, constrained by timidity,
Painfully introspective and unable to cope,
I winced in chagrin, bound by a febrile
Diffidence, awkwardly evasive. The misfit's onus
Shaped the poet's throttled cry.

                But have lately learned
(Though indubitably he paid his freight-hopping dues
On the Atlantic seaboard and the nearer Midwest)
His coast-to-coast junkets were something else;
Those awesome forays were accomplished in style.
As companion to the secretary of James J. Hill,
Founder of the mighty Great Northern Line,
He rode the millionaire's private car,
Vicariously rich, hobnobbing with swells,

For all his abstention the surrogate sybarite,
Living high on the hog.

                        And the disparity
Staggers me. From the pits of privation
To the couches of ease; from the hazards of the body
To the surfeit of the soul, the revolution is complete.
For fortune itself is parlous; one can survive its lack
But hardly its largesse: brazen ostentation,
The masks of pride, envelop the unwary;
Complacence and superficiality,
Its pretentious habiliments, cannot conceal
The stark anatomy of greed: the gut of gluttony
And the groin of lust; the salacious copulation
Of money breeding money. In his randy youth
Surely he sensed the sexuality of power
And was stirred—knowing, drifter-wise,
How to hedge his hand, make his pitch, his ploy.
Intercourse with heiresses was not that unthinkable:
In their cloistered world proximity itself
Was potent, and here he was proximate.
All one needed was entrance, right?
And once in hand, once cunningly caught,
The bird could be plucked....

                        O my father!
What angel of deliverance watched over your ways,
Protected your head, guarded your heart
And guided your feet? What power kept you pure
Through the dizzying concentricities of that life?
Nameless the nights, incalculable the days,
The fierce temptations, inordinate succumbings,
And the gall of their wrenching guilts.

Or was it rather the primal austerity
Of the American earth that wrought privation
Into your soul? For you, a city child,
Lacked the sustaining context of Nature
That nurtured me. And listening at night
I heard, confirmed in the wind,
Roaming the vast shelvage of the Pacific Slope,
What I sensed in you: the innominate loneliness,

The sacred solitude that sustains the world,
The austere power that purified your lips
(I never heard you curse); that kept you sober
(I never saw you drunk); that made you honest
(I never heard you lie); the fierce abstractness
Denoting a primal equity, the chime of an absolute
Intrinsic to man.

                    And women?
Which one seduced you, luring you out of that pall
Of birth-doom, to warm your blood
And shudder your heart? You were a faithful husband,
Scrupulously continent; but when I turned eighteen
You solemnly told me—the only sex instruction
You ever vouchsafed—"Go to a professional!"
Meaning, of course, a prostitute. It troubled me then
And puzzles me now. Whore-fucking
Is the last thing I can picture you doing;
But there it is, the sage advice
Of a lifetime's reflection! Which only shows
How little we know of our real life-sources;
How late we learn the reach of our roots,
Or the deeps of our blood's undoing.

But perhaps the thing is best understood
In the Victorian woman's view of herself
As invincibly chaste, inciting a corresponding
Violence in the legendary defloration,
Recalling Queen Victoria's rueful advice
To the British bride on her nuptial night:
"Close your eyes, my dear, and think of England!"
It threw the prostitute's amiable carnality
Into vivid relief, earning the visceral gratitude
Of numberless disenchanted males, her venereal sycophants.
From this point of view my father's
Hortatory admonition, far from denoting
A personal aberration, proved Rite of Passage
To a troubled generation.

He settled in time
In St. Paul, Minnesota, a Scandinavian enclave,
Where he found his trade: graduating as he grew
From street to shop, from newsboy to printer's devil;
Taken on as an apprentice compositor, novitiate
To the trade. Here he got his first education:
Typesetting, proofreading; learned the language in depth,
Plus the wide world of facts, to arrive
At journeyman's status, able to enter the skilled employ
Of any metropolitan daily in the country, a certified
Man of the stone.

But more to the point
Here too he found his calling. The distinction
Is vital. Just as his father
Sustained himself at the vulcanizer's bench,
But his calling was evangelical; so did the son
Sustain himself at the composing stone
Though his calling was music.

Vocare! To be called
Is the definitive gist of vocation, and its implications,
For sensual artist or ascetic monk,
Are largely the same: each broaches
The charismatic mode. For intuition and instinct,
The Spirit and the Flesh, merge together
In worship and in art, shaping the radical
Contour of the visionary quest,
Ineluctably governed, not by the mind's
Inveterate lust for logic, but by the powerful
Suasion of symbolic truth, the force of vocation
Fusing the substances of soul and psyche
To the archetype of God.

Call and surrender,
The dual foci of charismatic renewal.
Call is the first awakening of the self
To the stroke of potentiality. Surrender,
The abnegation of ego before the imperative
Of creative destiny, the clench of consummation.
No call, no surrender; no surrender,

No renewal. It is that simple.
And it can't be faked.
You have to wait for the call,
Wait out the terror of your helplessness
Before the deliverance of surrender.
Sometimes this takes years.
Sometimes, if you're lucky,
It takes decades.

⊡

How the call came to him
He never disclosed. A no-nonsense agnostic
Doubtless he never thought in such terms.
More than likely, hearing a band on a city street,
His being blazed, suddenly transfixed, an astounding
Awakening: the seizure of vocation
Coequals nature in elemental awe. I once saw a brace
Of Muscovy ducks, hatchery-raised far from a pond,
And fully grown before taken to water.
Shown the broad pool they crouched in distrust,
Must be shoved to the shore,
Nudged over the edge. But once afloat,
Overwhelmed by instinct, they gave voice.
What a long-deferred summons and what a surrender!
Such mad cavorting! Such diving and jubilant
Thrashing of wings! This, for my father, was music.
And music became his all.

In our beginning
Is our end. What he started then
He never forsook, never denied,
Never renounced. A true skald,
He was born to sing. In song
He lived, and singing
Died. Now I, his son,
Sing for him.

⊡ ⊡

CANTO THREE:
HIDDEN LIFE

DECEMBER 25, 1885, ADRIAN, MINNESOTA.

And the hidden life: a farm girl born on Christmas Day
Out on the frozen Minnesota prairie,
Near the small town of Adrian,
In a Roman Catholic enclave,
Founded by the visionary prelate,
John Ireland, Bishop of St. Paul,
Who, in his greatness of heart,
Sought to draw the immigrant Irish
Out of the congested seaboard cities,
Where, given the appalling squalor of their lives,
Faith and morals stood in fearful jeopardy.
Urging them back to the land
He hoped to restore their Old World stability,
Here on the fertile American earth, the New Eden,
Under the boundless providence of God, and the vigilant
Eye of the Church.

                    An unmitigated disaster.
One stupefying Minnesota winter
Was enough to convince the feckless Irish
That their visionary prelate, though doubtless a saint,
Was balmy as a crumpet. Abandoning their homesteads,
They sold the implements he had generously provided,
Pocketed the money, and beat a ragged retreat
Back to the slothful seaboard cities,
Letting faith and morals take their chances
Where a body could keep warm.
This left the field to the Germans,
A more resolute breed.

                    And both strains
Blended in her blood: the father, a German,
For tenacity and earthiness; the Irish mother,
For piety and imagination. The mixture
Proved benign: the fourth child of ten

She spoke of her earliest years as the gladdest.
Though life was hard and poverty crippling,
The rewards of righteous family life
Proved recompense enough for the bone-bruising hardships,
Not forgetting the awesome presence
Of primary Nature, the stupendous
Magnitude of the earth, the vast sky
Gripped at the edge by the steel horizon,
Rim of the world.

    ▣

                 For there was always the wind,
Streaming, blowing across the limitless prairies,
Rattling the corn and the sunflowers,
Crying at night round the eaves of the house,
Calling the ghosts of the buffalo,
Stirring the dust of the pioneers,
And the shattered, sanguinary tribes.

                       In the spring
She remembered the wonderment over her brow,
Over her heart and her hovering breath,
Touching her body in unfamiliar places,
Of which she knew nothing, had been told nothing,
Strange yearnings for otherness,
The undulant urge of the fated unborn.

For there was always the wind.
It came up from the Gulf, out of Mexico,
From the Texas stretch and the Oklahoma hollow,
Brooding womb of tornadoes, those savage
Wreckers of railroads and cities,
Scarring the groin of Arkansas,
Coiling where rivers spawn and divide,
And birds of the night,
Tracing the shining tributaries,
Fly dazzled into the dawn.

    ▣

Then tragedy struck.
In her ninth autumn the death of her mother
Tore the family fabric and the cold rushed in.
The father was forced to send them away,
Divide his soul-stricken darlings,
Parcel them out among strangers.

Some he placed in a St. Paul convent,
My mother among them, but that winter they sickened
In the strange city, and had to be withdrawn.
Undaunted, he searched and found a convent
Closer to home, but fate still fought him.
They'd no sooner arrived when it burnt to the ground.
The distraught father had no recourse
But to place his children in such separate homes
As were willing to have them,
No questions asked.

Her own drab lot
Fell to a single-child couple in Adrian,
Where, separated from her sisters,
Her life turned miserable. She lay by night
Listening to the wind prowl round the house,
Menacing now, to rub its muzzle on the window pane,
Its voice a troll.

Baptized a Catholic
Her natal creed proved anathematic
To that insular household.
She stopped attending Mass to keep the peace
And, in effect, was raised a Protestant.
But rejoining her sisters one summer vacation,
She received Confirmation and,
To the great indignation of her foster parents,
Returned to the Sacraments.
Soon active in her parish, helping the nuns
About the altar or in the catechizing of children,
She bore at home the irksome brunt of it,
And never wavered.

For prayer sustained her.
In the throes of that blunt familial estrangement

She found consolation in the Sacramental life:
Slipping into church on her way about town;
Making the dolorous Stations of the Cross
Saturdays after Confession;
Receiving Holy Communion in her Sunday best
At the weekly Mass; praying the Rosary
Each night at bedtime, her fingers
Sifting the beads like nuggets of gold
In the wilderness of God; the words
Lilting her lips, moulding the mind
Till sleep tied her tongue
As the divine mantra closed. Let the troll wind
Whine at the windowsill; in the warmth
Of her inner world she found her solace,
And could not be shaken.

                            At fourteen years
She'd been taken from school and set to work
In the local newspaper—prefiguring my father there,
The man she would marry—setting type
And reading proof, folding the printed sheets
For delivery. This, too, her surrogate education,
Broadening her farm girl's limited outlook
With some knowledge of the world.
Bright, resourceful, she rapidly matured,
And knew satisfaction, confirming her worth
In the labor force, coming of age in the new century
That would bring the man to her.

                                    He arrived,
As it happened, in the wintertime, unannounced,
A Norwegian by birth but with no trace of an accent,
Good-looking enough but not strikingly handsome
And short for his race. It soon developed
He was something special: the new bandmaster,
Belatedly hired by the town fathers
To present the next summer's concerts,
Always, before the advent of radio,
The focal point of community interest
Through the long summer months.

He had seen their ad in a city newspaper

And arrived for an interview. His credentials
Were impressive: he bore letters
From some of the best bands in the Midwest.
The salary was, let us say, adequate,
Provided they could secure him a place
On the local newspaper. It so happened they could:
The publisher, one of the pillars of the council,
Was pleased to oblige.

              He took the acceptance
For granted; it had become by then
A way of life: he had learned it thoroughly,
Knew it inside and out, and himself as well,
Taking care to contract for one season only,
Since no small town had ever claimed him long,
But diplomatically agreed to renegotiate in the fall,
If they liked him well and could come up with more money.

He would begin at once, whipping the callow band into shape
With weekly rehearsals toward the long summer program.
That same day, in the newspaper printing plant,
He slipped on his denim compositor's apron
And stepped up to the stone.

      回

              And so they met,
Each finding the other consummately attractive.
For her, he brought fresh air, liberating life,
To that small town confinement.
He was well-read and knowledgeable,
With a fascinating past and intriguing future.
Clean of speech and of thought,
He was supportive and helpful,
Occasionally unloading her composing stick,
Though she was perfectly capable of that herself.
Moreover, she enjoyed correcting proof with him,
Herself reading copy while he skillfully marked
The ink-pungent galleys of freshly-pulled print.

For him, he recognized almost at once

She was everything he consciously valued in women:
Her voice soft and low; cool, light laughter;
The gift of a keen sense of humor (a virtue
In which he himself was somewhat deficient)
But practical, too, adaptive and amenable,
Without affectation or self-preening vanity,
And implicitly honest.

                    In the spring he proposed.
Nor was she surprised; for though she lacked amatory
Knowledge of men; indeed, had only
Superficially dated, on church outings,
Funfests, and suchlike sociables, her intuition
Read the signs and read them aright,
Recognizing the butterfly winging in his breast
By the chrysalis stirring in her own.

But there were grave problems.
She was Catholic and devout,
He, a confirmed agnostic.
She was fifteen years younger than he
And two inches taller. To make matters worse—
Indeed, to make them impossible—
He acknowledged in his past a failed marriage,
An ugly divorce.

                    Oh, he could explain it!
Once, playing in a circus band,
He had fallen head over heels
For a female performer, a trapeze artist
And bareback rider, and they dashed into marriage.
He stressed the difficulties of circus life:
Incessant hoopla, the gypsy vagrancy,
Depthless euphoria and non-existent privacy.
And always crisis, crisis, the onslaught
Of the unexpected, from stampeding elephants
To irate farmers bilked of their money
By sideshow sharpers, the cry "Hey Rube!"
Sending stake-swinging roustabouts
Charging out front to clip the yokels
Before they could rally and wreck the tents.
Add to this the hornblower's gantlet:

Playing cornet on lurching bandwagons,
Chipped teeth, lacerated lips and blood
Dripping out of the spit-valve. All this
They endured; but when times worsened
And circusing declined, she wouldn't settle,
Refused to bear children, twice aborting his progeny,
Till contention soured them beyond endurance,
And they parted in disgust.

                    (Grounds for annulment
Under canon law, but difficult to prove,
And the diocesan chancery, given the options,
Declined to pursue it.)

                    Now he was alone,
Getting on in years, longing for a home
And the solace of a family. She, too,
Craved the love of a man and the wonder of a child,
And her heart was brimming, brimming.
But the thing was impossible;
The man didn't even believe in God.
To her credit she refused to lead him on.
She gave him no hope.

                    Then came the summer.
Every Saturday night he stood on that bandstand
In his smashing white uniform,
Before the whole town and half the county,
And held them spellbound. He had fantastic presence,
And magical authority over a band.
He was, moreover, a sensational singer,
Specializing in the art of the Swiss yodel,
A popular showpiece performance of the day.
In short, he set the town on its ear.

Nor was she indifferent to that glamour;
Nothing in life had prepared her for it.
He haunted her sleep, and his daily presence,
Dominating the composing room, was almost maddening.
Yet despite her obsession she could not yield,
Was even, sometimes, secretly relieved

He was forbidden her: he was that compelling.

As for him, when the music stopped at summer's end
And she remained adamant, he served notice and left.
He would not put in another such winter.
If religion was her choice, the devil take her!
He knew what to do: find another city, another gig,
And yes, if he must, another woman.

                              And the wind,
Blowing, took him away, gone across the prairie
In leaf-drift time, frost tracing the stubble,
Geese going south with the whooping cranes
In the smoky light of October.

CANTO FOUR:
THE HOLLOW YEARS

AUTUMNAL EQUINOX, 1905, ADRIAN, MINNESOTA

And so he was gone. And his absence
Imploded on that town like silence swallowing thunder.
She moved numbly through the shortening days;
Not an hour passed at the printing office
But his absence accosted her. She looked at the men,
Seeing them stripped of their value,
Utterly ordinary, tedious in their humdrum insufficiency.
Where had the light gone? The light
And the life?

        At the Mass,
Recalling his kisses, her prayers
Were cotton in her mouth. The keen-eyed nuns,
Who had not failed to note the tell-tale signs of one
Who could not say yes with her lips
But would not say no with her eyes,
Shook their heads and privately opined
That having dared to dance with the incubus
And tasted his lips, she must pay
Demon's debt with her pain.

        And the pain came.
At Halloween a letter from a distant city
Limped in, for all the world like a bedraggled valentine,
All dejected spirit and wounded pride,
The rude awakening of the rejected swain.

He acknowledged himself miserable.
Never before had a woman so compellingly unstrung him.
He was sorry he had been so beastly precipitate.
If he could get back his job—that amenable
Bandmaster-compositor arrangement in Adrian,
Could he still be her friend? And if not
(And here the mask slipped), since she obviously preferred
A life of prayer to living in love,
Could she find it in her heart, say,

To pray for him?

          It was a low blow.
Stung to the quick she shot back in anger:
Sorry that he suffered, but could he not understand
She was suffering too? Certainly she would pray for him,
Had been praying for him; but if God in His wisdom
Were to claim his wife, freeing him
(What dark expedients cross the mind when the heart is torn!),
Would he have gumption enough to pray for himself?
Let God be her judge if her bitter thoughts
Brought pain to anyone!

    Thus two Victorians
    Trammeled in the karma of the Great Divide
    That separates the sexes.

In confession she learned that this correspondence
Was sinful. For her, the man must be outside the pale.
The least compromise was dangerous.
Put him out of your mind, girl. You are flirting
With the loss of your immortal soul.
The stakes are that crucial.

               She wrote in distress,
One final time, begging him not to reply.
Still, he responded. Ignoring her admonition
He wrote bursting with news: the renowned
Saint Olaf's Band of Newbridge College
Was slated to tour Norway, celebrating
The coronation of the new king, Haakon VII,
And the country's final independence
From the sovereignty of Sweden.
Louis had been approached to go, presumably
As a sort of *ad hoc* resource person,
His years as a barnstorming bandmaster
Marking him a natural for backup director,
Pinch-hitter and trouble-shooter par excellence,
Not to mention on-deck vocalist when occasion permitted.
Such virtuosity could prove a Godsend
For a musical organization traveling abroad.
This would be his first return to native turf,

And he thanked God for the chance, the rare opportunity
To prove himself to his people. How he wished
She could stand by his side
When he yodeled in the fjords of Norway!

                                 Francelia
Was not amused. The irony of his thanking God
Had not gone unnoticed. How could she rejoice?
She had no such prospects: only the emptiness,
Only the grate of her dry thoughts
Abuzz in her brain; the past
A mocking memory; the future
A coffin and a corpse.

      ▣

                     She did not reply,
Determined to get on with her life.
Before she would hear from him again
Years would go by, her life would change,
Trouble would come to her, unhappiness deepen.
But she carried his memory and its meaning
Intrinsic to his being, wakeful within her,
His presence kept alive by what could only have been
Essentially her own: the substance of her faith.

      ▣

For in the mating ritual of humankind
Priority of option resides with the woman:
The man can only ask. Why this should be so
Is a mystery of Nature. But reflection suggests
The mechanism of reproduction governs the game:
The fundamental uterine placement
At the base of the sentient being. It is her consciousness
As the eyes and ears of the womb
That sets the sovereignty of selection
In the woman's hands. Of the working out
Reason may concur or demur: it makes little difference.
Before it can even weigh its options,
Instinct has chosen, based on a swift

Connatural recognition, the subtle
Impact of an affinity like bonding,
Or the biological mystery of imprinting.
It is as father of her child
She chooses her mate. So here.
Before the ideological imperative preempting volition
Francelia chose Louis that I might be.

    ⊡

Do I go too far? Overstep the protective zone of humility
That garbs the psyche, preserves the soul?
But the quick of my life is the myth of my engendering.
Something was meant, something awesome and foreboding.
It tells me the gods are alive, they watch and are listening.
To live one's myth is to think in its terms.
To fulfill one's myth is to suffer through to its source.

    ⊡

That winter she sickened. It seems
One of her lungs had festered, the left one,
And she coughed up phlegm. No one could say
Just why, but later in her life she attributed it
To a casual incident in her middle teens.
At play with companions, she was frolicking
Around a kitchen table, girls with boys,
Playing tag, pushing and shoving,
When a lusty lad, reaching across the table,
Grabbed her arm and jerked her toward him.
She felt a tearing under her rib,
And in great pain she left the game,
But the hurt never healed though the pain ceased.
As time went by the matter worsened
And the doctors feared tuberculosis.
In any case, they advised, get out of Minnesota,
With its terrible winters. Go to California;
See what a change of climate can do.
This counsel daunted her, but in time she acquiesced,
Writing ahead to kinfolk in Los Angeles,

Alerting them she would be on her way.
When the time came she boarded that train
With a heavy heart, and left Minnesota forever.

          🔲

Of the journey itself we know nothing.
She arrived in Los Angeles, presumably without incident,
Found lodging with her kin, and looked for work.
Presently she attended a beauty college,
Learning to be a manicurist, but forever afterwards
Kept mum about it. I couldn't imagine why,
But have lately learned that in those days the position
Was an adjunct of the barbershop, a masculine preserve,
Necessarily involving a certain presupposed
Intimate contact with casual men,
And though innocent in itself, it attracted
The demimonde who, like the parlor masseuse
Of our own day, exploited that intimacy
To turn a trick.

                    Whether small town naïveté
Led her into it, she never said, but given her morals
That is the likeliest explanation. But it's just possible
That the contagious surge of big city freedom
Awakened her wild side, and, bridling
At the reins of respectability
She took her fling at living dangerously—
As a manicurist! Or perhaps her move
Was simple expedience: a way to meet men.
In any case she never acknowledged it. Her sisters
Spoke of her secretiveness (actually a close-mouthed
Capricornian attribute) and this is an instance of it,
Which she never quite lived down.

                         Be that as it may,
It seems that her eyes began giving her trouble,
And she took to wearing glasses.
Later on, at a rooming house, the resident manager
Proved a Christian Scientist, one of the adept
Practitioners certified by the church. This woman

Persuaded her to set the troublesome glasses aside.
After an interval of prayer and meditation
Her eye problem cleared. Given a girl with a bad lung
This event proved eye-opening indeed. What is more,
Given a girl hopelessly in love with a man forbidden her,
Eye-opening intuition overnight became tunnel vision.

For the lady had faith. She herself had been healed,
And her countenance confirmed it: a spiritual aura
Pervaded her presence. For the girl Francelia
Faith was the indispensable requisite, the substance
She lived by. Then, too, other church members
Frequented the house, offering testimonials
Equally engrossing and no less credible.
For the church was strong in California. In fact, nation-wide,
It was at tide-crest, seizing the energies of the new century,
Its sensational novelty ripe for the times;
The electrifying news of its cures and conversions
Astounding the nation. In a very few days
Francelia attended her first service—
An act forbidden by her own church. And then began
Her first reading of *Science and Health* (also proscribed),
The controversial text of Mary Baker Eddy,
Charismatic founder and spiritual guide
Of the vital new movement.

                              Francelia was fascinated.
Familiar enough with the genre—Christian piety
And spiritual exhortation—she was unprepared
For what she found there: a singular earnestness
And down-home directness that were quite winning.
Reading on, she recognized clearly the faith-source
Of her landlady benefactress: the work rang true.
Couched in trite ecclesiastical diction, it concealed
An energy of startling originality:

> *Prayer is not to be used as a confessional to*
> *cancel sin. Such an error would impede true*
> *religion. Sin is forgiven only as it is destroyed*
> *by Christ—Truth and Life. If prayer nurtures*
> *the belief that sin is canceled, and that man is*

made better merely by praying, prayer is an
evil. He grows worse who continues in sin
because he fancies himself forgiven.

At first she had been nonplused by the title.
Was it disingenuously misleading? The unwary reader
Handed a putatively medical text
Only to be regaled with religion?

As for the book's more problematical issue:
The Catholic charge of a radical
Quasi-Manichean denial of matter and the flesh
Contradicted by the Incarnation, she was too unsophisticated,
Too intellectually and critically undeveloped,
To take its measure.

                Rather, the more she read
The more she realized that here was a remarkable
Religious intelligence, a profound attempt
To restore the cutting edge of Christianity
To its original uses, powerful in its attributes
And decisive in its effects: a consummate achievement.
She was immensely impressed.

                      But her commitment lay elsewhere,
And she knew it. Still, in all fairness, she owed it to herself
To objectively appraise the new challenge.
Buckling up her resolve she confronted the alternatives.
It did not take her long.

             What the old church offered
She knew well enough, but its reward lay in the Afterlife.
What the new church offered was the same Afterlife,
The same God and the same Christ, but held out the promise
Of a healing here and now, on the strength, moreover, of a faith
She already possessed! The argument
Was irresistible. And her scrapped glasses,
Like hapless relics of defunct theologies,
Confirmed her deliverance.

              True, her confessor,

Shaken by her patent transparency of motivation,
Pleading with her to reconsider. No upstart heretical sect
Could possibly replace the certitude
Possessed by the Church of Rome. No Mass. No Sacraments.
No Liturgy. No Saints. And most telling of all,
No proven history of salvation. But when she remained
Obdurate in her resolve, withholding absolution
He would have sorrowfully given her his priestly blessing,
Wishing her well, and wondering what the Providence of God
Had in store for such an earnest soul, so young and so vibrant,
Yet given over to such abject self-deception.

                        🔲

What Providence had in store was a whole new scenario,
That was yet as old as the hills.
How Francelia and Louis found each other
We do not know, but find each other they did.
A photograph survives, taken "about the time
Of their marriage." It shows them in a park,
Presumably in California, on a Sunday afternoon—
One of those postcard pictures roving photographers
Took on holidays in public places,
Then sold you the print for fifty cents.
It was warm on that day. Louis, in shirt sleeves,
Has folded his coat across his arm,
And wears his straw hat back on his head
To cool his brow. His stance has the virility
Of a man sexually sure of himself, caught in a moment
Of unconscious definition. Francelia stands tall,
A little behind and above him, her superior height
Augmented by a slight rise in the ground.
She wears an old-fashioned seersucker dress,
White and cool-looking, and holds her hat before her
With both hands—not the token of repression,
Like the fig leaf of Eve; but rather as a mandala,
Constellated at the zone of generation:
Passion's pit and the cleft of her fault.
Later, in her achieved maternity, other photographs
Will reveal her the classic madonna,
But now, on the eve of her nuptials,

The force of a subsumed freedom redolent in her figure,
She complements the man with a perky insouciance.
They are an impressive couple. I recall nothing
Quite like it among the family memorabilia.
It gives me an insight into something
Pondered a long time: one of the hardest things
The Oedipal son must come to understand
Is what the mother sees in the father.
For me, here it is, large as life:
What they found in each other. I own myself
Proud to be the spawn of this coupling.

回

They were married in Yuma, Arizona, on March 26, 1909,
Before a Justice of the Peace, and took up housekeeping there,
But not for long. Like an engendering flood the years
Swept them up and, circling, left the eventual
Flotsam of their lives tracing their trek, the nightfalls
Of their sojourning. In 1910
Their first child, a girl, Vera Louise,
Was born in Phoenix, and the following year
Found them in Bakersfield, California, where I was conceived,
To be born William Oliver at Sacramento in 1912.
My brother, Lloyd Waldemar, saw the light of day
Only thirteen months later in Turlock.
When 1914 found them still farther south
In Fresno County, where the small town of Selma
Proved hospitable and warm, Francelia sensed
That this was the place and put down her foot.

Events proved her right: the famed
San Francisco-Panama Exposition of 1915
Saw the Selma Band in the main parade.
My father's hit tune, *Selma the Home of the Peach*,
Proved sensational, confirming at long last
His sense of identity with a specific locale,
And the wanderlust abated. He then relinquished
His newspaper job to found his own press,
The Everson Printery; but not until

They had purchased a lot and built a house
Did my mother feel we were home.

⊡

So came to a close the formative years
That set the stage for my entrance into life.
As I write, my feeling is one of awesome destiny,
But fearsome mischance as well:
One could so easily not have been born!
You tentatively feel of yourself,
Just to make sure you are really here,
That you do exist, the events of your life
Did actually happen, arriving at terminus
Ineluctably confirmed in the eschatological
Reckoning of who you are, to leave in your passing
As hidden increment, like quartz of the sea
On the glimmering strand, the pure distillate
Of the engendering flood.

⊡ ⊡

CANTO FIVE:
THE BLOOD OF THE POET

SUMMER SOLSTICE, 1914, SELMA, CALIFORNIA

My first remembrance: the yard of our earliest
Selma sojourn, corner of Logan
And Gaither streets, on the east side of town.

The occasion: a bevy of neighborhood children
At play on the lawn, myself among them,
And no doubt my sister, though I can't recall her.
Certainly my brother is still a mewling babe-in-arms,
Which goes far to explain the conspicuous
Absence of my mother; she is seldom without us.

Instead, a couple of neighbor women, standing by in supervision,
Complete the scene. No men around. At so early a date
In the new century, the nursery syndrome precludes it.

Suddenly the lazy summer stillness is shattered by a scream.
It is my own. I have stabbed my foot on a piece of broken bottle
Hidden in the grass. How long it has lain there,
Like a serpent coiled to strike, no one can say,
Least of all a two-year-old kid,
Sheltered by his mother from accidental mishap
Or archetypal malice, till the rude day dawns,
To find him unready.

       Heedless as a pup
I frolicked with my kind, ecstatic in that animal
Abasement of the self before the power of the pack,
Till the mother's untoward absence
Exposed the flaw, and in my child's
Fear-benighted reckoning the serpent
Found my foot.

      Or did my foot
Find the serpent? In the cloudy womb of causation
Who nudges whom? Falling to the ground
I twist in terror at the seizure of my blood,

Shrieking to high heaven, bringing the scared children
And the alarmed adults crowding about me.

Someone fetches from the near back porch
A white enameled basin, full and slopping over
With pure tap water—a household utensil
Familiar enough to the ubiquitous back porches
Of small town America; but this time it threatens.
Scrambling frantically up on my useless leg
I look wildly around for my mother. But when these sudden
Strangers seize my ankle and thrust in my foot,
I yell bloody murder.

                    But I quickly recover,
Brought up short by the awe-struck faces
Clustered about me. I blink back my tears,
Too paralyzed by pain to see what they see,
But too rapt in the grip of the simmering archetype
Not to feel what they fear.

                    Then my vision fixes.
For out of my fragile, fang-pierced foot
Pulses the wellspring of my fugitive blood,
A ribbon of red, unfurling in the pellucid water,
Beautiful in its sanguinary loveliness,
Solemnly performing its surrogate office,
The changing of water to wine, as earnestly intense
As the serenade of life or the swan-song of death.

Years later, under the rubric of the castration complex,
I will read it as the sleeve of a lady's favor
Tangled on his helmet where her knight lay dead
(Slain in defense of her precious honor),
But eased by the solace of the jongleur in her bed.

So does the symbol, latent in the stuff of life,
Reconstitute its truth. But for now,
It spells only terror: this it is that fastens every eye,
Victim and lookers-on alike, in the portentous drama

Unfolding here.

          So the wound bleeds on
Picking up passion as it flows, compounding
    its enigmatic purpose
Till that humble and hallowed icon, the basin,
That once on Golgotha caught the veritable
Gore of God, source of its numinous efficacy, only to become,
By virtue of what grave default, the World Ill's
Stinking bucket of blood.

              But the ills of the world,
By God's clear injunction, are to be reckoned
Implicitly benign. His vivid signature, dazzlingly
Calligraphed on trees, rivers, rocks, buttes and benchlands,
The ordeal of life is the measure of its meaning.
Perdurably opportune, the hostages of pain
Never fail to evince the quantification of value
In the substance of the soul.

               It will be roughly
Twenty more years before the tongue of this poet
Finds its true tenor. But the centrality of vision,
Which the presence of his peers, in their invincible naïveté,
Evoke within him, will, in God's good time,
Given the centrifugal passion at the heart of things,
Confirm his destiny.

            Nor do I cry anymore,
But watch with amazement the limpidity of water
Undergo its savage metamorphosis,
To become before my astounded eyes,
Stunned in the existential verge of the Real,
A token of the poet's inimitable
Credential—his consecrated blood.

NOTE:

The title of Canto V is taken from a statement by Hugh Fox in a review / article: "The jagged cut image—for all its pain, it's really the only way you bleed, isn't it, and poems are, arn't[sic] they, the Blood of the Poet?" This statement is found among Everson's papers and was being used as the source for an alternative title for *The Masks of Drought*, namely, *The Jagged Cut Image*.

In a tentative acknowledgment, Everson attributes the statement to Hugh Fox but does not specify the title of the periodical in which Fox's review / article appeared. As of now, the periodical has not been identified.

Everson was born September 10, 1912. The year attributed to the incident recounted in Canto V is used by Everson with late typescripts of the poem. However, the year might have been 1915. The earliest note regarding the incident appears to be a journal entry from 1956, wherein he writes, "My earliest memory is having cut my foot as a baby...." In a 1978 preliminary but unfinished attempt to write the poetic account, he refers to himself as "three years of age." An undated and uncompleted verse, entitled "The First Memory," includes the phrase "not three years old." And here, of course, Everson refers to himself as "a two-year-old kid."

From a 1983 recorded interview with the poet, Bill Hotchkiss has provided the following excerpt regarding the incident:

HOTCHKISS: Could you make a guess as to how old you were at that time?

EVERSON: We weren't there [in the Eversons' first Selma house] too long, I don't think. That would be 1914 when we arrived there, and I imagine it was fairly soon after we arrived. I'd say that would be 1914, and with the shoes off, that would be summertime. Maybe the summer of 1914 or at the most 1915. Probably 1914. That'd put me only two years old. Is that feasible?

AMERICAN OCCASIONAL POETRY:
William Everson

As a genre the so-called "occasional poem" is not extensively practiced in American verse. Incurably romantic, we extol the seizure of inspiration and abjure the set performance, which constitutes so fundamental an element in the British tradition, where a formal elegy like Milton's "Lycidas," written as an entry in a school competition commemorating the death of a fellow student, emerged in time as perhaps the finest poem in the language. Moreover, the idea of a Poet Laureate, in the sense of an official Bard subsidized by the State to memorialize civic occasions, is repugnant to us. Lacking the security of the British social structure, our journalistic attempts to identify "America's Leading Poet" do keep us almost obsessively preoccupied with rank; but the notion of an official verse functionary at the top, an appointment nominally expected to produce significant verse on specific occasions, for us is abhorrent.

Still, the place of the occasional poem, intrinsic to the history of poetry, will not be denied. Despite themselves American poets are compelled to address their talents to significant occasions of general import, for poetry is "public" as well as "private" speech, and as such it cannot reluct from its ancient office. (As a case in point, Robert Frost's appearance at President Kennedy's Inaugural may be instanced.) For out of the guts of the body politic we do respond, and sometimes it is truly moving, as seen in Whitman's powerful "When Lilacs Last in the Dooryard Bloom'd" on the death of President Lincoln in 1865. Sometimes it is speciously contrived, as was James Russell Lowell's stilted but splendid "Ode Recited at the Harvard Commemoration," inspired by the ending of the Civil War, the same year. The important thing is that on such occasions the poet is forced to rise out of his subjective interiority where his individual strength customarily resides, and reach for the public voice. This requires a true break in plane, and, when successful, effects a transcendent emergence.

I was almost fifty years old before the requirements of a public event swept me above my native prejudice and compelled me to write my first occasional poem. That was "The Poet Is Dead," an elegy on the death of Robinson Jeffers in 1962. James Schevill, director of the Poetry Center at San Francisco State, commissioned it for a Poetry Festival in the Civic Auditorium that spring. Later in the decade Mayor Joseph Alioto appealed to me to present something at an event commemorating the anniversary of the 1906 earthquake, and I responded with an extended poem called "The City Does Not Die." That same spring of 1969 a drive to get San Franciscans to relinquish their handguns, the metal to be cast in a statue of St. Francis of Assisi by Beniamino Bufano, and dedicated on the first anniversary of the death of Robert Kennedy, inspired me to write a rhyming lyric poem "Melt Down the Guns." These appearances, nationally televised, brought me my widest public exposure, but also led to an immediate backlash. For as an ostensible reward Mayor Alioto proclaimed me "The Unofficial Poet Laureate of San Francisco," which produced not a few hoots from my peers, stemming from the prejudice noted above, but also because such designations lend themselves to political attribution, and the hapless "laureate" finds himself rising and falling with the fortunes of his sponsor. Thus when I left the Dominicans that fall in order to marry, the opposition press professed moral affront and proceeded to smear "Alioto's Poet Laureate." Such are the perils of the public arena.

Be that as it may, when the students of the first graduating class of Kresge College, the University of California at Santa Cruz, to which I had recently affiliated myself, asked me to compose a poem for their Commencement [June 17, 1973], I was not without prior experience in the awkward genre of the "American Occasional Poem." I had only seventeen days before the ceremony, but the foregoing occasions had accustomed me to writing verse against a deadline, and I plunged ahead. Aware that the essence of American poetry is not specified in pattern as much as in energy, I applied myself to the spacious outdoor situation of my anticipated audience, situated on the elevated Santa Cruz campus, so typically Californian with its open knolls over the sea and its majestic stands of redwood, as well as to the general relief at having just emerged from the most sodden winter in the history of the state—not to speak of the fact that two of our women students had been raped and murdered that year, for us at Kresge the most poignant of the series of local female victimizations that had prompted the District Attorney to speak of Santa Cruz as "the murder capital of the world." Jeffers had extolled the Coast's penchant for violence ("This coast crying out for tragedy like all beautiful places"). Certainly I wanted to utilize that penchant but without searing the souls of my hearers by references to events best left unspoken.

To obviate, therefore, a somberness almost built into the occasion, I chose as title a captious newspaper headline taken from an article attributing the extraordinary weather of that year to variations in the so called "jet stream," the upper current of air flowing from West to East around the globe. Then, groping for the archetype below all rites of passage as the symbolic key to the meaning of graduation, I began to recall the sobering self-examination of most Americans in that lamentable Watergate spring, and apply what I intuited of its implications, not as pertaining only to the Class of Seventy Three, but to all Americans in whatsoever year of our history.

In looking back upon my Ode now, five years later, I perceive in it the awkwardness of a genre not conspicuously amenable to the American psyche, but also a certain moral ruggedness inspired by the ghastly local events, no less than the depressing political situation of the time. These elements I take to be both its weaknesses and its strengths. In recompense I hope that as an Ode, something of the British tradition of formal public speech inheres in it, even as public declamation it evokes the raw energy of the American potential. For all our awkwardness with the form, the American poet must learn its uses. Sooner or later, and despite its hazards, he must find his private fulfillment in public utterance. This the poet has traditionally done across the history of the race.

WILLIAM EVERSON

June 17, 1978
Kresge College
The University of California, Santa Cruz

AFTERWORD:
THE KINGFISHER'S CRY
Bill Hotchkiss

[Note: the first three pages of the essay which follows are devoted to a brief chronicle of a friendship, a witnessing, so to speak, but with significant glimpses into the later career of the poet, in process. For this reason, the impatient reader may wish to turn ahead to the first division point to begin a critical consideration of the poet's art, theology, and aesthetics.]

As I write these words, it's early spring of 1999, and the poet has been gone for nearly five years. As my fingers play on the keyboard, the stunning unreality of Everson's death floods over me. Indeed, a quarter of a century and a bit more have passed since Bill and I became friends. At that time in my life, I was a young man with a brand-new doctoral degree—I'd written a dissertation on Robinson Jeffers, and Everson's *Fragments of an Older Fury* had been the source volume I most relied upon and was the critical work with which I felt most nearly in tune.

Actually, Everson (as Antoninus) and his poetry were closely associated in my mind with my introduction to the work of Jeffers himself—in a course on major American authors, University of Oregon, 1963, under the direction of the late Bill Nolte. At just about that time, as either fate or chance would have it, Antoninus gave a presentation in Eugene and read, among other pieces, "A Canticle to the Waterbirds" and "The Poet is Dead," his magnificent ode to Jeffers. I was working toward an M.F.A. then, doing a novel for a thesis but secretly committed to poetry. I was astonished by Antoninus' charismatic presence. Never before had I heard such a compelling and demanding and lightning-punctuated reading.

Eleven years later, when my doctoral dissertation was accepted and the degree completed, I mailed a copy to Everson, then teaching at University of California, Santa Cruz, and living (with his young wife Susanna and their son Jude) at a former California Division of Forestry station near Davenport, a property owned by Bud McCrary and Big Creek Lumber Company, north of Santa Cruz.

Shortly thereafter Judith Shears and I visited Kingfisher Flat for the first of many times. As the years of friendship went on, I brought various of my students at Sierra College, as well as personal friends, to meet Everson—including such authors as Stan Hager, David Carpenter, K'os Naahaabii, Gary Elder, and Bill Harryman. The last of these visits occurred just a month before the poet's death. With a gaggle of students, Stan Hager, and Judith Shears present, Everson was more than up to the undoubted stress of the visit—and despite damage to his vocal cords and the advanced Parkinson syndrome, succeeded admirably in communicating with his visitors.

During those final months, when Everson was able to return to Kingfisher Flat after his protracted and near-fatal pneumonia, he was visited and cared for by many, including his son Jude, Steve Sibley, Dan Stolpe, Janet DeBar, and James Chadwick. Rose Tannlund came to visit, as did Gary Young, Bruce Owens, Felicia Rice, Mort Marcus, Al Gelpi, Peter Thomas, Jim Houston, and Fr. Finbarr Hayes (Antoninus' one time printer's devil at St. Albert's), who administered Extreme Unction—and who was ultimately to conduct the memorial mass at St. Albert's and to preside at the funeral and subsequent re-interment on what would have been Bill's eighty-second birthday, September 10, 1994. Mary Fabilli and Susanna made telephone calls, and so did David Carpenter, Allan Campo, George Fox, Lee Bartlett, and publisher and long-time friend Robert Hawley of Oyez Press. Indeed, I have no idea how many people made contact with Everson during his final days, but the number was large.

Bill Everson's birthday each year, with a fire beneath the huge twin redwoods of Kingfisher Flat, and with the poet's favored hanging tenderloins sizzling over the flames, provided many a rendezvous. It was at one of these, as I recall, that Al Campo, Dave Carpenter, and I decided to put together and publish our 1978 volume, *William Everson: Poet from the San Joaquin.*

From 1974 through 1991, I never missed that weekend in September in honor of the poet's birthday. Only on his eightieth, when a large gathering showed up and Bill and Susanna (a shock to all) separated after twenty-one years of marriage, did I fail to make an appearance, my daughter Jennifer, granddaughter Brittany, and I visiting instead a week later—the poet lodged for a time with artist and close friend Dan Stolpe.

There were also get-togethers when the Eversons drove inland, across the Big Valley, and we were off to the mountains—to visit poet Cornel Lengyel at the latter's hermitage above Georgetown, to go on camping expeditions to Grouse Lakes Wilderness, to the areas nearby Carson Pass or Sonora Pass, or to Kings Canyon or Yosemite. A few times we had get-togethers beside the pond at my place near Newcastle, complete with poetry readings attended by gangs of my students from Sierra College and by former students and friends—including poets Ken Hancock, Randy White, Edith Snow, and Gary Elder.

Now those years are gone, and the man who was alternately
William Everson and Brother Antoninus lives in his work; since the
poet's death, Allan Campo and I and others have worked steadily, with
the firm commitment and backing of John Martin at Black Sparrow
Press, to see through to publication the poet's long-suppressed spiritual
autobiography, *Prodigious Thrust*, as well as those three volumes of
collected poetry which constitute the body of his life's work, *Residual
Years*, *Veritable Years*, and *Integral Years*. Everson trusted us, and I
hope our efforts have been adequate to a responsibility we willingly and
humbly accepted.

Poet from the San Joaquin, Beat Friar, and Sage of Kingfisher
Flat—he belongs to the Ages now. Not even Whitman or Jeffers was
more committed to *ars poetica*. Now Everson stands with these two;
and as a reviewer said more than twenty years ago, searching for just the
right expression, "William Everson IS poetry."

🔲

The Integral Years contains the verses of the final quarter-century
and more of the poet's life, a period (or sequence of periods) during
which he emerged from the Dominican robes of Brother Antoninus and
became once again William Everson—not as the anarchist conscientious
objector he had formerly been but as a man profoundly religious in his
orientation, devout both in terms of his Catholic faith and in terms of
the "pantheistic sources" that informed the work of *Residual Years* and
Veritable Years as well, one who had returned to the secular realm and
to "Woman" and the life of the family, after eighteen and a half years as
a monk. Significantly he did not go back to the vineyards of the San
Joaquin, the region that had brought him to manhood, but rather he
chose to be situated near the heaving Pacific that inspired his mentor,
Robinson Jeffers. Late, then, he came to the profession of teaching. As
poet in residence at Kresge College of U.C. Santa Cruz, Everson taught
his "Birth of a Poet" course and handpress printing as well, establishing
the Lime Kiln Press and issuing, with the able assistance of a sequence
of gifted and devoted students, a series of books that are now valued
collectors' items—they are, that is, the work of the master. Thus
Everson found his own "inevitable place" at Kingfisher Flat, beside Big
Creek, a clearing in the redwood canyon where he and Susanna raised
their son—a mile or so downstream from trail's end at the pool beneath
Stone Face Falls. This "zone of contention," as he might have called it,
became the microcosm of *Archetype West* (the title of his seminal

exposition of the nature of the defining paradigm of Western American literature).

The sound of Big Creek, flowing among granite boulders, informs many of the poems in *The Integral Years*—and so does the eldritch cry of the kingfisher, resident spirit of the place, in some ways the untranslatable voice of the Divine, the bird a feral objective correlative to the questing spirit of the Fisher King, intent upon grasping the entirety of *Mysterium Tremendum*, and yet unable even to ask the fated question, unable to do more than to screech out through an insufficient avian beak, and yet capable of *being* His verification (to use phrasing from "A Canticle to the Waterbirds" in *The Veritable Years*)—witness these lines from "Stone Face Falls":

> Suddenly a kingfisher swoops between.
> In midflight he sees us, veers sharply,
> Utters a sudden electrifying screech,
> The ineluctable tension cruxed at the heart of things
> Splitting his beak, the mystery
> Out of which life springs and from which it passes.
> Three times he circles, skirling his fierce
> Importunate cry, then climbs the thermal,
> The lazy updraft transcending the falls,
> And disappears up the canyon.
>   ...
>   Far ahead,
> Beyond the stone face of the falls,
> The cry of the kingfisher
> Pierces the noon. (158)

For Everson, nature is a grand "inscape," and each object or living creature is "a mouse [that] is miracle enough to stagger sextillions of infidels," to use Whitman's wording. At the roots of Everson's earliest poetry was a pantheistic presumption regarding the nature of things, even though in "Circumstance," in *The Residual Years*, the Divinity is portrayed as a type of vexing half-sentience to which one might pray but which will ultimately answer no prayers. Beauty, though sometimes terrible, is present, but behind that façade is a Something akin to Hardy's "crass casualty."

Yet, with his conversion to the Catholic faith, came the *thing* for which the poet had previously cried out in vain—for now he found *purpose* as the underlying dimension, and that purpose meant *good* and revealed the existence of the Divine, was a shuddering demonstration of the existence of God—if only the sentient human awareness were capable of seeing what lay just beneath the surface, disguised by and yet revealed through material reality.

In a poem called "In All These Acts"(*VY* 188), the poet subscripts the title with these words from the apocryphal "Gospel According To Thomas": *Cleave the wood and thou shalt find Me, lift the rock and I am there!* The Divine Entity is present within the grain of the wood and beneath any rock that might be lifted from its resting place. A single grain of sand has implicit within it the entire geological history of the planet and shines with the light of God—if, that is, the viewer were willing to open himself, to look with the wondering eyes of a child. For the pantheist, God is everywhere and in all things. For the *Christian* pantheist, grace, the progenerative force, and Christ's "sweet reprieve" are also palpably evident: birth and death and the wonder which unites them.

"In All These Acts" depicts the occasionally frightening though beautiful aspect of natural process, the usual norms being *violated* through a momentary eruption of the immense potential of natural process, and an elk is torn nearly in half by scissoring logs brought down by the tremendous force of a wind storm. Even in such moments of violence, and perhaps indeed more vividly in such moments, a terrible beauty reveals itself. Individual lives may be winked out, and yet the force of life itself, the force of God effusional from within matter, pours outward and onward without cessation:

> The many-faced splendor and the music of the leaf,
> The copulation of beasts and the watery laughter of drakes,
> Too few the grave witnesses, the wakeful, vengeful beauty,
> Devolving itself of its whole constraint,
> Erupting as it goes.

> In all these acts
> Christ crouches and seethes, pitched forward
> On the crucifying stroke, juvescent, that will spring Him
> Out of the germ, out of the belly of the dying buck,
> Out of the father-phallos and the torn-up root.
> These are the modes of His forth-showing,
> His serene agonization. (*VY* 189)

Perhaps in such lines Everson's ultimate rejection of the peace and quiet
(protection, insulation) of the monastery, in favor of the realm of the
wild, was subsumed and restrained, hidden, germinal but inevitable.
The poem falls about halfway through the *Veritable Years* sequence, but
it hearkens back to the aftermath of a violent storm that struck
Waldport, on the Oregon coast, during the time of Everson's detention
there as a conscientious objector during World War Two.

God, as Everson had come to believe, exists in everything and in
every action—and knows all pain and suffers the death-pangs of
creatures great and small. Yet the life-force itself, an Infinite Fountain
of Light, pours forth whenever a piece of wood is cloven or a rock is
lifted.

We find the same informing principle as backdrop for the merely
human (and occasionally pornographic) action depicted in "River-Root,"
with the description of the beginnings and gatherings of "the great
torpid river" that flows south in the night close by where the lovers are
in their process of mutual rediscovery and unification:

> River-Root: as even under high drifts, those fierce
>   wind-grappled cuts of the Rockies,
> One listening will hear, far down below, the softest seepage,
>   a new melt, a faint draining,
> And know for certain that this is the tip, this, though
>   the leastest trace,
> Is indeed the uttermost inch of the River.
>
> Or on cloud-huddled days up there shut in white denseness,
> Where peaks in that blindness call back and forth
>   each to the other,
> Skim but a finger along a twig, slick off the moist,
> A mere dampness the cloud has left, a vague wetness.
> But still you know this too is a taking, this too can be sea,
> The active element, pure inception, the residual root
>   of the River.
>
> Place a hand under moss, brush back a fern, turn over
>   a stone, scoop out a hollow—
> Is there already, the merest wet, the least moistness,
>   and is enough—
> No more than this is needful for source,
> So much is a start, such too makes up the rise of the River.

Even this, even these, of little more, of nothing less,
Of each, of all, drop and by drop, the very coolness
     priming the wind
Alone suffices: this in itself, for all its slightness,
     can birth the River.

And hence such wetness gains liquid body and cups a spring,
Lipped down from a crevice, some stone-slotted vein
     of the mauled mountain,
A jet of liberation, and in so much is swiftly away.
And the spurt makes a trickle, channeling out an edge for itself,
Forming a bed of itself as it goes, a bottom of gravel. (*VY* 119)

In his "Foreword" to the 1976 softcover edition of the poem, work
that had gone unpublished for nearly twenty years, Everson / Antoninus
wrote the following:

> ...like a seed it lay dormant in the earth until the conditions set
> vibrating in the bicentennial awakened it from a long sleep to
> stand up and manifest the energies it celebrates. Written in the
> monastery where, as Brother Antoninus, I was even then
> participating in that creative emergence called the San
> Francisco Renaissance, it hoarded its germ of relevance for the
> opportunity of today's historic occasion.
>   Not that the time itself was sterile. Allen Ginsberg's poem
> "Howl" was making its way in the world, transforming
> attitudes. A new birth in consciousness was stirring, old
> restrictions were collapsing. (N. pag. [7])

I believe it was fall of 1975 when Everson first showed me the
typescript for "River-Root," a poem which he had purposely not brought
forward during his tenure as Brother Antoninus—perhaps for fear the
work might not have received its *nihil obstat* from the Church and
possibly for fear of the controversy and even notoriety as well, had such
a book been published by a Catholic monk.

Since asked, I encouraged Bill to go ahead with his tentative plan to
publish—and hazarded a surmise that "River-Root" might eventually
become his best-known verse. Judith Shears and I both made
annotations on the typescript and urged publication. Various others, I'm
sure, did much the same.

Among my fellow Everson scholars, I have heard "River-Root" referred to as both the best and the worst of the poet's work. The matter remains to be determined, I believe, whether *pornographia* can ever fully take its place as a portion of the body of great literature. But my point here is simply that, for Everson, Eros and Thanatos alike are subsumed within the restless earth and the movements as well of glaciers and rivers and the great storms which join the oceans and the emergent bodies of land. Erotic and Spiritual partake of a oneness, a joining, a *syzygy;* they are coupled—even as "Over and over He dies and is born."

In 1970, shortly after that fated night at University of California, Davis, when Everson announced that he intended to leave the Dominican Order and to marry young Susanna Rickson, he began work on the critical study that was to be published in 1976 as *Archetype West* (Oyez Press), in which he attempts to get at the defining, species-specific characteristic of Western American literature:

> The vast literary prolixity of the West defies synthesis. Schools and trends abound, some with the blessing of remote sages. Movements are born and die overnight. Individual writers loom like unexplored islands out of the sea of Western words, to disappear in a decade. This essay, therefore, claims to be no more than a tentative probe into the underlying ethos. (xi)

Once upon a time in American history, as we're all aware, the land west of the Sand Hills of Nebraska was mythically *huge,* its brooding physical characteristics as yet shrouded in mystery, a land crossed by such imaginary rivers as the Buenaventura and the Multnomah—it was truly *terra incognita*, populated by warrior societies on horseback and by grizzlies and buffalo and mountain lions. Then came the fur trappers, the gold-seekers, the cattlemen, the loggers. The great mountains shouldered the sky, and rivers flowed at the bottoms of impossibly deep canyons. The land was untamed and incipiently violent. It impressed itself indelibly upon the psyches of those who lived there, and it does so still. If one has ever seen Mt. Shasta, for instance, the image of that giant will be imprinted forever upon the mind.[1]

---

[1] Once when Everson, Dave Carpenter, Judith Shears, and I were returning from a Robinson Jeffers Festival at Southern Oregon University, Bill wished to stop at the Klamath River—so that he might dip his wrists into the water of that stream. We watched two great blue herons engaged in a territorial dispute, each having taken position atop rocky formations on either side of a ravine. After what appeared to be demonstrations of shadow boxing, one bird realized itself outdone, and, with a fearful squawk, flew hurriedly away. The other began immediately

For Everson, Joaquin Miller (in whose *Life Amongst the Modocs,* Mt. Shasta is arguably the half-hidden central character of the autobiographical epic) "...emerges permanently as the West's first literary autochthon"(*AWest*, 175). But it was Robinson Jeffers in whose work "apotheosis" would be most fully achieved:

> The important thing here is that the negative facet of the American psyche did not achieve apotheosis until Jeffers carried it to the ultimate, and opened up the pantheistic affirmation inherent in its skepticism. Only then could the divinity caged in the nuclear material entity, the numen, show its true face, and the Godhead blaze through. Whitman is the sunrise in the East, but Jeffers is the sunset in the West. It is bloody and violent, but it is the last light given us. We deny it at our peril. (*AWest*, 77)

In "Hymn to the Cosmic Christ," the poet cries out to the "Dark God of Eros," to "Christ of the inching beam...":

> Groping toward midnight in a flinch of birth,
> The mystic properties of womb and earth:
> Conceived in semblance of a fiercer dream,
> Scorning the instances of things that merely seem. (14)

No longer shielded, so to speak, by the institutional givens and directives enforced by the wearing of a Dominican habit, the poet seeks to discover within his own Western American being an identity that would both suit his psychological needs and sustain him as he ventures out into the indeterminate realms of the secular life. In "The Scout" he tells us that, passing a leathercraft shop in Mill Valley, he sees "Yellow buckskin, long undulant fringes, / Lazy stitch beadwork of the Plains tribes, / Strong, tawny wear of the old frontier"(82). He seeks a new "habit" to replace the "black and white [now] worn by another"(82). The buckskin coat, duly purchased, takes the poet back, by virtue of imagination, to the archetypal past, where he meets the mysterious figure of an Indian:

---

to preen itself. Later, just at sundown, we drove past Mt. Shasta, a pale red fire of late light glinting from the glaciers high up on the huge volcanic peak. Everson, utterly entranced, muttered as a sort of litany, "God! God! God!"

```
     ...a mounted figure
Abruptly accosting. The single
Eagle feather of the scout marks him Protector,
Watcher of the Spirit, Guardian of the Sacred Mysteries,
     Keeper of the Pass. (83)
```

The poet gives the sign of recognition and of peace, "palm forward," but the Keeper of the Pass turns his mount and disappears, leaving the narrator "touched by a strange foreboding." There's potential danger here in this turning from the archetype of the monastery to the archetype of "shaman to his time," and, as he says, he smells "danger at the divide"(83).

"The Scout" may well be seen as a prologue to "Black Hills," a vision poem partly of dream and partly of waking—waking yet still attended by the dynamics of the dream, an intrusion of the surreal into the real. The trail is an "old" one which the mounted protagonist follows in his attempt to search out and befriend the male archetype whose potential rejection he fears, perhaps the very God the Father from whom he had turned away in the act of coming under the influence of Woman and of leaving the Dominican Order—up-slope, until he reaches "the ancient tree-burials of the Indians," a place of massacre transformed into a burial site by other bands of Indians the following spring.

In dream the rider's horse "balks unmanageably"(85). The poet-speaker gropes forward on foot and comes to "a spill of shattered boulders" from whence a "torrent of hatred," masculine, seems to pour. As a counterforce, the speaker calls up "the composite visage of all the great chiefs." He cries out, "Father! ... Return to our lives!" Finally he shouts, "I love you!" But the force of hatred merely increases—until "suddenly the rain begins"(87).

Once again the poet-pilgrim conjures up the faces of the great chiefs. Only when these images fade does the pilgrim wail in utter anguish and exasperation, "God damn it, I love you!"(88)

The poet's own shouts of despair awaken him, and he finds himself "rigid beside my young wife"(88). In these hours before dawn, the poet rises, still living through the implications of the dream, and ultimately he steps out into the moonlight, which "embraces" him. Moonlight reveals the "unsullied present," a realm seemingly exempt even from the implications of Sin Original, "eternally reborn." The moonlight "envelops me, and blesses me," and the poet imagines that "standing there in the doorway, / All Indian at last, / I lift up my arms and pray"(90). To become "all Indian" is to enter into a kind of prelapsarian world of Rousseauvian noble savagery, wherein peace, harmony of the male and female principles, the faith that somehow precedes faith itself, may be accessed and internalized.

But the poet realizes that "it is too much," the goal having been achieved too simply, too easily, and he turns back to bed. He has confronted the hatred of the Father archetype and been granted momentary succor by the Mother archetype. But here a kind of human, everyday "reality" intrudes, almost comically after the scenes that have been played out on the waves of vision and post-vision. He steps on a "plastic toy, / The dropped plaything of my wife's infant child"—the son that he has not yet seemingly claimed as his own. The poet has cut himself on a *giuegaue*, and the scratch bleeds: "I feel blood on my thumb, / Where the bones of all the buffalo / Gashed my heel"(90). In some sense, then, he has been transformed into Chiron, the wounded centaur, half horse and half human, the mounted pilgrim, so to speak, of the opening stanzas of the poem. Body and soul are now bonded in the ritual of blood sacrifice.

The buckskin coat, acquisition of which is described in "The Scout," is here depicted as hanging in the moonlight: "I have placed it high on the wall, / As my religious habit, hung high on the door of the monastic cell, / Stood sentinel there / Against the intrusion of the world"(89). The frontier style coat, which came to be Everson's most characteristic item of clothing, has both replaced the meditative religious habit of the Dominican and at the same time has become the habit of a primitive and nobly savage and autochthonous species of Catholicism. In trying to possess the Elder Godforce, that which in Everson's mind initially generated the Judeo-Christian religions, the questing pilgrim is turned away; in sensing and accepting his own inadequacy, however, he is embraced by the Woman-Moon Force, the feminine aspect of the Divine (imaged, so to speak, by the *anima*, differing in degree but not in kind), and becomes, at least momentarily in the meditative aftermath of his dream of attempted expiation, "all Indian at last"(90). That which the questing pilgrim sought and which was denied by the Grand Patriarch at the dream's climax, is now granted by the Grand Matriarch in the half-waking aftermath of the dreaming—not because the pilgrim has sought out and mastered, but rather because he has inadvertently made himself vulnerable to the healing force of the moonlight.

Was it the prospect of final vows, the full psychological implications of turning away permanently, and in the eyes of God, from the vanity fair of the temporal world, that first lured Antoninus into the arms of Rose and then of Susanna? Whatever the case, once the decision was made not to take those final vows, a distancing from the Dominican Order was inevitable—a distancing and a severance: "A fugitive monk and an unwed mother / Making love in the solstice weather" ("Socket of Consequence" 46).

Divested of his Dominican habit, the poet sought a new one, new symbolic attire, and the buckskin coat became precisely that. It fit Bill Everson well, extremely well. But the guilt engendered by turning away from God the Father—though he never did except *apparently*—persisted for years thereafter. At unpredictable moments, perhaps walking from the house to the great redwood trees, perhaps standing in darkness beside a drought-bitten stream in the High Sierra, perhaps staring reflectively off across the wild Pacific, he would vociferate in the most mournful fashion the words, "Forgive me!"

There was indeed, as he said in "The Scout," a certain, terrible "danger at the divide."

▣

Without an academic degree of any sort, Everson had accepted a part-time position, poet in residence, at University of California, Santa Cruz—and thus, lacking the traditional degreed certification, he entered academia. His reputation as poet, as fine press printer, and as a staunch individualist were sufficient reasons for the university to bring him aboard, thus setting into motion Everson's "Birth of a Poet" course (extremely popular among the students) and his workshop in handpress printing and the subsequent emergence of The Lime Kiln Press. Oddly enough, as university records reveal, Everson was never given a stipend for the latter course, though the publishing imprint became world famous.

This world of academia was new for Bill, and he pitched into it with characteristic energy and abandon. But as a result, he went through a creative drought, a poetic aridity that is truly broken only with the onset of the physical California drought of 1976-78.

Everson and I had discussed the matter of his "writer's block," and I suggested his going back into previous work, revising, in an attempt to seduce the muse. It was during the summer of 1975 or perhaps in September, at the time of our get-together to celebrate Bill's birthday, that I asked if he might have some unpublished poem I could use in *Sierra Journal*. We walked out to the printshop; Bill went through his files and ultimately handed me a worn manuscript page, asking, "What about this?" I scanned a piece called "Snowflake: The Death of Jeffers," the subtitle something Bill may have written in at the time. Elated, I accepted. I immediately thereafter typed a copy to take with me, replacing the original in its manila folder. My memory (though memory cannot always be trusted) is of an inked-in notation at the bottom of Bill's typescript: *Jeffers dies, January 20, 1962.* Bill later told me he'd written "Snowflake" immediately after learning of RJ's death—and that he really hadn't intended a further treatment of the subject. He subsequently explained he'd walked for hours that night after his relationship with Rose had been terminated, mulling his future, and that he'd learned of RJ's death in the morning. At the time (January 1962) he was still legally married to Mary Fabilli. In any case, as a Dominican lay brother, Antoninus was obliged to keep his relationship with Rose almost totally to himself. "Snowflake" does not mention her—beyond the mysterious reference to "Mal Paso: / The difficult divide," which could be taken as an allusion to Jeffers' "Tamar," "Fauna," and others, this being the name of a creek south of Carmel— where several crucial scenes in Jeffers' narratives occur. Mal Paso is the *bad crossing*, the "difficult divide," as Everson denotes it, and with only a minimum of associational extension the Spanish name might also be thought of as *Mexican Cross*, a term he uses to describe Rose, with himself "nailed to the Mexican Cross."

But in both "The Thing-Death" and "Rose Recreant," a pair of poems I take to be derivative from the original creative impulse, the references to Rose and the fractured relationship are not hidden at all— since, thirteen years and a lifetime later, they would have no reason to be hidden.

"Snowflake" concludes with these lines:

Mal Paso:
The difficult divide.

All night long
The dark brooding,
Mute pall,
The black foreboding.

Emptiness: lack of light.

All night long
Shut silence,
The pang of that foregoing.

And over the hogback
One coyote

Splinters the dawn with a yelp out of hell:

Abrupt finale.

The death of the master—and the end of Antoninus' love affair with Rose: the two events were incongruously joined. But after a time, the great elegy, "The Poet is Dead," came pouring out, first read at the San Francisco Museum of Art poetry festival, June of 1962—see Everson's note to the Auerhahn edition of *The Poet is Dead*, 1964, reproduced in *Fragments of an Older Fury* (Oyez, 1968. 165-166).

"Snowflake," "The Thing-Death" and "Rose Recreant," are all included in the "Eros and Thanatos" segment of the present volume, Appendix A. As Allan Campo has determined from the poet's papers at the Bancroft Library, the initial drafts of the three poems all bear the date of June 22, 1975. The subsequent typescripts are undated with the exception of a "Snowflake" typescript bearing the notation, "corrected July 5, 75." None includes the subscripted phrase, "The Death of Jeffers."

The matter of dating remains a great puzzle to me. If "Snowflake" were written in January of 1962, why are there only drafts from June-July, 1975—especially given the poet's practice of keeping all drafts of a poem together in a manila folder? The two-drawer filing cabinet out in the print shop, from whence Bill produced the copy of "Snowflake" for my consideration, was eventually moved to the re-built A-frame that housed books and printing press during the last years of the poet's life. But then, in the aftermath of Bill's death, the filing cabinet, with all the folders full of Everson manuscripts, was missing. It still is. Papers were sold to the Bancroft during the months preceding Everson's death, and so the folders containing manuscripts may be there. Allan Campo has found many things, but others are missing. The typescript of "Snowflake" from which I typed copy has not surfaced.

🔲

In "Steelhead" the scene of *The Integral Years* changes from Stinson Beach to Kingfisher Flat, and the poem depicts the poet's time of creative low-water. A steelhead is stranded in a shallow pool in Big Creek, the stream flowing directly behind the poet's home.

Then, in a dream, the poet arises and gropes his way to the creek, where, by dim moonlight, he discovers the big fish, "Alone on the bottom like a sunken stick— / No, like a God-stoned monk prostrate in his cell— / That enigmatic shape, sleeplessly intent..."(110).

With the coming of dawn, the poet rises, repeats his dream-trek down to the pool, and observes that "Giddy with delight the moths fly double. / In a spasm of joy the mayflies breed..."(111). In a world of procreant energy, he says, "Only myself, / Stooping to fathom his meaning here, / Know the tightening nerves..."(111).

The fish (symbolic of the former Catholic monk, one presumes) is trapped, will die there in the shallow water: "Ineluctable pariah, he burns in my dream / And calls me from sleep."

But morning light reveals "his scattered remains / Where the raccoons flung him: tore gill from fin..."(112). What persists is "The faint skeletal imprint—as fossil / Etched in stone spans time like myth— / The glyph of God"(112).

In "Kingfisher Flat" we find the essence of the masks of drought, as "The starved stream / Edges its way through dead stones, / Noiseless in the night"(128). The Eden-Garden where the great redwoods grow suffers from the intensity of drought, and "Impotence clutched on the veins of passion / Encircles our bed, a serpent of stone"—the curse that comes upon the marriage of December and May, "around the loins, like a fine wire, / The cincture of nerves"(128).

And the poet tells us, "I think of the Fisher King, / All his domain parched in a sterile fixation of purpose, / Clenched on the core of the burning question / Gone unasked"(128).

"Oh, wife and companion!" he calls out to her, "The ancient taboo hangs over us, / A long suspension tightens its grip / On the seed of my passion and the flower of your hope"(129). And he envisions Merlin and Niniane, "wisdom and delight / Crucified in bed..."(129).

Desire drew the poet away from his monastic cell, and now the continued fulfillment of that desire is denied. The irony is, so to speak, complete, for the poet is wrenched away from the needs of the flesh and at the same time is cast up and into the presence of the Divine.

In "Bride of the Bear," the poet reflects upon the insidious, implacable, insistent passage of time—the mortal span vanishing so quietly and inevitably that the human creatures are stunned to find it has happened. The poem is set in the High Sierra, a warm summer night during the height of the drought. A ranger warns of bear sign, and, as it turns out, the poet has brought along a bearskin, a "belated wedding

gift."[2]   The poet and his wife "drink late wine," and "Back by the fire /
You have fallen asleep, dazed with wine..."(132).

The young wife slumbers, and the protagonist fetches the bearskin,
puts it around her: "I have folded you in the bear's huge embrace," and
she snuggles "happily under it, sighing a bit.... / Thus have I made you /
Bride of the bear"(132).

The speaker reflects upon the days of their courtship, "Crazy monk
and runaway girl, / Panting in discovery, goading each other on, /
Wildly in love"(132-133). The time of their lives together is passing,
evaporating all too swiftly: "Whatever happened to time? / When we
pulled down our packs / The night lay before us. Now, in another hour,
/ Night is no more"(133).   As light traces the eastern peaks, out there
somewhere, beyond the "starved stream," the bear, powerful, masculine,
and "gorged on raw bacon / Sleeps off his jag"(133).   Of himself, the
poet says, "I, greybeard, nurse my drink and suck my pipe, / Watching
the stars expire"(133).[3]

⊡

"Stone Face Falls," which I've already briefly considered, is among
the most delicate and beautiful of Everson's poems.   In the "real" world
of Kingfisher Flat and Big Creek Canyon, the lay of the land is, I would
say, hugely significant.   The stream comes down from the backs of the
Santa Cruz Mountains, dropping over a sheer stone bluff about a mile or
a bit more up the canyon, above the poet's home.   Below the falls is a
lovely pool, easily large enough to bathe and splash about in.   The trail
leading upstream along the creek effectively ends there, just below the
falls.   The stream is an impressive torrent at its winter maximum, but
merely a thin white veil of mist and falling water during summer.   To

---

[2]   The bearskin in question, according to Susanna Everson, was a gift from John Carpenter—
who presented the couple with a wolfhide as well.   Lee Bartlett also made the gift of a
bearskin.   Hence, in the real world, there were two "belated wedding gifts."

[3]   This poem was derived from a camping trip to Grouse Lakes in the northern Sierra.   In
reality, there were a number of us present.   An older couple came up from Carr Lake and
reported a bear foraging along the water's edge.   Stan Hager, pistol in hand, drove his pickup
to Carr, got out, and fired a shot or two into the air.   The bear, Stan reported, stood up and
seemed not at all inclined to leave.   Stan got back into his truck and honked the horn a few
times.   The black bear grudgingly moved off into the forest.   As darkness closed in, we sat
around the campfire, drank wine, and told bear stories for the delectation of the kids present.
When several tales had been told and the night grew quite dark, we asked a couple of the
children to go down to the creek to get water.   They laughed loudly but would not budge.
Susanna slept in the Jeep that night, and the rest of us talked until nearly dawn.   In truth, I
cannot remember whether Bill had brought the bearskin or not.

one side, above the falls, is a stone formation which, from a certain
angle, does indeed suggest a human face—the face of an Indian chief, as
the poet sees it. To follow the stream yet further toward its source is
more than merely difficult, for that would involve working one's way up
over the nearly vertical stone formation, hand over fist, ledge by ledge,
in order to achieve access to the narrow ravine above. The waterfall,
then, provides a beautiful and effective barrier to human passage. In
some way it's as though the world ends right there, boundaried by
magic.

As the poet sets the scene, he and his beloved have come "in the
white heat of noon" to the foot of the falls, "Under the salmon-stopping
cliff." The spawning salmon and steelhead can go no further, and
neither can the two lovers. The poet recalls "those thunderous torrents
of the past, / When the wild cataract drove everything before it," but
now the waterfall is like a bridal gown, as "the diaphanous film /
Ripples down the rock, maidenly, a silken / Scarf, the veil of a bride, as
virginal / And as lovely"(157).

This scene is indeed one of Eden in its prelapsarian state, wild
loveliness in its fullest incarnation. The lovers are there alone, and
though we may see the graybeard poet and his young wife, we are also
encouraged to see them as reincarnations of Adam and Eve.

The woman stands under the waterfall, nude. In effect, she wears
the waterfall which is, in turn, "the veil of a bride"(157). Above them,
the stone face stares northward,

> Ten thousand years from the Bering Strait.
> And the mystery keeps, the indomitable spirit
> Guarding the secret where the water pulses,
> The source, the slowed rhythm at the timeless center,
> The heartbeat of earth. (158)

As the speaker moves to meet his beloved, "Suddenly a kingfisher
swoops between," and "Three times he circles, skirling his fierce /
Importunate cry..."(158).

The narrator drops his clothes and wades toward his beloved, Adam
to Eve:

> It is the longest walk—
> Out of the glacial
> Past, through the pulsing present,
> Into the clenched
> Future—man to woman

Through time-dark waters. (157)

The quest for oneness with the Wild God, the juvescent Christ Who
"crouches and seethes" through all of nature in "the modes of His forth-
showing" and "His serene agonization" is effectively here complete.
Although "Spikehorn," is placed next in the sequence, the poem
was, I believe, chronologically the first of the *Masks of Drought* volume.
It is based on an incident that Everson told me had occurred shortly after
he and his family moved to Kingfisher Flat—though David Carpenter,
on the basis of Everson's own dating of the various poems, places it late
in the sequence.[4] "Spikehorn" is spoken in first person plural, the
occasion being that of the poet and an unnamed companion (in actuality,
this was his close friend and publisher, Bob Hawley of Oyez Press)
coming upon a dead deer, shot by a poacher—dead there in a field
whose fence enclosed a pair of young Hereford bulls.
That night the coyotes find the deer's carcass:

> We heard from afar
> The yelping chorus, clamoration of the feast,
> High sung litany to the winnowing of time,
> The brevity of life. (159)

By the next day a flock of vultures has gathered. Two days later
"The sentinel bulls stand over the torn and scattered remains, /
Bellowing, lugubriously lowing, solemnly lamenting / The passing away
of all slotted-hoofed kind..."(159).
Scavengers of various kinds perform their work until little remains
at all. Weeks pass by, and the season turns into autumn:

> Then the changing year
> Brought a leaf-flurry. Equinoctial rains
> Replenished the earth. In the body-print of the buck
> The first green grass quickened the bronze.

> And we said:

---

[4] I discuss this poem briefly in my essay in *Poet from the San Joaquin*, written fall of 1977.
Internal evidence suggests that the events upon which the poem is based could not have been
later than summer and fall of 1976—but probably were three or four years earlier. The poem
was originally entitled "Rite of Passage," subsequently changed to "Spikehorn" for inclusion
in *The Masks of Drought*. Possibly the re-titling accounts for the late date the poet would
subsequently assign when sequencing the verses for Carpenter. Campo notes that "All the mss
of the poem are dated in October, 1977."

The cycle is complete,
The episode is over. (160)

Yet, as the poet observes, "silence...hung about that place," and the
two friends are "unwitting acolytes,"

...there in the immemorial clearing,
The great listening mountain above for witness,
The sacrificial host between the river and the woods. (160)

The disintegrative aspect of God is here not so dramatic, and
neither is the progenerative aspect.   But both processes continue,
mysteriously replicating, engendering life out of death.   No torrent of
hate pours from a spill of broken boulders, and the little spikehorn,
unlike the bull elk of "In All These Acts," is merely shot and, having
run until the darkness takes it, dies there in the meadow—its remains
ingested by scavengers.   Likewise, we are not shown any "staggering
rush of the bass," but rather the autumn rains work their subtle
chemistry upon the parched sod which has absorbed nutrient from the
dead deer. *It* (the process of the Life Force, the inscape of the Divine)
works through an inevitability of gradualness as the seasons pass and
the years spin on.   The mountain above stands witness, and the mystery
continues.   It is significant, perhaps, that in this treatment, the element
of the Feminine (Archetypal Woman) is not present.

In a poem entitled "Cougar," one of the *Masks of Drought* verses in
terms of its seminal derivation, even though it had not been written as
yet when that book was published, Everson describes a brief sighting of
a mountain lion—an event that indeed occurred there at Kingfisher
Flat.[5]

The mere presence of the big cat was miracle enough, momentary
though it had been.   The magic remained, persisted, a lingering,
profound presence.   The poet tells us,

We never saw him again.
But the single print in the set clay
Retains its distinctness,

---

[5] I recollect, vividly, receiving a phone call from Everson. I believe we had been to Kings
Canyon and had gone our separate ways at Stockton, so that Bill and Susanna arrived home
just about the time I did. It was near sundown when they reached Kingfisher Flat, and the
poem records the rest of the story. The excitement in the poet's voice was indeed intense—as
though something of unusual significance had occurred. It had indeed, because of the inherent
meaning which the poet profoundly sensed—and which served to generate the poem.

As tangible as the stunning presence
In the hushed afternoon, the solemn moment
When the veil was rent, the earthly music
Suddenly fell still, and the god,
Imperious, gathered us into those wakeful eyes,
And was gone. (170)

The moment is one of epiphany, deeply religious. Spirit, a Platonic essence, has somehow spilled over into the normative realm, and the force of the Divine stands in full demonstration—as the Sacred Archetype is revealed in material manifestation, an incarnational presence, a specific inscape of *Mysterium Tremendum*. The big cat is real, and feral, and continuously present even after it has disappeared into the forest surrounding the cabin and printshop. The natural condition of the place is partially in abeyance, owing to the human presence, but wildness is there, waiting, waiting. The human being, pious neophyte, is stunned—for it seems to him that the Ideal has, in this instant, become the Real. Divine Essence, eternally contained within living substance, has fully (if passingly) divulged itself.

In "The High Embrace" the poet contemplates the aboriginal condition of the place, of the great redwoods growing, living, and in some incomprehensible way sentient, beside the perpetual oceanward movement of Big Creek:

Watching giant grizzlies scoop gravid salmon on the spawning
     bars below,
And tawny cougars stalk for fawns in their leaf-dappled shade.
They heard the kingfisher chirr his erratic intemperate cry,
While over their tops the slow-wheeling condors circled the sun,
Drifting south to their immemorial roosting-ledges in the
     Los Padres peaks. (155)

In the poet's mind and essential being, the unexpected appearance of a cougar is a sudden proof of the ever-present God—and a revitalization of the necessary bond between the human and the Divine. That bygone age envisioned in "The High Embrace," an era of grizzlies and condors and cougars is, after all, not only time past but time present as well. If the world (subscript *human*) were not too much with us, as Wordsworth reflected, we would be more capable of sensing (because more open, more vulnerable) the Divine Instress, as Hopkins called it, in all things.

⬓

I drive northward through the Sacramento Valley this morning in the first week of March of 1999—puzzling, in fact, as to how I might draw my essay to conclusion. Almond and pear trees are in full bloom, and the Arctic swans, snow geese, and Canada geese have already vanished from flooded rice paddies. The Coast Range has snow at lower elevations than I can ever remember, and the Sutter Buttes (*Estawm Yan*, the place where Maidu legend contends mankind was created) are almost transparently gray—the big, ragged hills seem hardly real. The year moves on toward its time of resurrection, of full renewal. I find myself wishing, quite irrationally, that Bill Everson were here to witness the beauty of the place—the way in which light seems almost to pass through the otherwise substantial Middle Hills.

I recall a summer morning at Kingfisher Flat some years back, in 1983 to be exact. Judith Shears and I were recording some interviews with Bill [dated July 10th], and one of us thought to ask the poet what his very first memory might be. He shrugged and then after a moment told us of his recollection of an accident—yes, that was it—a summer day, himself nearing either his second or third birthday. This memory trace (or spot in time) was to be transformed into "The Blood of the Poet," placed in this collection as the last of his published poems:

Suddenly the lazy summer stillness is shattered by a scream.
It is my own. I have stabbed my foot on a piece of broken bottle
Hidden in the grass. (217)

Hands are placed upon the child, and his foot is forced into a basin full of water—to cleanse the wound. The laceration continues to bleed, and the child grows quiet, fascinated by the filaments of crimson oozing out of his own flesh into clear water. He watches the "savage metamorphosis" and is stunned:

...in the existential verge of the Real,
A token of the poet's inimitable
Credential—his consecrated blood. (219)

AFTERWORD:
THE LONG, LONG POEM
Judith Shears

We had the definite sense of entering another reality—first that terrible road in the headlights, dirt, deeply rutted, winding with breathtaking steepness up and up and up as if forever, and then back down, a stunning drop—Douglas fir and madrone and into the redwoods, their roots sometimes overhanging the road, ferns and sorrel clustering among them. And finally, at the bottom, on the flats along Big Creek, an old Forest Service station, two small wooden buildings beneath towering redwoods in the soft darkness of a coastal night. For a moment we were a bit disoriented, unsure which building to approach until a tall figure emerged from one—archetypal, streaming silver hair and beard, gaunt, slightly stooped even then—and stood at the bottom of the steps to a small, rose-twined porch and gestured us to park there. The welcome was warm, as was the little house where Bill and Susanna lived, fragrant with the dinner that Susanna was cooking and the scent of madrone wood crackling in the cone fireplace, the walls hung with various mandalas, animal furs and feathers, a certain elegant, literary untidiness in the piles of books and papers on the wooden picnic table in the front room. Another reality, perhaps, but a most gracious one, a place of beauty and spirit and hospitality.

And that was my first meeting with Bill Everson; surely no human being ever looked or lived more the part of the poet. I was awestruck—a mere undergraduate lit student in my twenties and here, in such a setting, meeting a genuinely great poet, one whose works I had studied and whose art had already stunned me with its genius, actually welcoming us into his home for dinner just as if he were an ordinary mortal. We had called only a few hours before—we were in the Bay Area, and Bill Hotchkiss, who was to become my husband, just finished with his dissertation on Robinson Jeffers, had hoped to meet and talk with Everson about Jeffers; Everson, with characteristic hospitality, responded to the phone call with an immediate invitation to dinner and even to spend the night if we wished to—we who were, essentially, strangers.

My second encounter with Everson was at a poetry reading he gave at Sierra College; I feel safe in saying that anyone who ever saw Everson give a reading will never forget the experience, for he was, simply, a

master of the stage—resplendent in his post-Dominican "habit" of
fringed buckskin jacket, full bearclaw necklace, gray wide-brimmed
western hat with beaded band, and that great mane of shining hair, that
beard.... And he transfixed us with silence, pacing like a long-legged
waterbird himself, pausing to turn and ponder us, the audience, a silence
palpable, solid, almost unbearable in its intensity—and then, abruptly,
breaking forth with his chant: "Clack your beaks, you cormorants and
kittiwakes...," subsiding almost to a whisper as he recounted to us, an
audience of strangers, the most painfully personal details of his life and
somehow made them universal, a part of the poetry.

I recall Everson in many other settings, for a friendship developed
between the Eversons and the Hotchkisses: at treeline in the Sierras,
gazing from a pass on a hiking trail out over glacial stone bejeweled
with numerous small lakes, and murmuring, "God!"—just that one
syllable. And the next moment, uttering what we came to recognize as
his perpetual mantra, "Forgive me...."

Or Everson at a campfire out under the great twin redwoods at his
home, sometimes on his birthday and sometimes not, fussing over
hanging tenderloin grilling in a rack that he held by hand at just the
right height over a fire of just the right degree of heat, with just the right
amount of Doug fir bark on the embers for just the right flavor—for in
that, as well as in his writing and his printing and his readings, the
thing had to be done *right*, done according to the proper ritual and with
the proper results. He was a perfectionist—he would attribute that
fussiness to his Virgo nature, and could laugh about it. For he also had
a wonderful sense of humor, part of the beautiful hospitableness of his
nature. Another of my fondest memories of the man is Everson sitting
on a stump by the campfire after we had devoured the tenderloin and the
bread and the salad, trading more than slightly off-color jokes with
David Carpenter, bent over, eyes closed, face squinched up in a
paroxysm of wheezing laughter.

So many aspects of the man Bill Everson / Brother Antoninus—for
he was a remarkably complex being. I suppose I thought of him
primarily as a holy man, although he himself might have denied the
title, for he had a profound humility and a torturing sense of his
shortcomings. But to me he was a holy man nonetheless—not so much
in the sense of a priest, although he certainly had, at times, that stature,
that oracular presence, but in the sense of a sincere seeker of God, a
pilgrim on the spiritual path. All other aspects of his life and his poetry
were secondary to that pilgrimage, I believe; he spoke consistently of his
poetry as his vocation; but his life was his primary poem, and the
written poems were the chronicle of that archetypal journey—a journey

that he *made* archetypal and then shared with us through the writing in a gesture that was profoundly courageous and unselfish.

🔲

The Integral Years—by that title, Bill Everson meant this third collection of his life's work to be the integrating vision, a synthesis of the contrasting—almost, one would think, contradictory—spiritual and poetic philosophies that brought forth the two previous collections—the pantheistic vision of *The Residual Years* and the Catholic mysticism of *The Veritable Years*. This third chapter was meant somehow to bring together the segments of his life, marked by two profound schisms—the first his dramatic conversion to Catholicism and entry into the Dominican Order, and the second his equally dramatic departure from that Order and re-entry into domestic life nearly twenty years later.

Bill Everson was a master—on the stage, on the printed page, and in his life as well. With Bill, all things, all acts, had meaning and deserved concentration and one's best effort.

🔲

Last night I played a tape by another master, Native American flautist Carlos Nakkai, his *Canyon Trilogy*. In the work, Nakkai utilizes echoes to weave intricate and beautiful strains, interlacing new phrases with repetitions of phrases from the moment before, timing the interlacing with great precision to create exquisite harmonies—and sometimes exquisite dissonances. The melodies themselves are drawn from nature—bird songs, coyote music, the music of water falling over canyon rocks—but the method of interlacing echoes, I realized, creates, not just harmonies but dimensionality as well—the overlapping echoes create in the mind, in the inner ear, in the very air, the illusion of physical space—you can *see* those canyons, can *hear* them as the music rebounds apparently from wall to wall, returns and is deepened each time by new melody and rebounds and returns and is rewoven again. At times it seems not only to transform space but time in those weavings.

The method seems simple, perhaps like all genius, but it creates a richness and a depth far beyond the linear melody one expects from an unaccompanied flute. And it struck me also that this final volume in Bill Everson's life collection draws an analogous richness from a similar method. It is not so much synthesis of the two apparently divergent streams of his earlier poetic and philosophic credos, but a new harmony

created from the echoing, the point / counterpoint, and often the very
dissonance of those two threads. Like Nakkai's canyon music, it creates
its richness and a sort of temporal dimensionality by incorporating
echoes from the seemingly dissonant melodic threads of the past and
weaving them into something new, not a synthesis but a new kind of
harmonic.

The pattern which Everson attempts to create out of these echoes is
nothing less than the harmony of matter and spirit—the early essentially
atheistic pantheism which attempts a celebration and esthetic
appreciation of pure matter, and the contrasting poems of *Veritable
Years*, which swing to the opposite pole and seek the purely spiritual
through the celebration of the God of traditional Catholicism. This is
not to say that either the materialism of *Residual Years* or the
spirituality of *Veritable Years* is unalloyed—for certainly the pantheism
of the early poems often hints at an inherent divinity in nature, and the
finest of the ecstatic religious poems celebrate God through nature.
Perhaps the greatest expression of this latter correspondence is the
magnificent "A Canticle to the Waterbirds," in which the very birds
become both the instruments and the medium of praise to God.

It is in the mature poetry of the present collection that Everson
makes the integration of these two threads his central concern. It is
frequently a poetry of contradiction, for the echo does not create an easy
and automatic harmony; the dissonance is not really resolved—for such
is the problem of mind attempting to understand that which is beyond
mind—often, the poems here are an expression of agony, a tacit
admission that reconciliation may in fact be impossible between matter
and spirit, archetypal mother and father, God and nature.

For after the surge of erotic energy loosed following the long years
of celibacy and expressed in several of the poems in the *Man-Fate*
volume, most notably "Tendril in the Mesh," the poet seems often to
find himself questioning and even repenting his decision to leave the
contemplative tidiness of the Order and to re-immerse himself in the
often chaotic energy of domestic life. In the midst of such an intensely
erotic expression as "Tendril," the sexual celebration is fraught with
guilt; the erotic fire blazes forth in darkness—both man and woman, in
the mythological language of the poem represented as Pluto and
Persephone, the archetypal May-December mating, are helpless, not so
much celebrants as victims of the sensual energy kindled between them.
The woman, although she "smiles, / The pomegranate seed in her
pouch," is portrayed as victim despite her apparent consent—the seed is
"her jewel of rape"(6). The act is symbolically incestuous, and both
participants are helpless before the power of the violation—the woman

less consciously so, in a sense the aggressor, the conqueror of the man's more conscious but helpless moral qualms. In the very recounting of the "rape," the poet / speaker decries the profound violation of the act:

O sing
Of all sires, whose passion, Plutonic, gnarls in the heart
In the immemorial fashion
Of fathers, and groan of the unspeakable thing. (6)

But despite full knowledge of the act's violation of the deepest human moral injunctions, there is no hesitation in carrying it through— "But fight through to the forcing"(6).

And the woman / daughter, in her violation, "smiles," and the man ultimately cries out, "Oh my God the terrible torch of her power!" It is a poem of profound intensity, and a great part of its intensity is in the dark layerings of guilt with the white heat of its sensuality.

In Freudian terms, Everson's abrupt and dramatic turning from the Order was a turning from the Father to the Mother, always the area of greatest psychological conflict for the poet. He was unable to be at ease, ultimately, in either world, if one believes the poetry to be testimony to the life—and in Everson's case, that is, I think, a fairly valid assumption to make.

"The Narrows of Birth" recounts an archetypal dream which vividly dramatizes the danger the poet felt in returning to the mother's world— ultimately, the young man is made a sacrifice and castrated by the power of the Mother. Waking from the dream, the poet / speaker comforts himself by touching his young wife and hearing her infant son in the next room, and the poem is brought to a conclusion thus—the dream is dispelled in the solidity of waking and the comfort of domesticity. But this conclusion does not truly represent a resolution. The sacrificial "son" of the dream becomes in waking life the "father" of both the young wife and the young wife's son, and by extension the son is the next in the endless chain of Oedipal dilemmas.

Having left the world of "God the Father" in leaving the Order, and finding himself in an extraordinarily problematic relationship with the world of the Mother, the poet sought in various ways to reconcile himself with the Father; "Black Hills" is another dream chronicle— almost a "bookend" with "Narrows of Birth," which dramatizes the experience of rejection by the Father-energy. Like "The Narrows of Birth," "Black Hills" seems to offer a resolution. The speaker wakes from the dream in which the Father-energy, in the form of the great chiefs of various Indian nations, returns only waves of hate for every protestation of love on the part of the "son." The wakened dreamer experiences a kind of benediction of moonlight, a "past-dispelling love" of "the beautiful, unsullied present." But Everson, master of symbolism, knew full well that the benediction of moonlight, of the "present," is a benediction not of the father but of the mother, and the wound he suffers by proxy from the son is, again, a continuation of the Oedipal chain— the father is wounded by the son as the son is wounded by the father in competition for the mother. So, again, there is no resolution but only a returning.

The individual mind, born of matter, enmeshed in the material, cannot find God on its own, cannot find resolution of the problem of spirit and matter. This is the lesson of all mystical traditions. The mind runs like a hamster in its wheel, endlessly revolving the same problems, endlessly returning to the point of origin, never progressing beyond a certain level despite its ceaseless activity. The ultimate lesson of intellect is that intellect will never find an answer; the answer lies beyond the scope of mind because it contains mind within it.

What emerged in the poetry of *The Integral Years*, according to several Everson scholars, was essentially a shamanic vision, and there is a good case to be made there. One finds the invocation of nature in a shamanic sense in many of the poems of *Masks of Drought*. The poet looks to the elements for meaning—the drought in nature is reflected by and reflects the internal drought of the poet. The movements of birds are studied for messages, as in "Goshawk." The "glyph of God" is written in the bones of a fish; but the meaning of all these messages is left indeterminate in the poems—presumably because these messages, these writings of God in the medium of nature, are ultimately beyond the ken of human intellect.

It is, indeed, the work of the shaman to balance the worlds of spirit and matter. He is the bearer of the message from the world of spirit to the human dwellers in the material. He attempts to shape the message that he receives into a form that is accessible to the ordinary person, the one who is concerned, for example, with harvests and hunting, with rainfall and the movements of animals on the very practical level of daily survival.

What is the message written in God's hand, the "glyph of God" mentioned in "Steelhead"? The poet does not translate that hieroglyph for us, at least not directly; but from the evidence of the poem itself, it would seem to deal with the urgency of life proceeding around and about—and oblivious to—the agony of the stranded and dying fish, which represents, on another level, the God-seeker himself, the "God-stoned monk prostrate in his cell," the sacrificial victim and hence the

Christ. But to have said this is to intellectualize the symbol, to reduce it, and it could as well be said that the Christ-sacrifice is a symbol of the meaning of the steelhead; that is, the Christ-sacrifice is a shorthand for the whole meaning of death and rebirth, the cycles of nature represented here by the fish. It is the business and probably the character of the intellect to seek a shorthand way to categorize, to encapsulate, to make tidy that which is truly beyond its scope—primarily, one suspects at times, so that we won't have to deal with the irreducible, the great and overwhelming facts that are specifically beyond intellectualization.

The fish, as monk, as sacrifice, is "segregate, wrenched out of context...out of place and out of purpose..."(111). In this sense the fish serves, of course, as a surrogate for the speaker and his deeply conflicted feeling over leaving the monastic order. But the poet's ultimate and greatest response to the visitation of the agonized and dying steelhead is reverence—"...in this recondite presence / I am favored in my life—honored in my being..."(111). And it is only this, this reverence, which is capable of understanding the glyph which the intellect can only gnaw at as the raccoons gnaw at the steelhead itself. It is the attitude of reverence which bestows upon the poem its profundity and its grace.

We tend to think of the gift of the shaman to the people as a special knowledge, but I wonder in fact if the shaman's true gift and true power does not lie in this special reverence rather than in specialized and arcane lore. In the poems of the *Renegade Christmas* collection, the shamanic vision dominates. In "Cougar" the visitation from the great feline is a gift from the Divinity: a "revelation," "the glimpse of something / Long withheld that we needed to know, / Something given purely for our own well-being; / A glimpse of the god"(169).

In the long essay that I wrote for *Perspectives on William Everson*, the volume that was published in celebration of Everson's life in his 81st year, I attempted to make the case that the poem "Mexican Standoff" represented a sort of reconciliation, at least in psychological terms, of the two strands of Everson's life and poetic vision, the Christian and the Pantheistic. Bill Everson was a little stunned by the idea—he said something like "I didn't think of that as a serious poem." I said something like "Oh. So I guess I'm way off base." And he most graciously replied, after one of his consummate long pauses, "No, you've convinced me."

But now, a little further along my own life path, I am less convinced. In fact, if there is a synthesis, it is not anything obvious. I am still profoundly moved by the poem's assertion of the human heart against the moralistic and taunting voice in the dream, which perhaps represents "God the Father" in its negative, disciplinarian sense, or even the castrating mother of "Narrows." I am moved by the poet's final ability to assert wholeheartedly the need for "ecstasy" rather than mere preservation of the physical—the half-humorous but heartfelt affirmation "I am a poet, for God's sake! / Use without passion is for the birds!"(176). Along with the poet, I "salute the old inveterate female heart which... / Never defers"(176). But I doubt, now, that I was justified in seeing that poem as representing a true synthesis or resolution of the conflict at the heart of Everson's vision.

In a sense, resolution is the need of the intellect, and of the lesser intellect at that. It is the desire to have everything final and tidied up. But the music of the poetry, like Nakkai's flute music, like the music of life itself perhaps, is in the lack of resolution. The music lies, rather, in the echo, in the unresolved, in the dissonance and returning that makes its own non-intellectualized harmony out of disharmony.

After I listened to the Nakkai tape, I still wasn't asleep. My mind had been too active, I suppose, churning over this essay, trying in its hamsterlike way to make that wheel go *somewhere*. I went out onto the porch of this little house on Pueblo land here in the canyon country of New Mexico. I heard a different music there, a wild yelping and shrilling of coyotes. They echoed each other, got the dogs going, had a grand old time. And I thought, "Thank you, God. There's music, for real." And Bill Everson, the Everson who looked out across the bare glacial stone and the tiny lakes of the high Sierras and murmured simply "God," would have agreed. There is the synthesis, right there—it is only the mind, which is perhaps the least part of us, grand as it can be at times, that can't comprehend the true harmony.

🔳

This is not a scholarly essay. I have written my scholarly essays on Everson elsewhere. Let this be a celebration, rather, of the man, his life, and his poetry. It is a bittersweet experience to see this final volume of what Everson envisioned as his life trilogy coming into publication, for although it represents what he envisioned as the final, synthesizing chapter of his life work, gathered and presented finally as a whole, it also means that the life itself is over, for the final chapter could not be published until there was no more to add. He clearly envisioned it that way himself.

It was a curious thing about Bill Everson; he lived his life perhaps more fully than most of us—it was truly a poet's life, full of profound and dramatic changes, not a life lived safely or simply, but led by the heart and the mind through stunning and revelatory turnings into places that could not have been envisioned and that would never have been imagined, let alone followed, by a more mundane or cautious spirit. He followed his heart; he dared to live his profound beliefs. And he loved life; he loved the gatherings of friends, he loved the feasts, he loved good wine and music and beautiful books, he loved ritual, he loved the company of women. But on the poetic level, he was also capable of looking at his life with a curious detachment, as an artifact. And so he was perfectly comfortable in perceiving the necessary symmetry of his life in terms of three major collections, the third, of course, not to be complete until his death, and so one that he himself would never see. It was a necessary part of the larger poem he was producing, the one called his life.

That recognition actually came to me many years ago, when I was typing the poems for *The Integral Years* onto computer disks for the poet. Bill Hotchkiss and I were a little baffled by Everson's apparent reluctance to follow with publication of the collection at that point until it dawned upon us that he was still writing, and that he had in mind to include everything from the end of *Veritable Years* to the end of his life in the third volume of the life trilogy. And so of course it could not be published until his death—he wanted no loose ends, no additional poems lying around, no scrawny afterthought of an additional volume to collect those poems. The proper number was three—thesis, antithesis, synthesis; Father, Son, and Holy Ghost; beginning, middle, and end. Period. Well, he was a Virgo.

And now to my final memory of Bill Everson. He wasn't really there—or at least not in the usual sense, for the occasion was his final burial, timed to coincide with his birthday, at the Dominican cemetery in Benicia. A small multitude of his friends and admirers had gathered to say their final good-byes to the poet—among them at least three of the "women in his life." It is a beautiful cemetery on a hilltop overlooking Carquinez Strait, windswept and grand. Many people stepped forward to lay small tokens of love into the grave and to offer remembrances of the life of the man. My very fondest memory, though, is of Rose, Everson's own "Rose of Solitude," stepping forward to sing "Happy Birthday." That, and the hawk that soared over just as we were leaving, circling low over us to get a look, or perhaps to say good-bye as well. It was a nice ending to the long, long poem.

A SELECTION OF UNCOLLECTED AND UNPUBLISHED POEMS 1975 - 1994

INTRODUCTION:
ALLAN CAMPO

As with our previous volumes, *The Residual Years* and *The Veritable Years*, we include a "Selection of Uncollected and Unpublished Poems" drawn from the period encompassing the present volume, *The Integral Years*. Actually, no such poems appear among William Everson's papers until 1975, from which time they are to be found until April 1994—less than two months prior to his death on June second.

The uncollected poems are those poems which, though published, Everson never included in his own collections throughout the period nor in his plans for the culminating volume. Although in number they are few, with the exception of "Seventy Suns" and "For the naked heart," they join with several others to make for an interesting story.

As for "Seventy Suns," this poem was written by Everson in November 1975 for inclusion in *Voices from the Southwest: A Gathering in Honor of Lawrence Clark Powell*—a *festschrift* celebrating the renowned librarian on the occasion of his seventieth birthday. Everson wrote "For the naked heart" while preparing the Preface for his collection of interviews, *Naked Heart: Talking on Poetry, Mysticism, and the Erotic*, where the poem appears as the Preface's conclusion.

The other uncollected poems—"Tarantella Rose," "Snowflake," "The Thing-Death," and "The Fountain of Pain"—must be taken in tandem with "The Vindication," "Rose Recreant," "Cinquain," and "Runway East." Everson's original intention had been to print these, together with six earlier poems, as the project for his Lime Kiln Press workshop in 1976, under the title of *Eros and Thanatos*. The project did not meet with success, however, and was abandoned in mid-1977. The poet then offered the collection to John Martin of Black Sparrow Press, but that possibility was superseded by the publisher's decision to go forward with the publication of Everson's *The Veritable Years*. In 1979, Herb Yellin's Lord John Press prepared to publish the collection, but that project, too, came to naught. Thus, the eight poems languished for some fifteen years. The story of how these poems—intended at one point for incorporation in that collection of poems from 1949 to 1966—came to be written in 1975 is told by Everson in an introduction he wrote for the projected Lord John Press publication. Using Everson's

259

manuscript we have included that introduction and his listing of contents with the "Eros and Thanatos" segment of this Appendix.

In 1992, Peter Thomas, a former student of Everson's handpress workshop, received the poet's encouragement to produce a fine press printing of six of these poems ("Cinquain" and "Runway East" being the excepted poems). In 1994, after his return from the hospital, on several occasions Everson reviewed the typescript of the poems with Thomas before the printing was executed. Peter and Donna Thomas proceeded to carry out this project successfully, and *The Tarantella Rose: Six Poems by William Everson* appeared in 1995. In his introductory note to the volume Peter has this to say:

> William Everson wrote these six poems in [1975] for a manuscript titled *Eros and Thanatos*. That text combined these new poems with several others written earlier in his career. Everson described to me his confidence in this creative act. "Once you find the archetype you can go back into a poem years later and pick it up again and change it and the reader won't be able to find the seam."
> ....
> Everson began printing *Eros and Thanatos* in 1976 at the Lime Kiln Press, where he taught a course in fine printing for the University of California at Santa Cruz. Due to a number of problems at the press, the book was never completed.... When Everson's poems were collected as *The Veritable Years*, the problems presented by the pre-dating of these six poems proved to be an overwhelming editorial dilemma and the plan to integrate them into his collected work was never employed.[*]

Thus concluded a particularly difficult and disconcerting episode in Everson's publishing career.

---

[*] *The Tarantella Rose: Six Poems by William Everson* ([Santa Cruz, CA:] Peter and Donna Thomas, 1995). N. pag. The Thomases had earlier produced a fine press printing of Everson's *The Poet Is Dead* (Santa Cruz: The Good Book Press, 1987). Our editorial insertion of 1975 as the year of composition corrects the "1972-74" used by Thomas as the period given him by Everson. Considering Everson's condition in 1992-1993—the aging process exacerbated by the ravages of his longtime Parkinson's disease—faulty recollection or communication is understandable. In addition to pertinent letters from Everson, the dated manuscript drafts of these poems confirm that they were written in 1975. The one exception in this regard is "Runway East" (not included in the Thomases' printing), which was written in 1977. In his Afterword to the present volume, Bill Hotchkiss makes a case for a 1962 dating of "Snow Flake." "Cinquain" was omitted from *The Tarantella Rose* because, according to Thomas, Everson did not think it "strong enough" to be included. "Runway East" was omitted because it is of a different character from the other poems.

As for the remaining unpublished poetry printed in this Appendix, it is drawn from some thirty pieces, in various states of composition, found among Everson's papers housed at the Bancroft Library. Some of the poems had been kept in separate folders by the poet, others were scattered here and there among his papers, and some were contained in his "notebooks"—the legal tablets he kept at the ready, wherein may be found prose efforts, correspondence, miscellaneous notes, and drafts of verse.

There is a real poignancy in the perusal of these notebooks as, with the passing of seasons and years, especially as one reaches the later 1980s, the handwriting steadily deteriorates so that into the 1990s illegibility becomes all too often the norm. Hence, though here and there the writing recovers clarity, our inclusion of the later unpublished verse is sometimes seriously pockmarked by notations of words difficult to ascertain or quite illegible. By the end of his recorded verse, "Jackboot" and "Hallucinations," both written in April, 1994, only the bold capitals of the titles are readily readable. "Hallucinations" is barely other than a title and some ten lines of almost sheer illegibility. We have included a photograph of this, the last poem, for, unreadable as it may be, it is a graphic testament to Everson's unremitting perseverance in the pursuit of the vocation to which he was called sixty years earlier when he picked up a volume of the poetry of Robinson Jeffers in the Fresno State University Library.

Nonetheless, the poems included here contain genuine delights for the Everson reader. Rejected Preludes for his autobiographical epic. Segments of the unfinished Canto VI. His attempt, following his eightieth birthday, to capture in verse the thunderbolt of marital collapse. Flashes of sharp imagery, the presence of the erotic, concerns of the spirit. Though the unpublished inventory amounts to less than half of that available from the corresponding poetry of the earlier periods, reflecting the quantitatively lesser body of published poetry during this third period of Everson's long career, it is not lacking in interest.

As regards the editorial logistics involved, a few comments are in order. The poems are arranged in approximate chronological order, with the date or period of composition in brackets at the end of each poem. For purposes of reference, a poem left untitled by Everson has been titled by the opening words of its first line and distinguished as such by the use of quotation marks.

In order to deal with the vagaries of manuscript transcription, we have used square brackets to indicate what the reader should know. A blank space within brackets indicates the fact that a word or words are missing. A word within brackets indicates an editorial insertion. A bracketed word that is preceded by a question mark indicates an editorial opinion as to a word that is difficult to read. An isolated question mark in brackets indicates an illegible word. Correction of spelling errors and the appropriate insertion of missing punctuation are not noted. Finally, where the poet indicated the accent pattern of an as yet unchosen word, we have placed such accentual marks unbracketed within the text.

The printed appearances of previously published poems are cited in the appropriate footnotes and credited on the copyright page. All of the unpublished poems, as well as Everson's holograph copy of his introductory note for *Eros and Thanatos*, are from the Everson papers maintained at the Bancroft Library of the University of California, Berkeley, and we express our gratitude for the permission to print them here.

We are also grateful to Janet DeBar for her responses to various relevant questions. We especially thank Peter and Donna Thomas for permission to quote from Peter's introduction to *The Tarantella Rose*; for the fact of that book's publication, which provided an authoritative text to complement our use of Everson's typescripts; and for helpful information that Peter Thomas passed on to us.

回 回

From *EROS AND THANATOS*
NOTE by WILLIAM EVERSON*

Of the many volumes of poetry I have published over the years none is more improbable than the present one. Everything I have issued has a certain inevitability, a certain directness of composition, that proceeds in an undeflectable chronological line. Not so this one. Welded together of disparate elements, some new, some old, it was tailor-made to a specific editorial situation, and was perhaps misconceived from the start. That it failed in the task it was conceived to accomplish is undeniable. But that does not mean that it is thereby lacking in interest. The misbegotten is not without its own kind of truth.

In 1975 when I began to assemble *The Veritable Years*, my collected poems of the conversion and monastic period, I was compelled to face a problem I had long put off. This problem had to do with the final placement of two important poems that seem to stand apart from the sequence of the period in which they were created. For me the early sixties had almost entirely been taken up with writing *The Rose of Solitude*, which of course is a celebration of Eros. But in 1962 I found myself estranged from the Rose and in that estrangement suffered a period of depression. In this depression "Missa Defunctorum" was written. Shortly thereafter the death of Robinson Jeffers precipitated the writing of *The Poet Is Dead*, as described in the [Note] to the Auerhahn Press edition [1964]. These two poems formed the core of the Thanatos accent that interrupted the flow of the larger narrative. They were not included in the published version of *The Rose of Solitude* [1967], and it was their placement vis-a-vis that sequence that arose in the makeup of *The Veritable Years* in 1975. To put them before *The Rose of Solitude* would break up the chronological sequence and confuse the reader. To put them afterward made no dramatic sense. What to do?

The decision I came to was that obviously both *The Poet Is Dead* and "Missa Defunctorum" ought to have been incorporated in their chronological place in *The Rose of Solitude*. The task, then, that I set for myself in 1975 was to re-immerse myself in the mood of that period

---

* The following text is transcribed from a holograph of Everson's introduction to a proposed publication of *Eros and Thanatos* to be issued by Lord John Press. The project was not carried out. The manuscript is undated, but it was probably written in 1979—the year during which preparations were being made to publish the collection.

and write the series of poems that could meld them into the larger narrative. Thus *Eros and Thanatos*. Putting myself back in the monastery, re-experiencing in memory the period of alienation from the Rose, the [?] incident of "Missa Defunctorum," and the upheaval of *The Poet Is Dead*, I began to build a new section that would perform what I should have written in 1962.

When it was completed, I typed up *The Rose of Solitude* with the new section added and prepared to incorporate it in *The Veritable Years*. However, certain doubts would not go away. There was the persistent feeling that these new Rose poems did not carry the same vibration as the rest of the series. There was something extravagant about them, something forced. Moreover other people with whom I discussed the problem felt that *The Poet Is Dead* was too big a poem to be encapsuled in *The Rose of Solitude*. It was not comfortable there. It was pointed out that these Thanatos poems could be placed before *The Rose of Solitude* but dated back when they were written, allowing the reader to make the adjustment himself. At last I concurred. The placement was not ideal in that it broke up the transition from "In Savage Wastes" to the opening of *The Rose of Solitude*, but at least it rescued *The Poet Is Dead* from the larger narrative.

There remains only to narrate the history of this edition. At the Lime Kiln Press, the student workshop I teach at the University of California [Santa Cruz], the students asked if I had a manuscript of poetry to print and I bethought myself of *Eros and Thanatos*. A beginning was made but the work did not prosper and it was eventually abandoned. Then Mr. Herb Yellin was looking over those sheets and asked if he might not issue them through his Lord John Press. He spoke of asking Jack Stauffacher, an old friend, to print them at his Greenwood Press. This seemed like a happy solution to an unhappy problem, and so I concurred. These poems will have an especial interest for those who are familiar with *The Rose of Solitude*. Let them ask themselves whether or not the sequence as given here should have been retained in that narrative, or whether the solution as given in *The Veritable Years* is proper.

CONTENTS*

回 回

---

* This is a typescript listing of contents for the projected Lime Kiln Press edition of *Eros and Thanatos: Fourteen Poems of Love and Death*. The poem titles accompanied by an asterisk were so marked by Everson to indicate the poems to be carried forward into *The Veritable Years*. The poems so marked are of course not included in this "Selection." Following the termination of the Lime Kiln project, Everson offered the collection to John Martin of Black Sparrow Press, but it was superseded by the decision to publish *The Veritable Years*.

THE TARANTELLA ROSE*

Sackcloth and ashes.

Dust in the mouth,
Lime on the lips,
The splint-slit eyes,
The brass-bound brow.

On this bed of denial
Silence, the tarantula's
Vice-like embrace,
Grips the monastery.

High overhead the summer moon
Gibbous, cresting toward full,
Soars and floats on.

Out in the cloister-garth
The fountain of youth
Splays on, ejaculating
Its myriad contents,
An unremitting orgasm,
The splurge of infinite excess.

Where does she fly,

---

* *New Catholic World*, CCIX, 1309 (January-February 1976), 46. Included in *The Tarantella Rose: Six Poems by William Everson* ([Santa Cruz, CA:] Peter and Donna Thomas, 1995).

Like a bird through the night,
Dancing toward dawn?

With what recklessness does she run
In her fierce tarantella,
Leaving behind her the searing memory
Of one man's passion,
His fabulous love?

Where and how far?
Why and with whom?

Dancing, dancing.

What possesses her?

Dancing, dancing.

A night without end.

How can she
Justify
What she has done? *[July-August 1975]*

THE VINDICATION*

Justify?

She does what she does.

Brooking no denial,
Neither asks nor requires.

The simplicity of decision.

Or rather,
As the illusion of rapture
Shimmers veils and scarves,
Evoking response?

Begone!

A going out of taut space,
A running reach,
The steep summit,
A glimpse of the beyond.

The emphatic foot
Stamped against confine,
The proud, fair features
Arresting in their authority
Of purpose, of sheer decision.

Dancing feet.
The peal of laughter.

High overhead the autumnal moon,
Gibbous, dying past full,
Sags and slumps down.

Out in the cloister garth
The fountain pounds on,

---

* Included in *The Tarantella Rose.*

Pounds on,
Excessive as the ravenous stream of life
Smashing its boundaries.

And the emptiness of the fall.

A splatter of water on water
Shivering the night.

Nothing more?

A shudder of dark on dark,
Fire on fire. *[Summer 1975]*

SNOWFLAKE:
THE DEATH OF JEFFERS*

One flake of snow and then the flurry.
Deep toward dawn, seeking his mate,
The poet goes over.

Seeking his woman,
His lost Eurydice,
Who beckons beyond.

All night long snow falls,
Rare on the ridge,
Heavy on the bridge:

Mal Paso:
The difficult divide.

All night long
The dark brooding,
Mute pall,
The black foreboding.

Emptiness: lack of light.

All night long
Shut silence,
The pang of that foregoing.

And over the hogback
One coyote
Splinters the dawn with a yelp out of hell:

Abrupt finale. *[June-July 1975]*

---

* *Sierra Journal* (Sierra College, Rocklin, CA), (Spring 1976), 15. Included in *The Tarantella Rose*. [See Hotchkiss' discussion of dating evidence, 236-238.]

ROSE RECREANT*

As taken back from breath
The presence,
Vanishing on its forever flight,
Leaves alone.

An emptiness?
A lack of light?

Yes.

Who goes is gone.
Who is not here
Is dead.

Is she not?

To the craving heart,
The eyes,
The longing lips?

Is she not?

Orpheus,
Probing the death-dusk,
Looked back and lost her.

She eludes him,
Laughing behind slit veils,
Fleeing the light.

Comes then the failing,
Comes a flagging of feet,

---

* Included in *The Tarantella Rose*.

The buckling of knees.

Where does she wander in that lovelessness?

O recreant Rose!

An emptiness
Herself creates
Out of its depth.

Why has she turned and plunged
Beyond the beyond,
Threading her dizzying way through mazes,
The labyrinthine core?

What lured her there?

No poet's passion,
No monk's shattered vow,
Compels her back,
Crying through hell.

Orpheus, the lure of what is lost,
Singing praise!
Praise!
His only blame:
That he looked back!

Gone!

Like a bird!
Singing beyond the sundown.

The illusive mocker,
Crying nightlong over San Francisco.

As who should say,

Holding scarves in empty hands,
Like rags, the last fragrance:

"My sin!"

And the lost reprise. *[June 1975]*

THE THING-DEATH*

In the death of all things
Heart clenches.

And the poet
Sings death, bitten by denial
(The going of the life-breath,
The spent venture.)

Sings.

A long surcease,
A pang of renouncement,
Deprivation in desire.

Even the great ones,
Tall heroes of song,
They too
Faint when their women fail:

Orpheus, love-blind in hell,
Looking back, longing back,
Singing, stumbling alone.

(Dismembered, torn asunder,
Female furies infesting the brain.)

Dante, heartbroken in exile,
Yearning his lost Beatrice,
The abandoned one,
Ethereal in heaven,
Dust in the grave.

Keats, coughing blood in Rome, his heart
Clutched on the soundlessness of a name

---

* *The Real World Press* (Santa Cruz, CA), (August 25, 1993), 9. Included in *The Tarantella Rose*.

Stabbed through him like a spear.

Mad Poe, broken, his child-bride
Sickened and fled on.
Clutching rags of remorse
He beats that bulging brow on the night.

Rosetti, shaken with grief (with guilt?)
Incomprehensibly daft,
Seeking her reincarnated shape
In deerwolf, woodchuck, the raven, the owl....

Rose!

And now great Jeffers, whose witness
Swept me into the following of song,
Dying tonight, seeking his mate, his lost Eurydice,
Crying under snowfall,
A gleaming shroud
Enveloping the coast,
Rare on the rocks,

Swaddling Pico Blanco,
Cloaking the riverbar at Big Sur,
Muffling the slant-steep
Streets of San Francisco,

Where the Rose, recreant,
Dances her stubborn way through hell.

Death and desire?
        Aye!
The brute dichotomy.

Snow falls.
Night turns. *

---

* No stanza break.

The great stars blacken.

But the Rose?

Flung petals.
Sea-spume on beach boulders.
Snowflakes in hell. *[June 1975]*

CINQUAIN*

Love sobs
In the sheets.
But the cold-closed eyes,
The calm, clean-shaven lips
Kiss death. *[July 5, 1975]*

---

* This poem remained unpublished. According to Peter Thomas, Everson had requested that it
not be included in *The Tarantella Rose.*

THE FOUNTAIN OF PAIN*

Desire and death.
And the cry of a woman
Disappearing under the knell of history,
Her bright lips a bloodclot
Burning the dark, live ember,
One ripple of sound
Where she sobs and vanishes....

                                        In my dream
I sense the woman-shape falling,
Death at her neck like a yellow beast,
A puma at a doe's throat.

I see the spill of dust,
The terrible scuffling,
One powerful paw
Pulling the muzzle over and back
To bare the silk-soft throat,
Then the ripping jaws.

                                    I awake in fear.
Far off in the night
A siren wails through the streets,
Threading sparse traffic,
Shrilling its weird hysterical way
Toward some blank intersection,
Where gargoyles of twisted steel
Perch on the broken throats
The smashed faces....

                                The siren dies away.
Out in the cloister garth

---

* *Hard Pressed* (Sacramento, CA), 4, (1978), N. pag. Included in *The Tarantella Rose*.

The fountain splashes in living pain
Interminably, like time to the damned,
Abstract, unchecked, insensible,
The waters of no beginning,
And of no end. *[July 1975]*

RUNWAY EAST*

The flight departs. Gaining air at takeoff
All the smashing sensation of ground-level speed
Drops away, and the great bird soars.

Looking down I see first the emerald-green bay, dappled,
Then the dark peninsula,
Shore-fledged marinas huddling its hem.

Beyond it the Pacific sustains the west, inscrutable,
The vast landlessness dividing the globe.

Soon, from under the tilting wing,
Crawls into view the singular city,
San Francisco, gleaming low morning light,
White-walled, tall-towered,
The steep ravines of its angular streets
Pitching down to the bay.

Beyond it shimmers the Golden Gate,
A girdle of bridge like the G-string of a dancer,
Linking hip to hip
The jeweled thigh of the City
And the sequined flank of Marin.

The plane points east.
I feel within me the old disconsolation,
The leave-taking ache,
The inexpressible pang of departure.

Tilting my head my eye listlessly traces
The nerve-chart of the city,
The long freeways crawling with traffic,

---

* This poem has remained unpublished. The text is that of a typescript dated June 22, 1977, and the poem is numbered as XI, which corresponds to its place in the "Contents" as listed by Everson.

The blunt trunk-lines, the thin thoroughfares.

Suddenly I see it: one familiar cloverleaf
Stemming off-ramp south.
And then, yes, the boulevard,
Straight-arming its way through twisting hills,
And then, by God, on a short sidestreet,
The house, pinpoint of pain—
It: the identical house!

                    O Christ and keeper!

Is she still abed, down there,
After the long night's rapture,
Asleep now, deep in her dream,
Exhausted at last of the long dance,
The fast-paced driving,
The ecstasy and the maze?

I cramp back that thought,
Stifle it down like a snuffed cigarette,
Crimp the burnt match-end that lit it,
And grind it out.

Let the past drown its contour in the waters of time!
Let the break come clean!
Let the bird fly free!

A sweep of coastline encircles my gaze and the
        big plane tilts.
Tamalpais, the maiden mountain, recumbent in slumber,
Defines the north.

Steeply below gleams the strait of Carquinez,
The narrow slot where fresh water and salt
Unendingly contend, the immemorial
Wrestling of the waves.

When moon motions
The sea withdraws and the pent river surges,
Its ochre torrent, a yellow phallus, stabbing the bay.
But at tideturn the ocean, inexorable, recovers itself,

Remorselessly repossesses the channel,
Clasping the groin and the squat headlands,
Lapsing and lolling its tongue in the cleft,
Lapping its spume.

It is the ancient warring within,
The eternally restless waters of the soul,
Muddy mind and sea-salt blood
Eternally contending.

The plane ploughs east,
Gains altitude,
Then levels out for the high flight ahead.

Now the stewardess approaches,
Coffee urn poised, a smile
Wreathing her lips,
A smile and a promise
She cannot fulfill.

I press my face to the vacant glass,
A sudden flex that shuts her out,
And she passes on, smiling, smiling....

Craning my neck I glance behind,
But the visionary coastline defining my world
Is quenched in space.

Then, suddenly, under the wing, inching into view,
Sacramento, city of my birth,
Seizes my sight.

Somewhere down there,
In a house that is no more,
I cried against dawn,
The brute pang of parturition,
Gulped giddy air.

What lies ahead?
Beyond the sterile flats of Nevada,
The waterless wastes,

The continental nape and the Great Divide?

> What will be
> Is.
>> What is
> Will be.

Like an exiled eagle we streak the Sierra,
Pierce the veil of the mythic east,
Birthmark of dawns.

For a little moment I gaze longingly back,
Then force my eyes ahead.
I must hush my heart, wean my blood
From the wine of the California sky,
The fine bread of its earth. *[February-June 1977]*

TRIAD*

There be
Three lifeless things:
The fallen snow...the dark
Before the dawn...the lips of one
Just dead.

"Love laughs"

Love laughs
Through the night.
But the sealed eyes
The sunk cheeks of the dead
Grow cold.

"No sound"

No sound
Trembles the dark
Even the coyote sleeps
Even the cat owl cannot cry
Tonight.

---

* The cinquains, "Triad," "Love Laughs," and "No Sound," as well as "Cinquain" in the
"Eros and Thanatos" section above, were all written on July 5, 1975.

SEVENTY SUNS—TO L.C.P.*

The lean face
    lazes in autumnal light;
a wintry wisdom flickers in the eyes.

But the springtime energies,
    the blood's delight,
flame sunrise in those Arizona skies.

And all the books
    his fingers ever touched
glow like the desert quartz in fancy caught.

And all the loves
    his ardent lips once brushed
bloom like the yucca in his winy thought.

The body *is* its beauty
    and the mind:
these, his two imperatives included,

Will shape quintessence
    of a keener kind,
the pall of sadly growing old precluded.

Now autumn rainfall
    quicks the desert green

And seventy suns, enjoined,
    glide on serene. *[November 1975]*

---

* The poem was included in Voices from the Southwest: A Gathering in Honor of Lawrence
Clark Powell, eds. Donald C. Dickinson, W. David Laird, Margaret F. Maxwell (Flagstaff
AZ: Northland Press, 1976), xv.

PRELUDE:
Dust Shall Be the Serpent's Food

Of the Self I sing, *Atman*, the human soul,
Of the spirit's invincible powers and the ordeal of its growth;
Sleeping its long dream of futurity, the years' vicissitudes,
Somnolent, patiently nursing its inner strengths, dreaming its dream.

How birth burdens it into the world, latent with racial wisdom,
How infancy buds the ego, *jiva*, the individual perceptive consciousness,
    sourced in the instancy of primary relationships, the mother,
    the father, but the soul dreaming its dream;
How childhood fans ego to flame, beyond the polarity
    of primal relations,
Feeds it on light, the marvels of the world, the stirrings
    of its latent powers; but the soul dreaming its dream.

How adolescence fans the enflamed ego to activation, conquest,
    seduction and defloration, intellectual activation, but the soul
    dreaming its dream.

How manhood releases ego into its own dimension, the power
    of decision, command, performance, loyalty, commitment,
    the finding of the mate, child-getting, the $\cup$ / $\cup$ energies,
    but the soul dreaming its dream.

And how, at the onset of middle age, at the apotheosis and
    crystallization of ego, at the grim passage, rounding
    the Horn of life, all hangs on the verge, the Self's long moment,
    its own birth hangs on the verge;
Until, gathering its deeps within it, it fights free and forward, emerges
    out of the cocoon of ego, outdistancing regressive fears, the tie-ins
    of all attachment,
To surge at last onward to the Port of God. *[October-November 30, 1975]*

"And what are its modes?"*

And what are its modes? More birdlike than manlike?
A windhover on a thermal, fluttering like an exultant moth,
    shrilling in the sun.
Or condor-like circling in the [?core] of heaven, on unalterable pinions
    focusing pure height?
Or more like the albatross, [?lonely ?lovely] in unspeakable depths
    of darkness,
Threading its solitary way through what quagmires of darkness,
Over what tide lies beneath it where oceanic currents, the rivers
    of the sea,
Form banks of edged foam to tell where they are,
Spanning Antarctic coasts of extremes to equatorial zones?
Or is it like the deep-diving grebe laterally flying through
    sea-deeps to find its food, as the shamans of old
    understood that totem in their own soul's descent?
Or is it a mockingbird on a midnight branch, drenched in the full light
    of [the] moon,
Pouring his bleeding heart of his love out on the world,
    singing and singing?
Or is it a loon cackling insanely out in the night, along the river
    verge where the tule stand shelters its nest,
Sobbing uncontrollably of its womanly woe, a crazy woman or a girl
    made mad of a lost love?
Or is it the stately blue heron, so airy in its flight,
    its broad bending wings
Sweeping its delicate body airborne in flight? *[February 1, 1976]*

---

* This untitled piece is filed with the "Prelude" poem and may have been meant as a continuation of that poem. In that case, the antecedent of "its" would be the Self.

TAKES-THE-PIPE[*]

The darkness was gone. All the world lay gleaming about him,
Glowing with a visionary sheen, a transparent and shimmering
    luminescence.
He saw before him the whole of the Absaroka, the land of the Crows.
To the west were the Big Belt Mountains and the Crazy Mountains.
To the north were the Bear Paws and the Little Rockies, the country
    of the Blackfeet.
To the south were the Bighorns, the Arrowheads and the Beartooth.
He saw the Yellowstone like a shining artery
Tracing the skin of the earth,
The Bighorn stemming like a branched vein.
To the east lay the plainsland.
He saw the vast herd of the bison, inexhaustible, ranging the earth.
He saw the camps of the River Crows below him and the Mountain
    Crows to the north.
He saw beyond the Absaroka the vast range.
He saw the dread valley of the smoking valley
Where the earth boiled, and no Crow dared to tread.
Then he saw the leaves turning yellow and knew autumn was coming.
Far away were hostile lodges, their braves on the horse raids.
One Crow all alone was riding to meet them.

"My son, do you see that horseman

---

[*] The poem is a versified account of a segment from "Takes-the-pipe, A Crow Warrior," a story written by Robert H. Lowie and included in *American Indian Life*, edited by Elsie Clews Parsons (New York: B.W. Huebsch, Inc., 1922), 17-33. Everson read the Bison Book Reprint (Lincoln: UNebraska, 1967). Accompanying the poem, Everson gives a summation of the story prior to the climactic segment which is the material of Everson's narrative: *The story of Takes-the-pipe begins with his infancy and follows him through his boyhood and youth as he becomes a Crow warrior. He receives his name when he reaches for the pipe, the symbolic act of bravery. In a vision he receives his medicine and is promised immunity in battle, but is warned not to eat kidney. On a raid his knee is shattered. He realizes that somehow he had violated his taboo* [for he had indeed eaten kidney during a feast preceding the battle], *and because he could never now cut a picketed horse, he could not be a chief. His life becomes miserable. Finally he goes again to the mountains for another vision, and offers a knuckle in propitiation. Three apparitions appear to him on successive days offering him boons. These he refuses, he wants to become a chief, but they cannot help him. There is one day left, and he faces it with desperation.*

Out there on the prairie with trailing sleeves?
He has broken loose.
His people could not hold him back.
He could not be a chief and wants to die.
He is a Crazy Dog."

The voice of the bear, entering the span of his vision,
Filled it without sound. All he could see now was the lone horseman,
    going to his doom, his feat of immortality.

The voice continued.
"He speaks backward.
He defies the will of the tribe.
He shits on the rules of the camp.
Where there is danger
He is the foremost.

Dress like him.
Do as he does.

You shall be great!

As long as there is a Crow nation
The people will speak of you.
The women will praise you.

This I give you if your heart is strong.

You shall be great!"

        ▣

The vision ended.
Takes-the-pipe could hardly believe it.
He lay there wondering, letting the significance sink in.
Overwhelmed by the sequence of possibility opening before him.[*]

---

[*] No stanza break.

Was it true? Could it actually be?
Then, suddenly, everything made sense.
He saw with incredible clarity the meaning of his life
And the destiny before him.
He saw the meaning of his birth and the moment of his first vision.
He saw the promise given him, and the break in his knee,
The blessing that put within his grasp the ultimate of realization.
And he laughed. He lay on the crest of the hill
And laughed in faith, in great exultation, and sheer relief.

He tried to get up and face the apparition that had enlightened him.
He was too weak. Overwhelmed he fell back exhausted,
Relapsing into unconsciousness.
And awoke with the day wide about him.

He stood up.
"Thank you," he whispered. "Ai-ee! Ai-ee!
Oh, father, father...
What you have shown me is very great.

I will do it.

I wanted to live and be a chief.
It cannot be.

Now I know what I am to do.
I will die a Crazy Dog."

And he limped down the hill,
Stone by stone, along the slopes,
Branch by branch through the forest.
Limping into the dawn.

By the next sundown
Takes-the-pipe could hardly crawl. With reeling brain
He faced the west, the sundown quarter, and drew himself to his knees.
Seizing his knife he chopped off another left-hand joint,
And held it aloft. The bleeding stump streamed blood on his face.

"Ai-ee! Fathers, holy ones, masters of life!*

---
*
 No stanza break.

This, I give you! Hear me!
Accept my offering! Make me a chief!"

Suddenly in the dusk he sensed something approach.
It came panting, shuffling grotesquely,
Shaking a rattle and singing a song.
Against the dull stain of the sunset
Takes-the-pipe saw it straighten and stand up.

Many a time he had watched the giant grizzly
Rear in confrontation, its paws folded on its breast,
Its weak eyes blinking, its keen nose snuffling the air,
The blaze on its breast like a badge of light
On a field of silver.

The singing stopped.

                    "I am the last,"
Whispered the apparition. "Though I am heavy and slow,
I have arrived."

Takes-the-pipe called out to him, fearfully,
Hardly daring to trust his vision.
"Ai-ee! Father, I knew you were coming!
Cure my knee! When I cut a picketed horse
I become a chief!"

There was a prolonged silence.
Takes-the-pipe saw a light waning behind the massive shape
Bleeding the west, like the evaporation of time.
A wind sprang up the boulder-strewn slope.
Behind him the black oak leaves began to turn in the breeze.

Finally the great beast spoke:
"My son, he who was your father is very strong.
He will not let you be a chief.
But I too am strong. If you are a man
I can help you. If you are faint-hearted
No power can make you great."*

---
* Stanza break.

"Ai-ee!" cried Takes-the-pipe, his heart leaping with hope.
Make me greater than others!
What matters if I die?"

The great beast dropped to all fours and moved to meet him.
Takes-the-pipe saw the humped-back shape against the west,
Ponderous, the gait powerful and slow,
Irresistible, the motion of total strength.

"My son, there are many chiefs.
Of *your* kind there shall be but one."

Suddenly he loomed above the crouching brave,
A thunderhead over the height of the hills,
Portentous and vast.

"Tell me," the grave voice, no more than a whisper,
Filled the night space, a soft sibilance about it,
The voice of infinite wisdom. "Have you seen the whole world?"

Without waiting for answer the presence swung his massive arms
      about him
And swept him to his feet, holding him high.
He caught the bear smell now, the cave-odor fetid and rank.

"Look!" he urged. "See it all, for once!
It is yours to behold!
Once you have seen it
Nothing can dim it!
Nothing can cancel the realization!
Nothing can deny you the knowledge of life!"

Now the darkness was gone. As an eagle turns in its gyre
Takes-the-pipe hung at the pinnacle of the [   ].
All the world lay gleaming about him,
Glowing, a softly radiant visionary sheen,
A transparent and shimmering luminescence.

                                    [*incomplete*]. *[July 1976]*

"I had smelt it first"

I had smelt it first, that odor of char and ash,
The aftermath of desolation,
On the East Fork of the Kaweah in the summer of '33.
I would know it again on the Alsea an exact decade later,
And on the Deschutes in forty four and the [   ] in forty five,
And on the Trinity in forty six, as if the wider war
Could not be complete without the final ordeal by fire.

Will I know it on Big Creek in '77? Only time can tell. *[August 1977]*

"Good morning"

"Good morning. You will be happy to learn—"
The voice of the newscaster, deflated and flat,
Seems almost regretful—"all fires are contained."
I think of the long lines of the weary firefighters,
Trudging blankly out of the hills, glancing [　?　] back
At the vast black desert of the extinguished burn,
Only a burning snag or a smoking root remaining
Of the mighty blaze. There is something about the finality of victory
Almost mournful, as if the quiescence of peace
Is never a match for the thrill of contest.
Or as two lovers, [　?　] shivering after climax,
Sink ever so regretfully into the rapture of rest.
What is the source of such passion, is it not divinity?
Is it not, surely, divine? *[August 1977]*

DROUGHT-BREAKER

The year died darkly. After the equinoctial rains
The drought regained its grip, and October passed parched,
Then sterile November of the cloudless skies banking the coast.
Toward solstice a quickening of south wind,
And the first of the storms trooped in from the south.
By year's end the creeks were running and the grass green.
Back in the Sierra the snow lies ten feet deep on Donner Pass.
Now in mid January, storm after storm has pelted the coast.
The San Lorenzo rolls to the [?]; all the coastal current
[?] yellow mud into the [?] of the sea.
We woke last night to another rain, wires down and no lights,
The dawn breaking grey and a warm monsoon.
Bucking the coast road
I drove the boy to school, then drifted back up the coast.
At Davenport Landing high tide smashed the cliffs,
Gigantic surf standing off shore three quarters of a mile,
The breakers marching relentlessly in, pitching logs, debris,
      the offscouring of the sea thrown into the land.
At Scott Creek beach the tide takes the channel,
Creekward backed up a good mile,
Inundating the land, the fallow fields of Brussels sprouts
A giant lake. I stand for a time watching the sea,
A rain squall walks in from the south. I look
Up at the sky and think: "This time it's for sure.
After all these months. Let it pour, let it rain.

                                              Go back home
And bed that woman." *[January 9, 1978]*

PARKINSON'S POEM

A small saw-whet owl found dead in the trail.
I took it home for an owl totem, thinking to skin it out,
But instead placed it on a window sill,
Till my wife protested. Unable to get to it
And unwilling to forego, I placed it in the cupboard
Over the back porch laundry where morning and night
I perform my ablutions, rinsing my face and brushing my teeth.

The days went by and I clean forgot it.
Even when maggots began to fall in the sink
I had no recollection what they might be,
Till a whiff of death brought the whole episode
Back to my mind, and I carried out the nauseous [?],
And buried it in sand.

          Shortly thereafter
A dizziness and tremors began to seize me.
I made no connection. The doctor called it a virus,
And [it] must run its course. Others spoke of it as
Labyrinthine vertigo, an affliction of the inner ear, common enough
This year. I thought of those [?] maggots crawling on the shelf
    near my false teeth but kept quiet about it.
After several weeks the dizziness passed but the shaking persisted.
I sought out a neurologist.
He questioned me closely, observed my movements, and pronounced
    the verdict:
What you have, sir, is *paralysis agitans*, better known as Parkinson's
    disease.
He spoke of it at length, described the symptoms, outlined the treatment.

Driving home afterward what I retained was that it is an affliction
    associated with advancing age, and that there is no cure.
Suddenly a kind of wild exultance ran through me,
A rising response of affirmation and challenge.
I said, "This is it. The issue is joined. The long ambiguity is over."
I thought of my poem "The Master" written thirty-five years ago,
First joining the issue of affliction,

But now, this is for real.

But that night I pulled out an encyclopedia,
Checked the disease and read the worst.

Suddenly the false affirmation drained out of me,
A terrible depression dropped over my soul.
I shut the book and stepped out in the night.
The great drought hung over the land
Like a giant hand on the brain of a victim,
Stifling the life, cutting off the fine flow of blood,
The veins in the arterials.

                              I thought of the dead saw-whet,
The gruesome maggots crawling the shelf by my false teeth,
And the hideous leer of a hideous face—a [?] old man, bent double
       and crippled for life, his face a mask,
His lips [?], speechlessly mumbling,
A shaking [*incomplete*]. [*February 20, 1978*]

ECSTASY LINE[*]

Roving the beach I chance on them,
Broad daylight, half-naked bodies coupled in rut, the man
Lunging from below, the woman
Straddled on top (no sand
In the cunt), the explicit apparatus
Flagrantly exposed, climax a knotted
Convulsion.

                    Seeing me,
They stare with dazed faces, like animals surprised,
Impassively regarding [me] until I pass by,
Then resume their rut.

                    And climbing the bluff
I look down the long shore, seeing the white line of foam,
The churn of breakers, the froth and spume of it
Seething in churn. It is the line of ecstasy,
Vibration of transcendence, beaten up into / ∪
Out of the primal confrontation:
Water and shore, the width of the ocean
And the rockwall of the continent.

It is the ecstasy line indeed when the grunion run.

But there is another such line, another tide and another synthesis.
For from behind the hills come the hordes of sun-seekers,
Pouring out of the cities across the mountains, all the bay-side
        peninsula,
And from the vast valley beyond. On weekends their cars
Thread through the passes, long serpentine lines of them,

---

[*] Accompanying the drafts of May 17, 1978, is Everson's note: *It was last Saturday (May 13)
I was giving a presentation at the UCSC Library called "The Day Is a Poem" on West
Coast writing, with Jim Houston. It was during this talk that the image of the coast as an
ecstasy line came to me, to be immediately, in a flash of intuition, matched in the mind by
another line, the ecstasy of the flesh, the copulation line, the eros-driven hordes drawn to
the coast. I have carried the poem around since to begin it today, being alone all day, and
free to reflect.*

And fair out along the [?   ].

                            Here they strip off their clothes
And run down to the sea, meet the ecstasy of the wave
With the ecstasy of the flesh, and thus, in the summer [?   ],
Begins the line of copulation, in the nooks and crannies of the cliffs
Little convulsive knottings of flesh, the sun looking down
      on the wave and women, on rockhead and male,
With sublime [?   ], calling and evoking, the [?   ] ecstasy.
                                   [May 17, 1978; July 7, 1980]

"We chose the stately alder"

We chose the stately alder at the trail-fork
For victim: the sacrificial offering
Rendered out of the roots of existence
For our pride's expiation.

                  It stands alone,
In its maximal fullness of growth,
No taint nor blemish, no disfiguring scar
Nor fire-burn at the base
Disfigures its perfection.
Self-possessed in the self's abundance,
Life's gift back to life.

                And I, ancient sacrificer,
Approach it reverently, lay my hand upon it,
Fondly, as a man reassures the woman he loves
In her night of defloration.

              Sharp is the saw and keen the axe,
There is no indecision nor wasted motion,
Clean and swift the work proceeds,
The rite unfolds.

          Suddenly the stroke takes.
A shiver runs up the stately frame.
The yearning top, that had reached for the stars,
Begins to sway. A kind of [raptured] shiver
Runs down it, a wince of anguish, then the awful agonization
Possesses it, a moment transfixed.

                Feeling it go
I step aside. Throwing back my head
I shout the long shout of acclamation,
The lumberjack's
Immemorial aria of consummation,

Alerting the woods:

"Timber-r-r-r!"

                                Far back at the house,
In the kitchen-close morning, my wife
Is stopped by that sound, electrified.
She will recall the fantastic energization
As if decades of years were stripped from me,
Restoring me to my own prime manhood,
As if the voice of the archetype
Blew through me, sacrificer, immolator,
Before the crash that will close it
Erases its note.

                        I myself am in awe,
Standing there in time's eye of whirlwind,
Watching the tall trunk teeter majestically,
On its quivering axis, and at last start to go,
Like a dancer, balanced on the ultimate aspiration,
While all about it the hovering light
Hangs in lofty suspension,
To then go down, a rush and cleavage of descending force,
And the shattering crash. The dust blows about me,
Softly settling, a grey nimbus, a mantle of death.

We lay our hands on the disheveled shape,
Prone now, exclaiming softly,
As on the African veldt the Black gunbearers,
When the Great White Hunter has brought down the Wildebeest,
Lay hands on him, the fallen trophy,
Touching and stroking, grinning and exclaiming,
The gutturals of admiration.

So do we now. But the moment
Eludes. We pick up our axes
And move to our work,
Lop limb from trunk,
And section the saw to the narrow gauge
That will render this god to cordwood. *[July/September 1980]*

"I lie panting"

I lie panting, half-sunken in sleep,
Still back in the legendary world,
With Arthur and Merlin and the good Sir Gawain,
Who out of *noblesse oblige*
Embraced the horrible Lady Granell
And discovered a bride. *[December 20, 1980]*

"The great blue heron"

The great blue heron paces the pasture,
A lordly gait, among the grazing cattle,
Stalking gophers, who have riddled the earth
With their tunneling trails, pulling short grasses
Underground to weave their nests.

Of all the birds that fly I *[incomplete]*. *[November 7, 1981]*

KILLER STORM

Early on in the wintertime
It struck without warning—
The heaviest storm in a hundred years—
Two gigantic cyclonic systems
Up from the south and down from the north
Lock off the coast and hold there,
Two centrifugal monsters coiled in rut, orgasmic spinoff
Drenching the coast.

                      All Santa Cruz county
Took the brunt. Mountain villages
Cut off from each other and the world,
No power, no light and no phones,
[?Monstrous] landslides down rain-slick ridges
Burying houses and all within. Before it was over
Nine lives lost.

The heaviest storm in a hundred years,
On the third day of deluge we were driven out,
To spend the night with our kindly landlords
Safe on the ridge.

On returning with daylight the first impression
Was confusing. The creek we had known
Changed character. As the waters withdrew
Exposing its banks I understood what it was:
A clear case of riparian shock. The banks were naked, stripped
    of undergrowth,
With here and there a swimming alder, but these denuded,
Their white flesh stripped clean
To gleam in the light like atrocity exposed,
The rage of the river stripping [?the] barks,
Logjams piled [?] haphazardly
To back up the torrent and face it sideways out of its channel,
Cutting out yards of the creekroad
Above and below us but the house spared.

For days I limped around slightly stunned,

Sharing the drama of dislocation in wild disarray.
But after a week the signs of redemption
Began to emerge. I caught the gleam of renewal.
Stripping the accumulation of a century,
Scouring the bottom of all its debris,
The light-bodied chalkstone whirled away
But bars of clean granite cobble, as polished as jewels
Arranged in renewal.

I thought of the snake
Sloughing its skin in the throes of renewal
To quicken in the light with its new integument.
The mangle of tortured logjams
Disfiguring the channel, but between them and among them
The shoals of new granite, blue, gleaming in the sun.
It gave a joy to be alive again, almost whole again, almost new
        in one's age,
Strangely new in one's old age. *[June 19, 1982]*

ELK

Prairie Creek Park: far north in the state
And we pulled in exhausted. We had traveled all day;
Our nerves were on edge and we were close to a quarrel.
I was adamant and intransigent;
You were morose and resentful.
The campground was full so we circled around to [?make] the beach
Which we were glad to find deserted, but time only
To pull down our gear from the road-sore jeep,
Cook a rapid supper, and turn in exhausted,
Too angry to talk.

All night long
The sea champed, unable to masticate the beach,
And in frustration withdrew to its den
Without solace.

The morning was bright,
No fog, the beach still empty of all but ourselves,
And adventure beckoned. We found an inviting trail
That left the beach through a narrow ravine
With a beautiful bank of fern on its northern side,
And [?] we started to climb.

After an interval of steady climbing
We stopped at the edge of a green meadow
To catch our breath. Still hidden behind a screen of pine
We looked in the meadow and [? ?],

What?

Elk.

A half dozen or so, all with their heads down
Happily [?] the green [?]
And so we approached.

We continued to walk. The trail wound past them

No more than forty feet [?   ].
The nearest, sensing our presence, lifted their heads,
Watched us serenely with [?quiet] liquid cool eyes
Only mildly curious. As we slowly walked on
Two others, and then a fifth, all cows
And all [?content], placidly munching.

But the highest elk, the one farthest from us,
Looked up last, and we saw the antlers just as he saw us.
Suddenly he sprang as if struck by a dart,
Panic in his startled eyes. It was an act that cried out
As loud as if he had spoken: "For God's sake, women,
Why didn't you say something! They're [?   ]!"
He slammed blindly into the barrier bush,
And reeled [?   ], shaking his head, antlers waving
        in desperation.
Then tried without success for another way out.
By this time the five females were all alarmed.
The [?   ] of the buck infecting them,
They swung in behind him, all of a piece,
And raced through the grass till he found an out
And they all disappeared. We heard their hooves
[?   ] and [?   ] on the [?   ] earth
[?   ] they [?   ] up the [?   ], and passed out of hearing
In the fragrant morning.

                    Back at the jeep
We loaded our gear and piled sheepishly in,
Outward bound in the bright morning,
Somehow confirmed in our human dimensions,
At one with each other in the pulse of nature,
When male and female in the rush up the ridge,
The single mode of sexual survival,
Broke even. *[February 8-9, 1984]*

"I stir fitfully"

I stir fitfully, half-asleep, and my arm
Begins that weird vibration, the [?scope] of my illness.
Parkinson's is a disease of consciousness.
We do not experience it when we sleep.
But half asleep is half Parkinson's territory
And the palsy and the paralysis
Play the field between them.
Sometimes the leastest chill from under the covers
Sets the nerves on edge, alert, like a Geiger counter that shivers
      its needle at the least uranium.
They are like geese
Alert in their farmyard.
Any approaching thing, rather any *strange* thing,
Sets a skirling of shouts among them, a warning clucking.
And let a man approach they gabble up a storm.
So it is with the palsy. Let the leastest chill
Slip between the blankets, through the wind's advance,
The agitation begins. Soon the flaw must be found and corrected,
Or else you will quake all night,
And the dawn find you exhausted.

In one of those [?seizures] [?]?] I [?so upset]
Bent double, my long back curved down to the earth.
I do not exercise—one of the precepts advised,
Nor do I know why, save that for me, a feeling-intuitive, by type
Find sensation and thinking the shadow area,
And given the inertia native to this affliction,
All the exercise proposed, be it ever so brief
Never gets accomplished. And year by year
The insidious advance of encroaching [?] creeps up
      through my body,
Possessing the soft muscles and the lank thews,
Bending the bones and making rigid the face,
The infamous Parkinson's mask,
That makes rigid the cheeks and the straightened lips.
Even the glib tongue goes stiff, [*incomplete*]. *[February 4, 1985]*

"The sacred distillate"

The sacred distillate of the new consciousness
That changes the world. In a word
The hero does not propose a new doctrine
And enforce it through his personal exertion.
He doesn't even know what the new consciousness is.
He knows only the urgence for consummation.
Thus Christ did not die to establish his doctrine;
He preached his Father's doctrine. What he died for
Was to disestablish death and replenish life.
So the poet in his poem
Does not propound his subject.
Prose could do that. What a poem *is*
Is the consummation in esthetic form
That replenishes life. Thus if the definition of a sacrament
Is a sign that effects what it signifies
Then vocation is a sacred calling
For it does nothing less.
Vocation is the mode that makes consummation effective.

[May 3, 1985]

"A shiver of silence"

A shiver of silence. In the offing
The quietude of lambent dusk
Swaddled the fields. Far off
Dogs barked, the jackass in the paddock
Brayed in concert with the tremolo frogs.
A time to accept. A time to assent.
A time to confirm. What the life prefigured
Is here put to the test.

                              A test,
What is the value of test? Why test?

To prove. Duration involves
Conviction.

                              A [? of ? ?]
[? ? ?]. A [?] of conjoining
Under the distancing of
Time and [?denial].

                              The agony in the garden,
The agony of the [?toiled] embrace of lovers.
Strong for consummation. The pure pleasure
Of [? ?] by the [?] of [? ? ?]
[*illegible*]
The soul [?] in the coign of its beatitude
Purging [?] like a skinflint
[?Choking] with [?] of pleasure. *[August 19, 1986]*

"Every poet is born twice"

Every poet is born twice—both nasty.
From the beginning you want to go.
You've been in there nine months
All cooped up.
[*illegible*]. [*July 27, 1989*]

PROLOGUE*
THE WONDER OF THE CHILD

The wonder of the child is the measure
Of the mind. Everything we can become
Is clenched in our initiating crisis, our first
Facing out, the break-in-plane between the centripetal
Waters of the womb and the centrifugal
Surge of the sun.

                    Our primal scream
Strikes the eardrum of our consciousness
With the shock of recognition. In the trauma
Of our birth we crawl the dark of the uterine tube
Through the terrible gate of sinew and bone,
To gasp in the light and gulp pitifully for air,
"Born," in the unsurpassable words of Saint Augustine,
"Between piss and shit."

                    Between the nerves of this comprehension
Smolders the fire of our grief, our pang of disappointment,
What we make of our lot. And having survived
Our ordeal of birth, nothing else that ensues is unfaceable,
        not even death.
For just as our fitness for survival we confirmed in our ordeal of birth,
So will our fitness for salvation be verified by the ordeal of our death.

For the law of inception as the maximum impulsion of power
Holds true across the span of polarity,
Binding birth and death in a dual insurgence.
The wonder of the child is the apogee of consciousness.
As Jesus declared in his homily: "Unless ye become as a little child
Ye shall in no wise enter the kingdom of Heaven."
Which translates into the surge of emergence

---

* This poem was written to introduce Book Two of *Dust Shall Be the Serpent's Food*. For a time it was designated as Canto VI and entitled "The Wisdom of the Child" prior to its placement as Prologue.

As the throb of creation.

                          For there is a certain
Falling off in the course of consciousness. Everything
Points to the spurt of origination as the decisive
Moment of the urge to be. All power
Is a kind of dispersal, a deceptive running down.
Our search for transcendence is pure nostalgia:
A passion for the recovery of what we had lost.

Every child, every birth, subsumes the instant of entelechy,
The spontaneous manifestation of prime reality. As adults
We desperately clutch the modicum of experience
As the habiliment of fundamental identity,
Unable to explain or account for
The disappearance of a richer life.

Distantly lost, unconsciously remembering to forget
How often do we trouble to remind ourselves
Of all we were, unable to reconstitute
The sacred integrity that shaped us? Until the tolling bell
Sounds the knell of our desuetude
And the facile attempts of our casuistry
Clot the hushed repository of our past. *[November 1990-August 1991]*

"For the naked heart"*

For the naked heart of the poet
Glides ever away, returning
To the dim swamp lands of the soul
Where Good and Evil, ancient antagonists
Like rutting dinosaurs in the freezing sloughs,
Savagely disembowel each other
As they copulate to the death. *[August, 1991]*

---

* This poem was printed as the conclusion to Everson's "Preface" to *Naked Heart: Talking on Poetry, Mysticism, and the Erotic* (Albuquerque, NM: U New Mexico, 1992).

CANTO VI*

The year: [1958]. On a cot in my cell,
Absorbed in the writings
Of the medieval Dominican sage, Meister Eckhart,
Searching for mystical clues, I hear a knocking at my door.
It proves a student priest, one of the newly ordained friars,
Completing their studies here at the House of Studies,
Before assignment to the apostolate.
Father Martin Gianini, dressed in clerical garb,
Black suit and clerical collar. "Brother Antoninus,"
He began before I could greet him,
I have something to show you!"
He held out a sheaf of paper,
"Amazing stuff!"

"What is it?" I ask.

....

I immediately knew my brain [was] in a senseless
     dream-trance,
The cathedral gone, and in its place
My home town, Selma, sat in midmorning quietude
Beginning its day.

I become aware

---

* "Canto VI" of *Dust Shall Be the Serpent's Food* first appears on some five holograph pages,
dated November 17, 1990. However, the text is so largely illegible that it would be
impracticable to attempt to reproduce it here. This draft recounts Everson's early efforts at
self-hypnosis, to which he was introduced by Fr. Martin Gianini, O.P., upon the latter's return
from an AMA conference on the medical use of hypnosis. The text printed here uses hardcopies
derived from a number of holograph draft pages and provided for the poet by his caregiver,
Steve Sibley. Although the poet uses "1960" in the latest hardcopy, he also uses 1958 and
even 1963 in the drafts. A journal entry of December 19, 1958, confirms the correctness of the
year given here. A journal entry of February 14, 1959, suggests that Everson did not
immediately persist in the use of hypnosis but took renewed and sustained interest after Fr.
Gianini brought him further material on February 11. The "cathedral" mentioned in the
second segment of our text was an image used to provide entry into the hypnotic state.
Everson's inclusion of "my first trauma" (see next page) refers to the incident recounted in
Canto V, "The Blood of the Poet."

That my sister and brother are with me, which presents
A certain problem;
For though by position we traverse the site
Of the Logan Street residence, our first Selma sojourn,
Bearing in its somnolent configuration the precious insignia
      of my first trauma,
The line of our direction suggests
As inception point our "A" Street family residence
Which would not be built until 1919,
Whereas the time-frame of the present action
Is clearly 1914-15.

                    But dreams are like that.
For factual objectivity they have little regard;
Whereas if it feels comfortable with a situation as here it cuts corners.
After all, the "A" Street addressed sustained the emotional
Core of the family for twenty-six years and it is not surprising
That, given the emotional experience to draw upon,
It should telescope its association.

                    Second Street
Ends at Wright for city limit, which we cross as well as a narrow bridge
      over a shallow irrigation canal.
Beyond it lay an open field sown to barley,
Sloping down to an apricot orchard beside a small tule pond so shallow
It only showed water in wet years [incomplete].
                    [November 1990/May 1992/April-June 1993]

AND MY LIFE COMES ROUND[*]

And my life comes round. On my 80th Birthday
My wife declares, "For twenty-three years
I have given my life to you
And can do no more."

In warm insouciant weather, the last days of summer
Lean on the land.

It had been an archetypal evening. Many guests,
Many old friends, and many old lovers
Had gathered round the campfire in the limpid dusk.
[*incomplete*]. *[September 17-18, 1992]*

---

[*] The poet's eightieth birthday celebration, September 10, 1992, became the occasion for the rupture of his marriage.

"And the emptiness"

And the emptiness recurs, no woman in my
      life now
To hold me together, the separate selves,
Querulously twittering, like flocking birds
Huddled together on their midnight roost,
Sleepily protesting, hardly aware that this [?oak-struck] [?   ]
No longer exists to hold them together.

On my eightieth birthday my wife
Unceremoniously kicked me out of the house
And out of the life we shared for twenty-three years,
To find sanctuary with a friend.

                              What had gone wrong?
I had thought to end my life in the bosom of my family,
In keeping with the expectation of a distinguished elder
[?Surrounded] in the company of many friends,
With the loving attention of my faithful wife.

Instead the [?   ] unexpectedly [?   ].
My wife's own family begged me to leave,
Insisting my life was in danger.
I was incredulous, but I was persuaded
When our son Jude arrived with his car,
To bear me away to sanctuary.

Lying in the dark the twittering flock of [?   ] birds
Became ghosts in the haunted house of my heart
Unhappily wringing their hands together
Questioning the reality of the fate
That had set them [?   ] from the power of life,
The force that had kept them in being.

I knew them now for the facets of unreality
We [?   ] in the world, images of the ego,
By which we confirm the substance of our hopes
But they [?make] no subsistent being in the world.
[incomplete]. [Fall 1992]

HOG WILD[*]

Knowledgeable locals
Quick to recall their first encounter with feral pig
In Santa Cruz County. Marked nine years back.

Lud McCrary, picking his way up a brush-choked draw with his horse
Snorted spooked stopped
Stark still.

Something was there,
Coyote? Cougar? He stood in his stirrups straining to see, to hear.
He caught a slight movement
In the thicket.
Suddenly the brush erupted with life,
And a fierce old mother sow charged out bristling with womb-fury, her
    eyes mean with anger, baleful with hate.
She was closely followed with her farrow of pigs scuttling with terror.
Bringing up the rear came the fierce old boar, 300 pounds of impacted
    fury, his boar mane bristling, his snout plowing the ground
    [incomplete]. [September 30, 1993]

---

[*] This poem is a verse rendition of a local interest article printed in the Santa Cruz Sentinel, September 30, 1993.

APPENDIX B

REGARDING
DUST SHALL BE THE
SERPENT'S FOOD

CONTENTS

Introduction by Allan Campo

回 回

INTRODUCTION:
Allan Campo

To provide an appropriate and helpful context for Everson's unfinished epic poem, *Dust Shall Be the Serpent's Food*, we are including several pieces that he wrote in regard to it. These include both published and unpublished texts—the latter from among the Everson papers at the Bancroft Library, UC Berkeley. What I wish to do in this introductory note is to clarify the chronology and the design of the epic—matters which are of some interest and, perhaps, importance—especially given the fact of the poem's unfinished state.

In his Foreword to *In Medias Res*, the 1984 Adrian Wilson fine press edition of Canto I, Everson attributes the inception of the epic to the course he presented as Poet in Residence at the University of California at Santa Cruz—"The Birth of a Poet"—beginning in the fall of 1971. Among his papers at the Bancroft Library, there is a manuscript of what was written as the Prologue to the epic, accompanied by an astrological chart for October 13, 1975, labeled "Inception of epic" (and included among the photographs in the present volume). The initial draft of this Prologue (the Prologue being included in our Appendix A) is dated October, 1975; and the first draft of Canto I is dated October 25, 1975. And it is 1975 that he uses in the Foreword.

In terms of the poem as we now have it, Everson's chronology is accurate. However, the actual genesis, the true inception, goes back further. Among his Bancroft manuscripts is a draft of a "Self-Interview," dated October 26, 1980, and it begins:

> Years ago I read E. M. W. Tillyard's *The English Epic and Its Background* and was immensely stirred by it. "There is nothing so exciting and so awe-inspiring in the world of letters," he wrote, "as the spectacle of a great spirit daring to risk everything on one great venture and knowing that in its execution he will be forced to the limit of what a man can endure." Inspired by these words I determined to write an autobiographical epic, using Teilhard de Chardin's *The Phenomenon of Man* as the model of a contemporary Christian cosmology.
>
> Nothing came of it....*

---

* The statement cited by Everson is from E. M. W. Tillyard, *The English Epic and Its Background* (New York: Oxford University Press, 1954) 11.

As it happened, in the fall of 1967 I was temporarily living in
Sausalito (a small town just across the Golden Gate from San Francisco
and noted as something of an "artists' colony"). At the time, Everson,
who was still Brother Antoninus of the Dominican Order, resided at the
Kentfield Priory while fulfilling his regimen toward becoming a vowed
religious. It was an easy bus ride from Sausalito north to Ross and then
a short walk to the Priory, and I spent various occasions visiting with the
poet.

Early on, Everson told me of his then recent reading of Tillyard's
work and of his determination to write an autobiographical epic. In fact,
he had already begun by writing an "Invocation" in the classical manner
and read it to me. As a model for his poem, he took Wordsworth's *The
Prelude or, Growth of a Poet's Mind*. Everson would set out to recount
his development as a poet—from the time of his parents and their
meeting and marriage, his childhood, his early poetic vocation, and on
through his life until his release from the conscientious objectors camp
in 1946. Unlike Wordsworth, however, Everson thought to adopt the
"heroic" attitude and to incorporate awarenesses derived from depth
psychology. He planned a work of ten cantos. His leaning toward
Wordsworth's poem as an approach may have been suggested by
Tillyard's observation regarding the Romantic poet's choice of subject
for an epic poem:

> When it came to the point Wordsworth could not feel so keenly
> about an imagined theme as about the things, big and small but yet
> wonderful, that had befallen himself; and plans for an objective epic
> had to give way to autobiography. (244)

After I left Sausalito early the following year, I heard nothing more
about the proposed epic until, in a postscript to a letter dated July 16,
1969, Everson wrote:

> The epic is launched, but I am shocked and dismade
> (dismayed!) by its beginning. I knew I was going to have to go back
> into some pretty hairy stuff and that's partly what held me up so
> long, but I never figured it was going to open up in the way it
> actually has. Now after a week I'm nauseated and every day gets
> harder to write. I didn't write at all yesterday and don't want to
> today either but I have to get on with it.

So it should have come as no real surprise that, while still at Stinson Beach (the community where, after leaving the Dominicans in December of 1969, Everson, his new wife, Susanna, and her infant son, Jude, settled for a year and a half until their move to Swanton), the attempt to further the poem—especially in regard to his father, with whom he had had a particularly difficult relationship—resulted in an upheaval of such painful memories and emotions that, as he later told me, he chucked the manuscript into the fireplace of the Stinson Beach house and let it burn. Unfortunately, the Invocation was among those pages and so was lost.

As a side note here, the composition of the powerful "Black Hills"—begun on May 10, 1970—is very likely related in part to the aroused father-issue with which Everson was grappling in this attempt to proceed with his autobiographical epic.

Out of sight, however, was not out of mind. The epic re-emerged in 1975 as a "new" project, flowing from his "Birth of a Poet" lectures, as Everson recounts in that Foreword to *In Medias Res*. Eventually, he took up *Dust Shall Be the Serpent's Food* (from the Book of Isaiah) as the overall title for the epic. In fact, back in 1963 the poet had selected that verse as title for his projected Collected Poems, not dropping the idea in favor of *The Crooked Lines of God* until the summer of 1975.

Once renewed, the writing of the epic continued, sometimes steadily, sometimes sporadically, through the summer of 1993. But the onset of pneumonia that fall, his nearly-fatal struggle in the intensive care unit, and his return home to Kingfisher Flat for the final months of his life left no energy for pursuit of the work, and it remained uncompleted beyond Canto V, "The Blood of the Poet," initially printed in the 1992 volume, *Perspectives on William Everson* (Grants Pass, OR: Castle Peak Editions). However, in November of 1990 he had begun Canto VI, incorporating his 1958 introduction to auto-hypnosis and the childhood memories he had recovered through that method. The poet continued to work on it until the summer of 1993. The fragment that exists is included in our Appendix A.

Another canto was perhaps also in the offing. During my visit with Everson in July of 1993 (my last such visit before his hospitalization), the poet recounted an incident from his mid-twenties. He had reluctantly been persuaded to accompany a friend to Berkeley for a seance. Prior to the seance, Everson had a personal palm-reading session with the psychic, who told him that one day he would write a poem "for him who carried the cross." With his pantheism and his antipathy toward organized religion, Everson scoffed at this incongruous Christian reference. But the significance of the prediction as it was borne out in his Catholic poetry could not be ignored. And his enthusiasm in our conversation about it, the importance of it to him, was a clear sign that it held the germ of a new canto—though one never to be written.

◨ ◨

I. "Self-Interview," October 26, 1980

[The following reflection is transcribed from two holograph pages.
The "years ago" time frame refers to 1967.]

Years ago I read E.M.W. Tillyard's *The English Epic and Its Background* and was immensely stirred by it. "There is nothing so exciting and so awe-inspiring in the world of letters," he wrote, "as the spectacle of a great spirit daring to risk everything on one great venture and knowing that in its execution he will be forced to the limit of what a man can endure." Inspired by these words I determined to write an autobiographical epic using Teilhard de Chardin's *The Phenomenon of Man* as the model of a contemporary Christian cosmology.*

Nothing came of it, or at least nothing has come of it yet. Perhaps it is not the American way. Whitman said it is not. In the Preface to the 1855 *Leaves of Grass* he writes, "...the expression of the American poet is to be transcendent and new. It is to be indirect and not direct or descriptive or epic." I've thought a good deal about that indirect as opposed to direct expression and have begun to feel that that just might be what I have been doing all along.

The indirect way is what I take to be [that] of the confessional mode, particularly the confessional sequence. In meeting the exigencies of my life, step by step, I have created an odyssey that delineates not the external frame of a sidereal universe, but an inner world, a "landscape of the psyche" in [Albert] Gelpi's phrase, a cosmology of the soul. Rexroth first pointed to it in his Introduction to *The Residual Years* (1968):

> Everson has been accused of self-dramatization. Justly. All of his poetry, that under the name of Brother Antoninus, too, is concerned with the drama of his own self, rising and falling along the sine curve of life, from comedy to tragedy and back again, never quite going under, never quite escaping for good into transcendence.... Everything is larger than life with a terrible beauty and pain.

---

* This paragraph was lifted from an interview with Everson conducted by Stephen Henry Madoff and included in the collection of Everson interviews, *Naked Heart: Talking on Poetry, Mysticism, and the Erotic* (Albuquerque: University of New Mexico, 1992), where the passage appears on page 146. The interview is dated 1983, but that is an error. Internal evidence makes it clear the interview took place in 1980. Evidently, the response to the interviewer's question provoked further thought, and the "Self-Interview" was a result. It is worth noting that, as of this point in time, Everson had given up the idea of an epic poem and looked upon his total body of poetry as his "epic."

In my Preface to *The Veritable Years* (1978) I was able to objectify
it in terms of the Trilogy of my life work, and define its shape. *Crooked
Lines* may not fulfill the [four] requirements Tillyard specified,
particularly that of *predetermination*. But sometimes unconscious
predeterminism, the adhesion to an obscure motivation, is more
purposive than conscious [?   ]. Not only so, as time goes on the
stakes are narrowing. As I near completion it's going to take a more
consistent [?] application of intellegence and [?], than [? ?] has
exacted of me. To bring off the *Integral Years,* [?   ] age and failing
health and waning powers, is going to take as much sheer determination
as ever the Masters were called on to complete their own epics. This
may sound like an old man's vanity, but Fate is at my face, and it's
eyeball to eyeball.

II. PROPOSED CONTENTS

[The following listing of the contents of the projected epic
reproduces a holograph manuscript dated July 9, 1982.]

Prologue
Canto One In Medias Res
Canto II Life of Father
Canto III Mother
IV   Early Life Brother [and] Sister
V   Edwa
VI   Vocation & Jeffers
VII War
VIII Mary Fabilli Prodigious Thrust
IX   Conversion
Epilogue

III. Foreword to *In Medias Res*

[The following Foreword was published with *In Medias Res*, Canto One of the epic, in the fine press volume issued by Adrian Wilson in 1984.]

FOREWORD

In Medias Res is the opening canto of an uncompleted autobiographical poem tentatively called *Dust Shall Be the Serpent's Food*. The idea of an epic, always latent in a poet's psyche because, historically, it constitutes the supreme achievement of the literary art, actually emerged from a course I taught at the University of California, Santa Cruz, where I served a ten-year stint as Poet in Residence. This auspicious, patently honorific [title], retains some of the prestige of the ancient office of poet, whereas the appellation of Poet Laureate has become so politically debased, in America at least, as to constitute something of a joke.* The distinction is important to the genesis of the poem, for I was induced to reflect upon the situation and role of the poet as a symbolic force in its own right, despite the various emphases of different times, whether classical or romantic, contemporary or futuristic.

The course in question, "Birth of a Poet," was designed to engage the problem of vocation at the stage of life when it is most problematical and hence most important: the college years. Our text was Joseph Campbell's *The Hero with a Thousand Faces*, tracing the mythological evolution of the Rites of Passage, wherein the hero, representative of the bearer of consciousness for the race, reenacts the ordeal of deliverance from the forces that hem humanity in. So I took the poet as bearer of consciousness of his time, and I stressed he must be prepared to assume the heroic attitude, or fail the archetypal ordeal which the Rite of Passage exacts, for the list of American poets who have cracked up is awesome. Society, the collective, cannot advance of its own; as Jung maintains it can only advance through the charismatic individual; hence nothing less than a heroic consciousness suffices if mankind is to go forward.

In introducing the course each quarter I began by narrating my own life story as exemplifying the ordeal of vocation; and thus it followed

---

* Apparently Everson had some misgivings about the harshness of his remark regarding "Poet Laureate." Later, in a draft of an Introduction for *The Engendering Flood*, he began with the opening section of this Foreword but then lined out the entire sentence.

that I must adapt to the role and narrate my life in specifically heroic terms. Since the mode of the hero is epic, my narration tended to directly accommodate the epic pattern as the continuity of my experience. This entailed a study of the epic as a literary form, which led to the present attempt, "in medias res," the classical formula for the epic as it has come down to us from the Greek and Roman heritage.

The Latin appellation is clear enough: "in medias res" means simply "in the middle of things." But in terms of the epic tradition it has also come to mean "the low point in the fortunes of the hero." Nor is it difficult to grasp why this should be so. In the bardic tradition the epic was invariably chanted, and the typical situation would be relatively informal: a great hall packed with people of every distinction, from noblemen and warriors to women and children. Some would still be eating and drinking, with the inevitable dogfight erupting from among the bones flung under the tables. It behooved the bard, then, to adopt a beginning that would instantly engage the attention of his listeners, and for this the low point in the fortunes of the hero proved ideal. For with the audience well in hand, the bard could bear off a point or two in intensity, and use flashback to recount how the hero got himself into such a fix; finally going forward to apotheosis and the redemption of the people through his efficacious deeds.

Thus the *Iliad* of Homer, an essentially barbaric opus, begins with the Greeks demoralized and in disarray after ten fruitless years before besieged Troy, with Achilles, their greatest warrior, refusing to fight anymore, sulking in his tent because Agamemnon, the nominal head of the Greek forces, had pulled his rank on the hero, appropriating his concubine. So too Homer's *Odyssey* finds Odysseus hopelessly astray on the long journey home from the sack of Troy, establishing the low point in the fortunes of the hero, even though we are first shown the crisis situation in the hero's home, where his faithful wife Penelope is badgered by greedy suitors, and his son Telemachus endures their insults. Virgil's *Aeneid*, the first truly literary, or "civilized" epic, begins with Aeneas shipwrecked on the coast of Carthage, the fateful diversionary episode that drives him from the arms of Dido to the founding of Rome. With Dante the focus shifts from the objective action to subjective clarification, the shaping of the psyche in spiritual purgation, what would later be called individuation, the long mystical centuries between Virgil's time and his own having effected the emphasis of contemplation over action, despite all the victories obtainable in the world. Finally Milton, in *Paradise Lost*, mythologizes the scriptural account of man's verge toward violational selfhood, thereby memorializing the Protestant ethos which created the modern world.

And so it was that, reaching a point in my life when a summing up seemed called for, I reflected on that journey and realized that the low point in the fortunes of *this* hero was indubitably the death of my father at the close of World War II. Impelled by the reconciliation of all it implied, I took up pen and started to write.

That was in 1975. Given such clear beginnings, what is the ethos governing the apotheosis of violational selfhood that I spoke of as constituting the way, standing behind the atomization of consciousness in the modern world? That is not something any poet can define. It works through him and of him, but strictly speaking, not by him: rather he taps another source, a dimension instinctively entered, seeking deliverance from a collective oppression holding his time and people in fee. In his creative night of the long sea-journey, his dark night of faith, he feels the ordeal write its meaning of passage through time, as his own unconscious, in its voluptuous dream, prefigures its destiny.

Be that as it may, the canto's early manuscript drafts showed a strong start but nothing conclusive; for whatever reason I had put it aside. Then in 1981 a local writer's group organized a Work-in-Progress reading and, having nothing else that qualified, I turned back to the canto and began to hammer it into shape, though by the night of the reading I still had my doubts. As it turned out the work was well received and, reassured, I continued to polish it. Not only so, I began the second canto on the life of my father, but how that one will fare is still unresolved. So I am content to let *In Medias Res* go to press, hopeful that even if no other cantos emerge to sweep the epic to apotheosis, it will at least have the substance to stand alone.

William Everson

January 22, 1984
Kingfisher Flat
Swanton, California

IV. Author's Note to *The Engendering Flood*

[The following "Author's Note," written in July 1989, appeared as Everson's introduction to *The Engendering Flood* (Black Sparrow Press, 1990), the publication of Cantos I to IV as Book One of the epic.]

AUTHOR'S NOTE

The Engendering Flood is the first book of an autobiographical epic poem entitled *Dust Shall Be the Serpent's Food*. It consists of four cantos, the first being called "In Medias Res," so named after the classical formula for the epic as it has come down to us from the Greek and Latin tradition. The words mean simply "in the midst of things," but more aptly have come to specify "the low point in the fortunes of the hero." For me that point was certainly the funeral of my father at the close of World War II in 1945, and so I have begun it.

The epic formula then calls for flashback to delineate how the hero got to that point. Thus Canto II, entitled "Skald," after the Scandinavian minstrels or bards of the Viking period, relates the life of my father, an immigrant Norwegian musician. Canto III, "Hidden Life," narrates the humble origin of my mother on a Minnesota farm in the last century, how she met my father and how they fell in love. Canto IV, "The Hollow Years," tells of the estrangement of the lovers, their eventual reconciliation, marriage, procreation, and arrival in Selma, California, where I grew up. Thus far, my immediate lineal background. Book Two will begin my personal odyssey.

W. E.

V. Unpublished Introduction
to *The Engendering Flood*

[The following selection is an amalgam of several typed partial drafts with handwritten revisions by Everson following his initial draft of the foregoing "Author's Note." The latter is dated July 1, 1989. The drafts from which this selection is formed were written during July and given a completion date of August 1, 1989. After these several drafts Everson returned to his original "Note" for publication. However, in the rejected drafts, he set out to broaden his introductory discussion of the epic poem, and it has seemed worthwhile to present his thoughts. Given the incomplete and even rejected nature of the material, the attempt here is not to construct a well-crafted essay, but rather to bring together the thoughts and approaches he was attempting to present. Except in the instances of inset quotations, a double space separation indicates a shift to a different segment from among the drafts.]

FOREWORD

The Engendering Flood is the first book of an autobiographical epic poem entitled *Dust Shall Be the Serpent's Food.* It consists of four cantos, the first being called "In Medias Res," so named after the classical formula for the epic as it has come down to us from the Greek and Latin tradition. The words mean simply "in the midst of things," but more aptly have come to specify "the low point in the fortunes of the hero." For me that point was certainly the funeral of my father at the close of World War II in 1945, and so I have begun it.

The epic formula then calls for flashback to delineate how the hero got to that point. Thus Canto II, entitled "Skald," after the Scandinavian minstrels or bards of the Viking period, relates the life of my father, an immigrant Norwegian musician. Canto III, "Hidden Life," narrates the humble origin of my mother on a Minnesota farm in the last century, how she met my father and how they fell in love. Canto IV, "The Great Divide," [i.e., "The Hollow Years"] tells of the estrangement of the lovers, their eventual reconciliation, marriage, procreation, and arrival in Selma, California, where I grew up. Thus far, my immediate lineal background. Book Two will begin my personal odyssey.

In writing my story the attempt will not be to measure the facts of my life against the contents of my books in order to accent a cause and effect relationship between them. In a sense that was already done in the long confessional sequences that I have published over the span of my years. I have always drawn heavily on my life for the subjects of my poems, and the sequence has been acknowledged to be primary in the registration of the immediacy of modern psychic life. [M.L.] Rosenthal and [Sally M.] Gall, in their breakthrough study, *The Modern Poetic*

Sequence: The Genius of Modern Poetry [New York: Oxford UP, 1983], argue convincingly for the sequence as the primary modern mode of the art. I have probably written and published more sequences than any other modern poet: true sequences like "Chronicle of Division, "A Privacy of Speech, and *The Rose of Solitude*, as well as several proto-sequences, or groupings of poems, each written as though to stand alone, but related through theme or mood—series like *The Hazards of Holiness* and *The Masks of Drought*.

The virtue of the sequence is that it permits the juxtapositioning of lyric intensity while obviating the flat-footed plodding of narrative prose, capturing the facets of modern sensibility, rather like a roll of still-photographs, each print sharp with a singular intensity, and each disparate, but not meant to stand alone.

Why, then, it may be asked, the epic? If the sequence is so right for the times, and your handling of it assured by long practice, why risk failure with the antique epic, the most difficult and forbidding of all poetic enterprises? So grandiose and presupposing [sic] as to shame our latter-day pretensions? An autobiographical epic seems even more suspect. What's the next step, self-canonization?

The charge is not new. I have always drawn heavily on my life for the subjects of my poems, justified by some but faulted by others. As Kenneth Rexroth wrote in his Introduction to *The Residual Years* [New York: New Directions, 1968]:

> Everson has been accused of self-dramatization. Justly. All of his poetry, that under the name of Antoninus, too, is concerned with the drama of his own self, rising and falling along the sine curve of life, from comedy to tragedy and back again, never quite going under, never escaping for good into transcendence. This is a man who sees his shadow projected on the sky, like Whymper after the melodramatic achievement and the tragedy on the Matterhorn. Everything is larger than life with a terrible beauty and pain.... Night alone, storm over the cabin, the sleepless watcher whipsawed by past and future.... Something terribly important and infinitely mysterious is happening.... It is necessary to hold steady like Odysseus steering past the sirens, to that rudder called the integrity of the self or the ship will smash up in the trivial and the commonplace. This is what Everson's poetry is about.... (xxii)

If this cannot absolve one from the charge of presumption for casting one's story in epic form I can't imagine what could. It seems made for the mold.

On the other hand, Tom Clark, no stodgy academic, is unconvinced. Reviewing Lee Bartlett's biography of me in *The San Francisco Chronicle*, he is visibly disturbed:

> The relations between poetry, fame and public relations in America is high-lighted here without critical judgment. So are this poet's use of women, and of the church, and the curious blend of spiritual submissiveness and violent phallicism in his work.
> There are cases where it is fair to ask of a biographer that he call the bluff of his subject at least part of the time, and I think this is one of them. Failing that, the story feels not only less than fully told, but oddly unedifying.

So, oddly unedified, once again I take up my pen to close, but not to bluff, reflecting that whatever a religious poet does to further his career is somehow seen as reproachful. Clark is displeased that when I went out from the monastery to give my readings I wrote my own publicity and printed my own posters. I did not conceal this from my superiors or my sponsors or my biographer. How, then, can it be construed as bluffing? Walt Whitman did not scruple to review his own books and get his newspaper cronies to publish them anonymously. We deplore this, but is Clark prepared to deny that today it detracts not a whit from his genius? I did not have to bluff. I didn't even have to exaggerate, for I had the press notices, the testimonials and the reviews to back me up. Tom Clark is a knowledgeable, thoroughly professional poet and critic, widely experienced in the literary field, but I fear my religious dimension is his stumbling block; then his objectivity deserts him, and he growls in exasperation.

Now I must close for sure. Clearly the time has come for an overview, which is one attribute of the epic—it comprises a summing up. Forged in the womb of the collective unconscious, sustained on the backwash of epochal event, annealed in the fires of holistic depths, the epic vision, like a migratory eagle, spreads its wings and circles the sun. The sequences spelled out my life as I lived it. Now I look to the epic for what it all means, though that can't be known until finally written down, for a poet does not learn what he knows until his tongue tells him. In the shaping of speech lurks the incipience of understanding.

—William Everson
August 1, 1989
Kingfisher Flat

APPENDIX C

WILLIAM EVERSON

September 10, 1912-June 2, 1994

◨ ◨ ◨

In the course of his long life, William Everson passed through three distinct phases as a poet. Growing up in the heart of California's San Joaquin Valley (in the town of Selma, not far from Fresno), Everson discovered his true poetic vocation in his 1934 encounter with the poetry of Robinson Jeffers—an encounter that led Everson to aspire toward the creation of a body of poetry drawn from the material of his valley, as well as from his own personal experiences. His initial use of the confessional sequence was twenty years in advance of the mode that ultimately gained currency from the late '50s onward. There in the Valley of the San Joaquin, the poet and his high school sweetheart, Edwa Poulson, were married following Edwa's graduation from Fresno State, and the young couple leased the old Wenty Ranch, where the poet tended grapevines and wrote. The Second World War interrupted this San Joaquin isolation when Everson was conscripted as a conscientious objector and spent over three years interned in federal work camps. At Waldport, Oregon (his primary place of internment), he was instrumental in the founding of the Untide Press and in the establishment of the Waldport Fine Arts Program—projects which were to contribute to the development of the San Francisco Renaissance of the 1950s. The War years saw the breakup of Everson's marriage to Edwa, and, after his release from "alternative service," the poet eventually settled in Berkeley with his second wife, poet and artist Mary Fabilli.

On Christmas Eve of 1948, Everson underwent a conversion from his proclaimed agnosticism to Catholicism; and, because the Church could not recognize their marriage, Bill and Mary were obliged to separate. In 1951, Everson became Brother Antoninus of the Dominican Order, at St. Albert's Priory, in Oakland, California, where he wrote *Prodigious Thrust*, a book destined to remain unpublished for forty years—until it was issued by Black Sparrow in 1996. Indeed, the post-conversion years gave birth to the second major division of his career. Through the publication of his three major collections of religious poetry and his readings throughout the country from 1958 on through the 1960s, Antoninus became known as "the Beat Friar" and achieved a measure of fame quite beyond that of the earlier period.

After eighteen and a half years, Antoninus' situation was, again, abruptly changed—this time by virtue of his leaving the Dominican Order in December, 1969 (a year short of his final vows), to marry Susanna Rickson.

Resuming his secular identity, William Everson, his new wife, and his adopted son, Jude, moved in 1971 to Kingfisher Flat, in Big Creek Canyon, some fourteen miles north of Santa Cruz. As poet-in-residence at Kresge College of the University of California at Santa Cruz, he spent ten years giving a series of meditative lectures and resurrecting the Lime Kiln Press. This latter project not only brought Everson new fame as a master printer but enabled him to nurture an entire generation of creative printers and artists. To match his earlier handpress printing of the *Psalter*, executed during his first years as a Dominican, Everson and his students at the Lime Kiln Press produced a series of acclaimed editions, including *Granite and Cypress*, a collection of Robinson Jeffers' poems in a volume that has been hailed as one of the masterworks of American fine-press printing—as, indeed, the *Psalter* had been twenty years earlier.

During these Santa Cruz years, Everson created more poetry, brought forth several handpress volumes, became a recognized first-rank critic and scholar of Jeffers' poetry, continued his public readings, and added further essays and interviews to his growing body of work—even as Parkinson's disease took its increasing toll on his physical capacity.

On the occasion of his eightieth birthday, Everson and his wife, Susanna, separated and were subsequently divorced. Struck down by pneumonia in the fall of 1993, the poet survived the nearly fatal attack and returned to his beloved Kingfisher Flat home where, a few months later, after an interval during which he was visited by a constant stream of friends, scholars, former students, and fellow poets, William Everson died in his own bed on June 2, 1994. Following a memorial mass and funeral services at St. Albert's Priory, he was buried in the Dominican Cemetery in Benicia, California.

Hailed by Albert Gelpi as "the most important religious poet of the second half of the twentieth century" and by Diane Wakoski as "one of the most essential and dynamic American poets of the mid-twentieth century," Everson received various honors and awards, from a Guggenheim Fellowship in 1949 to the silver medal of the

Commonwealth Club of California, the Shelley Award from the Poetry Society of America, and the PEN Center West Body of Work Award. Finally, and perhaps most heartwarming of all, Everson received the Santa Cruz County 1991 Artist of the Year Award.

William Everson has left us about sixty published volumes, including some forty of his poetry, several books of Jeffers scholarship and criticism, and various volumes of superb handpress work. At the time of his death, he had completed half of his projected autobiographical poetic epic, *Dust Shall Be the Serpent's Food.*

⊡ ⊡ ⊡

CHRONOLOGY:
WILLIAM EVERSON

For purposes of reference, the editors have compiled this sketch of the poet's life, set against a scattering of events of general historical significance.

1912:   The sinking of the Titanic. William Oliver Everson is born in Sacramento, California, September 10, 1912—at home, 2120 H Street—the second of three children, older sister (Vera), younger brother (Lloyd). He is the son of Louis Waldemar Everson and Francelia Marie Herber. The father is a self-educated Norwegian immigrant and a successful commercial printer (The Everson Printery), a local bandmaster in Selma, California, and a district Justice of the Peace. The poet's mother is of German-Irish farm background. Raised Catholic, she is fifteen years her husband's junior. She converts to Christian Science after the marriage.

1913:   President Woodrow Wilson is inaugurated.

1914:   World War I begins; President Wilson issues a proclamation of neutrality; Panama Canal informally opens to commerce, August 15; in California, Mt. Lassen erupts; John Muir, spiritual father of the environmental movement, dies.

1916:   The death of Ishi, the last "wild Indian" in America.

1917:   U.S. Declaration of war against Germany, April 6; Russian Revolution, November.

1918:   World War I ends, November 11; in California, Mt. Lassen ceases its eruptions.

1919:   Versailles Peace Conference; treaty is signed; the Eighteenth Amendment to the Constitution (national prohibition) is ratified.

1920:   The Nineteenth Amendment to the Constitution (women's right to vote) is ratified; President Wilson receives the Nobel Peace Prize.

1922:   A treaty of union, adopted on December 30, founds the Union of Soviet Socialist Republics.

1926:   Sinclair Lewis refuses to accept the Pulitzer; Byrd and Bennett reach the North Pole.

1929:   Great stock market crash, October 24.

1931:   The Depression worsens; nine million are unemployed, and 1,294 banks fail. William Everson graduates from Selma High School, Selma, California.

1931-2: F.D.R. is elected president of the United States. Everson attends Fresno State College for fall semester, 1931. The Fresno State *Caravan* publishes Everson's "Gypsy Dance," December, 1931. Everson drops out of college and thereafter works in local canneries.

1933:   The Twenty-first Amendment to the Constitution (end of national prohibition) is ratified by vote of ratifying conventions in each of the states.

1933-4: Everson works for the CCC (trail crew) at Cain Flat, on the road to Mineral King in the California Sierra Nevada, in Sequoia National Park.

1934:   Everson returns to Fresno State College and renews his relationship with Edwa Poulson, his high school sweetheart. He discovers the work of Robinson Jeffers; "It was an intellectual awakening and a religious conversion in one.... Jeffers showed me God. In Jeffers I found my voice." Everson begins to write *These Are the Ravens*.

1935:   Everson drops out of college "to go back to the land and become a poet in my own right, to plant a vineyard...." He publishes (through Greater West Publishing in San Leandro as well as through The Everson Printery in Selma) his first book, *These Are the Ravens*.

1937:   *Poetry* magazine publishes "We in the Fields" and "Dust and the Glory" (subsequently retitled "Attila") under the combined title of "The Watchers"; *Saturday Review* publishes "Sleep."

1938:   William Everson and Edwa Poulson are married. Shortly thereafter they move to the Wenty Ranch, where, after completing *San Joaquin*, he writes *The Masculine Dead, War Elegies*, the first *The Residual Years*, and *Poems MCMXLII*.

1939:   Publication of *San Joaquin*, introduction by Lawrence Clark Powell (Los Angeles: Ward Ritchie).

1941:   Japan bombs Pearl Harbor, December 7, and the United States enters World War II.

1942:   The Japanese take Manila; United States forces are driven from Bataan; Doolittle bombs Tokyo; the Japanese are defeated at the Battle of Midway Island and at Guadalcanal; U.S. bombers make their first raid on Europe; British and American forces land in French North Africa. Everson publishes *The Masculine Dead: Poems 1938-1940* (Prairie City, Illinois: James A. Decker).

1943:   Roosevelt enunciates the Allied intention to seek unconditional surrender of the Axis forces; saturation bombing of Germany continues; America defeats the Japanese at the Battle of Bismarck Bay; Allies invade Sicily and the Italian mainland. As a conscientious objector, William Everson reports for alternative service at Waldport, Oregon, January 21; six weeks later, Edwa turns to mutual friend Kenneth Carothers for companionship. Everson becomes director of the Fine Arts Project at Waldport and works with William Eshelman, Kemper Nomland, Adrian Wilson, and Vladimir Dupré, establishing the Untide Press. Everson publishes *X War Elegies* (Waldport, Oregon: Untide Press); the marriage of Everson and Edwa progressively deteriorates.

1944:   America defeats the Japanese in the Battle of the Marshall Islands; Battle of the Anzio Beachhead; Rome falls to the Fifth Army; D-Day, Normandy Invasion; Allied troops enter Paris; Roosevelt re-elected; Battle of the Bulge. Everson publishes *The Waldport Poems, War Elegies*, and the first *The Residual Years* [actually issued 1945] (Waldport, Oregon: Untide Press).

1945:   Roosevelt, Churchill, and Stalin meet at Yalta; Iwo Jima falls; U.S. troops cross the Rhine; President Roosevelt dies, and Harry S Truman becomes president; Germany surrenders, May 7; atomic bombs are dropped on Hiroshima and Nagasaki; Japan surrenders, ending World War II, August 14. Everson publishes *Poems MCMXLII* (Waldport, Oregon). Waldport closes, December, 1945; on December 26th, Everson reports to Cascade Locks to await demobilization.

1946:   While in San Francisco on furlough, in February, Everson purchases a Washington hand press; the poet reads Wilhelm Reich (first sustained exposure to depth psychology); at the beginning of July, Cascade Locks camp is closed, and Everson is sent to Minersville, in Northern California; the poet is discharged from alternative service at the CO camp in Minersville, July 23; he sets up his Washington in the apple dryer at Ham and Mary Tyler's Treesbank Farm, near Sebastopol; here he meets poet and artist Mary Fabilli; he associates with authors Rexroth, Duncan, Parkinson, Whalen, Lamantia, Broughton.

1947:   Everson lives in Berkeley and is granted divorce from Edwa; he works (for the next two years) as a custodian for the University of California Press.

1948:   Everson publishes *The Residual Years* (New York: New Directions); William Everson and Mary Fabilli are married, in Reno, Nevada, on June 12; Everson converts to Catholicism, Christmas mass, St. Mary's Cathedral, San Francisco.

1949:   Everson publishes *A Privacy of Speech* (Berkeley: Equinox Press) and is awarded a Guggenheim Fellowship; the poet and Mary Fabilli separate, June 30, when the Church rules against recognition of their marriage; Everson is baptized at St. Augustine's Church, July 23.

1950:   On June 25, North Korean forces cross the thirty-eighth parallel, initiating the Korean War. Everson moves to Maurin House, the Catholic Worker house of hospitality in Oakland, where he associates with Carroll McCool, an ex-Trappist monk.

1951:   Publication of *Triptych for the Living* (Berkeley: Seraphim Press). Everson is accepted as a lay brother (donatus) in the Dominican Order at St. Albert's in Oakland and receives the name Brother Antoninus.

1952:   Dwight David Eisenhower is elected to the presidency. Antoninus begins the writing of his spiritual autobiography, *Prodigious Thrust*; he works at printing the *Psalter*.

1953:   An armistice is signed, ending the Korean War, July 27. Antoninus continues work on the *Psalter*.

1954:   McCarthy hearings in U.S. Senate; the Senate censures McCarthy. Antoninus experiences a period of crisis of faith—

a "dark night of the soul"; he abandons work on the *Psalter* and
begins to study for the priesthood.

1955: Antoninus cuts short his attempt at the priesthood and returns
to St. Albert's. He issues his hand-printed edition of *Novum
Psalterium PII XII* (Los Angeles: Countess Estelle Doheney).

1956: Eisenhower wins re-election by landslide. Antoninus
experiences an interior break-through; he re-discovers depth
psychology, and, after a brief Freudian influence, through
Victor White (*God and the Unconscious*) he begins reading the
work of Carl Jung; he completes the writing of *Prodigious
Thrust*; he gives his first public reading under the persona of
Brother Antoninus, at San Francisco State College.

1957: The second issue of *Evergreen Review* announces the Beat
Generation. Antoninus writes *River-Root*, not to be published
until 1976 (Oyez) but subsequently included in *The Veritable
Years* (poems 1949-1966).

1958: The poet gives his first public reading outside the Bay Area—in
Los Angeles, at the Aquinus Institute.

1959: Antoninus publishes *An Age Insurgent* (San Francisco:
Blackfriars) and *The Crooked Lines of God* (Detroit: Univ.
Detroit Press); the latter volume is nominated for a Pulitzer
Prize. The poet gives readings in Detroit and in Chicago; he
appears on Irvin Kupcenet's television show, is featured in
Time magazine and is dubbed "the Beat Friar"; Archbishop
John Mitty of San Francisco attempts to "silence" Antoninus
because of the poet's contacts within the Beat Generation;
Antoninus is banned from further readings; the poet meets Rose
Moreno Tannlund, beginning an "intense relationship."

1960: John F. Kennedy is elected president. Archbishop Mitty dies,
and the "silencing" of Brother Antoninus is lifted.

1961: The ill-fated Bay of Pigs invasion takes place; President
Kennedy then orders the first American combat troops to Viet
Nam.

1962: America teeters on the edge of war as a result of the Cuban
Missile Crisis; first gathering of the Second Vatican Council.
Robinson Jeffers dies. Antoninus publishes *The Hazards of
Holiness* (Garden City: Doubleday).

1963: President Kennedy is assassinated, November 22; Lyndon
Johnson becomes president. Legal divorce ends the marriage of
William Everson and Mary Fabilli, May 13; Rose Tannlund
urges Antoninus to enter the Novitiate, and he does so—
Kentfield Priory, Marin County.

1965:   This year marks the final gathering of Vatican Council II.
         Antoninus meets Susanna Rickson.
1966:   Antoninus publishes *Single Source*, foreword by Robert Duncan
         (Berkeley: Oyez).
1967:   Publication of *The Rose of Solitude* (Garden City: Doubleday);
         Scott, Foresman issues *The Achievement of Brother Antoninus*,
         introduction by William Stafford.
1968:   Richard Nixon narrowly defeats Hubert Humphrey and is
         elected to the presidency. New Directions issues an expanded
         edition of *The Residual Years*, foreword by Kenneth Rexroth;
         Antoninus publishes *Robinson Jeffers: Fragments of an Older
         Fury* (Berkeley: Oyez); Antoninus receives the Commonwealth
         Club of California silver medal for *The Rose of Solitude*; he
         leaves Kentfield and continues his Novitiate regimen at St.
         Albert's.
1969:   On December 7, at a poetry reading given at the University of
         California, Davis, Brother Antoninus presents the love poem
         "Tendril in the Mesh" and announces his intent to resign from
         the Dominican Order and to marry Susanna Rickson. At the
         conclusion of the performance, he removes his Dominican
         robes and exits. Everson and Susanna marry in Mendocino the
         following Saturday, December 13, with Robert and Dorothy
         Hawley and photographer Allen Say present.
1970:   California displaces New York as the nation's most populous
         state. At Stinson Beach, Everson begins life with Susanna and
         son Jude; he writes "Black Hills" and other poems for *Man-
         Fate*, which he completes the following year.
1971:   Everson is hired by the University of California, Santa Cruz,
         Kresge College, as master printer and lecturer. He becomes
         Poet in Residence and begins teaching that fall. He and
         Susanna and son Jude move to Kingfisher Flat on Big Creek,
         north of Davenport. Everson begins teaching his "Birth of a
         Poet" course (which will run 1971-1981)—meditations on the
         poetic vocation.
1972:   Nixon wins re-election by landslide; the famous Watergate
         break-in occurs. Everson resurrects The Lime Kiln Press at the
         University of California, Santa Cruz; under this imprint the
         poet and his students issue *Gale at Dawn* (poems by Everson,
         Hitchcock, Korte, Veblen, Clark, and Skinner).
1973:   The Viet Nam War is concluded, January 23. Through the
         Lime Kiln Press, Everson issues *Tragedy Has Obligations*, by
         Robinson Jeffers.

1974:   Richard Nixon resigns, and Gerald Ford assumes the
        Presidency of the United States. Everson publishes *Man-Fate*
        (New York: New Directions).

1975:   Everson issues *Granite & Cypress*, by Robinson Jeffers (Santa
        Cruz: Lime Kiln Press).

1976:   Jimmy Carter wins the presidency. Everson publishes *River-
        Root* and *Archetype West: The Pacific Coast as a Literary
        Region* (both from Berkeley: Oyez).

1977:   Publication of *William Everson: A Descriptive Bibliography,
        1934-1976*, compiled by Lee Bartlett and Allan Campo
        (Metuchen, NJ: Scarecrow Press); Everson is given Poetry
        Society of America's Shelley Award.

1978:   Everson publishes *The Veritable Years, 1949-1966*, afterword
        by Albert Gelpi (Santa Barbara: Black Sparrow Press), and the
        Presscollection is awarded "Book of the Year" by the MLA
        Conference on Christianity and Literature; *Blame It on the Jet
        Stream!* (Santa Cruz: Lime Kiln Press); the first book of
        criticism devoted solely to Everson's work appears, *William
        Everson: Poet from the San Joaquin*, by Allan Campo, D.A.
        Carpenter, and Bill Hotchkiss (Newcastle, CA: Blue Oak
        Press).

1979:   Publication of *Benchmark & Blaze: The Emergence of William
        Everson*, (an anthology of critical essays about Everson's
        work), ed. Lee Bartlett (Metuchen, NJ: Scarecrow Press); the
        poet is honored as a Tor House Fellow (Tor House Foundation).

1980:   Ronald Reagan wins the presidency by landslide. Everson
        publishes *The Masks of Drought* (Santa Barbara: Black
        Sparrow); *Earth Poetry: Selected Essays and Interviews*, ed.
        Bartlett (Berkeley: Oyez).

1981:   Everson issues *American Bard*, a structural re-arrangement of
        Walt Whitman's prose introduction to the first edition of
        Leaves of Grass, rendered into verse following the
        characteristic Whitman rhythms—and thus presenting the work
        as a poem in its own right, with its presumed original form
        made evident (Santa Cruz: Lime Kiln Press); suffering from
        Parkinson's Disease, Everson retires from his position at U.C.
        Santa Cruz.

1982:   Viking issues a trade edition of *American Bard*, foreword by
        James D. Hart (New York); Everson is awarded a National
        Endowment for the Arts Fellowship.

1984:   Ronald Reagan is re-elected to the presidency. Everson
        publishes *In Medias Res* (San Francisco: Adrian Wilson Press);
        Renegade Christmas (Northridge: Lord John Press).
1987:   Publication of first full-length critical study of Everson's work,
        The Rages of Excess: The Life and Poetry of William Everson,
        by David A. Carpenter (Bristol, Indiana: Wyndham Hall).
1988:   George Bush is elected president. Everson publishes *The
        Excesses of God: Robinson Jeffers as a Religious Figure*
        (Stanford: Stanford University Press); Lee Bartlett publishes
        William Everson: The Life of Brother Antoninus (New York:
        New Directions); Oregon Institute of Literary Arts award;
        National Poetry Association Award for Lifetime Achievement.
1989:   The "Evil Empire" begins to crumble, with the satellite nations
        moving toward full independence. In May of this year Everson
        receives the PEN Center West Body of Work Award.
1990:   Everson publishes *The Engendering Flood* (Santa Rosa, CA:
        Black Sparrow Press); *Mexican Standoff* (Emeryville, CA:
        Lapis Press).
1991:   The United States is involved in the Persian Gulf War against
        Iraq, with decisive victory to the American-led forces under
        General Schwarzkopf; the Soviet Union is dissolved; on
        Christmas Day, the hammer and sickle flag is taken down in
        Moscow and is replaced with the tricolor of the Russian
        Republic; the Cold War, presumably, is over. Everson receives
        Santa Cruz County Artist of the Year Award and the BABRA
        Fred Cody Body of Work Award; he is a featured reader at the
        International Festival of Authors, Harbourfront Readings,
        Toronto, Canada.
1992:   William Jefferson Clinton is elected President. On September
        10, William Everson is eighty years old. The poet and his wife,
        Susanna, separate, with Everson filing for divorce. Everson
        publishes *Naked Heart: Talking on Poetry, Mysticism, & the
        Erotic* (Albuquerque: U. New Mexico); publication of
        Perspectives on William Everson (Eugene: Castle Peak).
1993:   Everson continues to live at Kingfisher Flat—editing
        manuscript and working on *Dust Shall Be the Serpent's Food*.
        The poet, a virtual invalid, is attended by Steve Sibley. The
        divorce from Susanna is now final. The last week in October,
        Everson is stricken with pneumonia—during a two-month
        illness, the poet is several times near death.

1994:   Everson, released from Dominican Hospital in Santa Cruz, is
         again at Kingfisher Flat. Publication of *The Blood of the Poet:
         Selected Poems*, ed. Albert Gelpi (Seattle: Broken Moon Press).
         After a long springtime during which Everson is once again
         able to receive visitors—and there are many, many of them—
         the poet finally succumbs to the debilitations of Parkinson's
         disease, pneumonia, and old age. He dies at home, Kingfisher
         Flat, June 2, 1994, and is buried at the Dominican cemetery in
         Benicia, California, with final interment occurring on his
         birthday, September 10, 1994, Fr. Finbarr Hayes presiding.

1995:   Publication of *William Everson: Remembrances and Tributes*,
         ed. R.J. Brophy, combined winter and spring issues of
         Robinson Jeffers Newsletter (Long Beach: California State
         University Long Beach UP); publication of *Quarry West 32,
         The Poet as Printer: William Everson*, ed. Rice, Weisner,
         Young, Vogler (Santa Cruz, CA: U.C. Santa Cruz Printing
         Services); publication of *Take Hold Upon the Future*, the
         correspondence of Everson and L.C. Powell, ed. William
         Eshelman (Metuchen, N.J.: Scarecrow).

1996:   Clinton is re-elected. Publication of *Prodigious Thrust*, the
         poet's long-delayed spiritual autobiography, the account of his
         conversion to Catholicism, written in the early fifties, ed. Allan
         Campo (Santa Rosa, CA: Black Sparrow Press); in addition,
         Black Sparrow schedules publication of a *Collected Poems* of
         William Everson in three consecutive volumes titled, in accord
         with Everson's expressed wishes, *The Residual Years, The
         Veritable Years*, and *The Integral Years*, with hitherto
         uncollected and unpublished poems to be included in the new
         editions.

1997   Black Sparrow publishes an expanded edition of *The Residual
         Years*, part one of Everson's life trilogy, *The Crooked Lines of
         God*.

1998   Black Sparrow publishes an expanded edition of *The Veritable
         Years*, part two of *The Crooked Lines of God;* Robin Price
         publishes *Ravaged by Love*, a transcription of Everson's 1975
         "return" reading at U.C. Davis.

1999   Clinton is impeached. The United States, in conjunction with
         NATO, wages an undeclared air war against Yugoslavia.

2000   Black Sparrow publishes this present edition of *The Integral
         Years*, the final volume of Everson's life trilogy, *The Crooked
         Lines of God*.

INDEX OF TITLES

352

INDEX OF FIRST LINES

THE PRINCIPAL PUBLICATIONS OF WILLIAM EVERSON

Verse

These Are the Ravens (1935)
San Joaquin (1939)
The Masculine Dead (1942)
X War Elegies (1943)
The Waldport Poems (1944)
War Elegies (1944)
The Residual Years (1945)
Poems MCMXLII (1945)
The Residual Years (1948)
A Privacy of Speech (1949)
Triptych for the Living (1951)
An Age Insurgent (1959)
The Crooked Lines of God (1959)
The Year's Declension (1961)
The Hazards of Holiness (1962)
The Poet is Dead (1964)
The Blowing of the Seed (1966)
Single Source (1966)
In the Fictive Wish (1967)
The Rose of Solitude (1967)
The Achievement of Brother
    Antoninus (1967)
A Canticle to the Waterbirds
    (1968)
The Springing of the Blade (1968)
The Residual Years (1968)
The City Does Not Die (1969)
The Last Crusade (1969)

Who Is She That Looketh Forth
    as the Morning (1972)
Tendril in the Mesh (1973)
Black Hills (1973)
Man-Fate (1974)
River-Root / A Syzygy (1976)
The Mate-Flight of Eagles (1977)
Blame It on the Jetstream! (1978)
Rattlesnake August (1978)
The Veritable Years (1978)
A Man Who Writes (1980)
The Masks of Drought (1980)
Eastward the Armies (1980)
Renegade Christmas (1984)
In Medias Res (1984)
The High Embrace (1985)
The Poet is Dead (1987)
Mexican Standoff (1989)
The Engendering Flood (1990)
River-Root: A Syzygy (1990)
A Canticle to the Waterbirds
    (1992)
The Blood of the Poet (1994)
The Tarantella Rose (1995)
The Residual Years (1997)
The Veritable Years (1998)
Ravaged by Love (1998)
The Integral Years (2000)

Prose

Robinson Jeffers: Fragments
    of an Older Fury (1968)
Archetype West: The Pacific Coast
    as a Literary Region (1976)
Earth Poetry (1980)
Birth of a Poet (1982)
Writing the Waterbirds (1983)

The Excesses of God (1988)
Naked Heart (1992)
Take Hold Upon the Future,
    [correspondence Everson
    & L.C. Powell] (1995)
The Light the Shadow Casts (1996)
Prodigious Thrust (1996)

355

Printed January 2000 in Santa Barbara
& Ann Arbor for the Black Sparrow Press
by Mackintosh Typography & Edwards Brothers Inc.
Typeset and layout via computer
by Bill Hotchkiss, Allan Campo, Judith Shears.
Design by Barbara Martin.
This first edition is published in paper wrappers;
there are 300 hardcover trade copies;
100 numbered deluxe copies;
& 26 lettered copies have been
handbound in boards by Earle Gray.

ABOUT THE EDITORS
& CONTRIBUTORS

🔲 🔲

ALLAN CAMPO
(Contributing Editor, Text Editor, Typographer)

Allan Campo's friendship with William Everson began in 1958—as a result of the poet's initial reading appearances in Los Angeles, his first readings outside the San Francisco Bay Area—and was sustained by numerous letters, phone conversations, and visits—including many to the poet's Kingfisher Flat home during the last twenty years of Everson's life. Campo was the editor of Everson's recently published "spiritual autobiography," *Prodigious Thrust*. He co-edited, with Lee Bartlett, *William Everson: A Descriptive Bibliography* and wrote an "Afterword" for Everson's *The Mate-Flight of Eagles*. He has also contributed several substantial essays to the study of Everson's poetry, including "The Sensuous Awakening" (in *Poet from the San Joaquin*), "The Woman of Prey" (in *Benchmark and Blaze*), and "The 'Agents of Perfection'" (in *Perspectives on William Everson*). Campo was born in Los Angeles in 1934 and remained a resident there until he moved to Toledo, Ohio, at the end of 1993. He holds both a Bachelor's and a Master's degree from Loyola University (now Loyola-Marymount).

🔲 🔲

DAVID CARPENTER
(Contributing Editor)

David Carpenter, Professor of English at Eastern Illinois University, has taught at Loyola-Marymount University, University of Oregon, and University of Bonn (as a Fulbright Fellow). Besides his *Rages of Excess: The Life and Poetry of William Everson,* the first critical biography of the poet, Carpenter has published poetry and fiction, as well as scholarly essays on such writers as William Everson, Gary

Snyder, William Stafford, Frank Norris, and Willa Cather. Editor of *Research & Review* at Eastern Illinois, Carpenter has served as a frequent book reviewer for *American Literature, Western American Literature, Dow Jones News,* and *Texas Books in Review.* He was co-author, along with Campo and Hotchkiss, of *William Everson: Poet from the San Joaquin,* and his work is included in *Perspectives on William Everson.*

Carpenter holds a B.A. and an M.A. from the University of California, Davis, and a Ph.D. from the University of Oregon. His close friendship with Everson began in 1975 and over the years included numerous visits to Kingfisher Flat.

◙ ◙

JUDITH SHEARS
(Contributing Editor, Text Editor, Typographer)

Judith Shears first met William Everson in 1974, becoming a close family friend thereafter, through numerous visits to the Everson home at Kingfisher Flat, camping trips to the Sierra Nevada, and attendance at various of Everson's poetry readings. Along with James B. Hall and Bill Hotchkiss, she was a contributing editor (as well as book designer) for *Perspectives on William Everson.* Working in consultation with the poet, she created and edited *The Integral Years* computer diskette which, along with Steve Sibley's subsequent version, served as the basis for much of the present text.

Shears holds the B.A. and M.A. from California State University, Sacramento, and the M.F.A. in creative writing, prose fiction, from the University of Oregon, where she was a teaching fellow for several years, both while working on the creative writing degree and while doing advanced graduate study in the doctoral program. Poet and novelist, Shears is best known as author of *The Russians.* Born and raised in Calaveras County, California, at present she lives near Santa Fe, New Mexico.

◙ ◙

BILL HOTCHKISS

(Contributing Editor, Text Editor, Typographer)

Everson's literary executor, Hotchkiss first met the poet in 1963. Eleven years later the two men became friends by way of their mutual interest in the work of Robinson Jeffers. Together, they edited the Liveright (Norton) re-issue of Jeffers' *The Double Axe* (1977). Hotchkiss was co-author, with Allan Campo and David Carpenter, of *William Everson: Poet from the San Joaquin*. With James B. Hall and Judith Shears, he was co-editor for *Perspectives on William Everson* (1992). He served as text editor and typographer for Everson's long-delayed spiritual autobiography, *Prodigious Thrust*, ed. Campo (Black Sparrow Press, 1996) and, with Campo, was co-editor for the Black Sparrow editions of Everson's *The Residual Years* (1997) and *The Veritable Years* (1998). Hotchkiss holds a B.A. from U.C. Berkeley, an M.A. from San Francisco State, and an M.F.A. and a Ph.D. from the University of Oregon. He teaches at Sierra College, in his home town of Grass Valley, California.

⬒ ⬒